Dedication

To my wife and best friend Kelly, my parents Don and Joan, and my daughter Zara.

I love you all, and I dedicate this book to you.

Authors' Acknowledgements

I'd like to thank David Grisman, Mike Compton, Marla Fibish, Chris Acquavella, Don Stiernberg, Rich DelGrosso, John Goodin, and Tim Connell for being the inspirations that they are and for sharing some of their mandolin expertise. Also a big shout out to Scott Tichenor, Mike Marshall, Richard Perlmutter, and Alan Epstein for providing some 'human interest' content to help break up the monotony of one scale exercise after another.

I am grateful for the editing team of Mike Baker, Steve Edwards, Ben Kemble, Andy Finch, Matt Flinner, and Arthur Stern who, against all odds, were able to turn my ramblings into something worth publishing.

Thanks to Stan Werbin and Dave Matchette at Elderly Instruments and Trevor Moyle at TAMCO for supplying photographs of rare mandolins. Thanks also to my friends Bill White, Fred Swaffer, Daniel Hansen, George Powell, and Adrian Bagale for lending instruments for the photographs and recordings used in this book.

I would like to thank all of the great mandolin players past, present, and future that inspire us to pick up the mandolin.

Publisher's Acknowledgements

We're proud of this book; please send us your comments at http://dummies.custhelp.com. For other comments, please contact our Customer Care Department within the U.S. at 877-762-2974, outside the U.S. at 317-572-3993, or fax 317-572-4002.

Some of the people who helped bring this book to market include the following:

Acquisitions, Editorial, and Vertical Websites

Project Editor: Steve Edwards

Commissioning Editor: Mike Baker

Assistant Editor: Ben Kemble

Development Editor: Andy Finch

Copy Editor: Kate O'Leary

Technical Editors: Arthur Stern, Matt Flinner

Proofreader: Mary White

Production Manager: Daniel Mersey

Publisher: David Palmer

Cover Photos: Trevor Moyle: The Acoustic Music Co.; Weber Fine Acoustic Instruments (www.webermandolins.com)

Cartoons: Rich Tennant (www.the5thwave.com)

Composition Services

Senior Project Coordinator: Kristie Rees

Layout and Graphics: Carl Byers, Carrie A. Cesavice, Joyce Haughey

Proofreaders: John Greenough, Melanie Hoffman

Indexer: Claudia Bourbeau

Brand Reviewers: Jennifer Bingham, Zoë Wykes, and Carrie Burchfield

Publishing and Editorial for Consumer Dummies

Kathleen Nebenhaus, Vice President and Executive Publisher

Kristin Ferguson-Wagstaffe, Product Development Director

Ensley Eikenburg, Associate Publisher, Travel

Kelly Regan, Editorial Director, Travel

Publishing for Technology Dummies

Andy Cummings, Vice President and Publisher

Composition Services

Debbie Stailey, Director of Composition Services

Contents at a Glance

Table of Contents

● ●

Foreword

*I*t is with great pleasure and a sense of pride that I welcome you to *Mandolin For Dummies*. Our unique little musical instrument – the mandolin – is one filled with limitless possibilities. Whether you're just learning or you've been working at it for a considerable amount of time, a wealth of valuable information awaits you within these pages.

The mandolin had its beginning in Europe centuries ago. During the natural migration of humans seeking new opportunities and a better life, people often took with them the family mandolin which was portable, unlike the bulkier guitar or piano. The mandolin found itself in new surroundings, mixing with unfamiliar music and cultures. New music genres were being born. The influence of Italian music took hold in Brazil and spread to other parts of South America. Europe's classical music found a good home in today's Asian mandolin orchestras. In the United States, penniless immigrants who had entered the country through New York's Ellis Island ultimately mingled with the descendents of African slaves to create new styles of soulful, hyper-charged folk music.

It's within this context that we celebrate the mandolin, which brings us to the book's author. Don Julin has dedicated his entire life to making great music on the mandolin. He's a musician's musician. At performances, Don might be trading solos with a Hammond B3 organ, cello, drummer or electric guitar. On occasion, you find him performing solo mandolin with a loop recorder where he layers his own back-up in real time. Don also works with everyone from folk singers to seasoned jazz professionals. As if that isn't enough, he leads ensembles of all sizes (including a mandolin orchestra), composes for film and television, has owned a recording studio and is widely recognised for his writing and teaching. In short, Don is a musician you won't find tied to or limited by any genre.

Diversity is Don Julin's strength. In him, we have the perfect author for *Mandolin For Dummies* and a terrific mentor to lead us forward in one of life's great joys – playing music. Enjoy!

Scott Tichenor
Mandolin Cafe (www.mandolincafe.com)

Introduction

- -

Mandolins heal the world! Recent scientific studies show that the mandolin has the amazing ability to reverse the ageing process, give temporary relief from depression and anxiety, and possibly even cure cancer. Experience the miracle of this diminutive yet powerful instrument!

*F*or many years this was the opening statement on my website (www. donjulin.com). Even though it may not be backed up by a legitimate medical study, this little sales pitch has put smiles on the faces of many people. I hope that it encouraged some readers to pick up the mandolin and begin to feel the healing.

From Mozart's 'Deh, Vieni Alla Finestra' to Led Zeppelin's 'The Battle of Evermore', the mandolin has brought that special something to a wide range of musical styles for more than 200 years. The instrument that started out serenading passengers on gondolas in Venice, Italy, played the leading role in the development of bluegrass in America. Although to some people the mandolin looks like a little guitar, hearing a few notes is enough to show that this is no guitar: the mandolin is much cooler than a guitar!

About This Book

You don't have to read *Mandolin For Dummies* from cover to cover, and I promise there's no test at the end! Think of this book more as a reference that allows you to go straight to the topic or technique you're interested in. If scales aren't your focus today, simply bypass those sections and jump to another topic. (Those scales or timing exercises may look (or sound) good in a few months.) This book has useful information for the beginner, but also includes some sage advice from some of today's top pros.

Here are some tips for getting the most out of this book:

- ✔ **Look carefully at the photos:** Positioning your hands properly is very important to obtain a good tone from your mandolin. The photos give you a better idea of what your fingers need to look like than just using the chord charts.

- **Listen to the audio tracks:** Music is sound, not paper, and so even though I use paper to communicate many elements of music, the end result is sound. I use the audio tracks to demonstrate many of the songs, techniques and exercises that I describe in this book. I recommend listening to each exercise a few times before trying to play it.

- **Read the charts:** I present the songs and exercises in tablature, rhythm patterns for strumming and standard musical notation. You certainly don't need to read music, but it's provided for those who already can. (Appendix B covers standard music notation.)

What You're Not to Read

Throughout this book, I mark some paragraphs as Technical Stuff. These technical bits aren't necessary to being able to play great mandolin but may give you a deeper understanding of the relevant exercise or concept.

Sidebars (shaded in grey) contain little nuggets of mandolin knowledge that you can use to impress people at social events. They may feature wisdom from a famous mandolin player, a story about a mandolin personality or a little-known historical fact. You don't have to read these sidebars, but they make for some fun reading while you're taking a break from practising.

Conventions Used in This Book

I use a few conventions in *Mandolin For Dummies* to help you navigate your way around the book:

- The Internet has made being a mandolin enthusiast more fun than ever. When I reference a website that you may want to check out, it appears in this very official-looking `monofont` type. Rest assured that when an address breaks across two lines of text, I haven't put in any extra characters (such as hyphens) to indicate the break. Just type exactly what you see in the book, as though the line break doesn't exist.

- I *italicise* important words that may be new to you, and define them nearby.

- Instead of writing 'picking hand' and 'fretting hand', I use 'right hand' for the picking or strumming hand and 'left hand' for the fretting hand. I apologise if you're left-handed, and ask that you read 'right hand' to mean 'left hand' and vice versa.

✔ The terms 'up', 'down', 'higher' and 'lower' have different meanings depending on which hand I'm referring to. I use 'up' and 'down' to describe the right-hand movement for strumming or picking. An *up-stroke* is the motion of picking or strumming where the pick is moving up (against gravity). A *down-stroke* refers to picking or strumming with a downward motion (with gravity).

I use these same terms a bit differently for the left hand. 'Up' or 'higher' refers to the note's pitch and indicates moving your left hand or fingers towards the body of the mandolin (see Chapter 1 for the different parts of the mandolin); notice that the sound gets higher. 'Down' or 'lower' also refers to pitch and indicates moving your left hand or fingers towards the headstock of the mandolin (notice the sound gets lower).

✔ I indicate minor chords with a lowercase 'm' after the chord name. So 'A minor', for example, is 'Am'.

✔ I use the US terms for indicating the length of notes, with the UK terms in parentheses. Therefore, I refer to *whole* notes, *half* notes and *quarter*, *eighth* and *sixteenth* notes. These US terms seem more logical and clear than the UK equivalents (which are *semibreve*, *minim*, *crotchet*, *quaver* and *semiquaver*, respectively). Check out Chapter 4 for more details.

Foolish Assumptions

The only assumptions I make about you are that you're interested in discovering more about playing the mandolin, that you're using standard tuning (G, D, A, E) and that you're playing with a pick. I don't assume that you can read music or that I know what style of music you want to play (or that you should be interested in only one style of music). I don't even assume that you own a mandolin yet.

How This Book Is Organised

Mandolin For Dummies is organised so that you can easily get to the information you want quickly, without spending a lot of time hunting around for it. The chapters are grouped into the following six parts, which are broken down into chapters, each covering a specific subject, skill or musical style.

Part I: Being Bitten by the Mandolin Bug

This part is for mandolin beginners or those needing a reminder of the fundamentals. Chapter 1 contains an introduction to the mandolin family of instruments, and all the various parts and their names. Chapter 2 shows you how to get the mandolin in tune, and in Chapter 3 I guide you towards finding a comfortable position, holding the mandolin, when sitting and standing.

Part II: Starting to Play the Mandolin

In Part II, I get down to playing the mandolin. I suggest that you take things slowly: discover and practise a few techniques, and have fun with some tunes. When you feel confident about what you've picked up, maybe go back and pick up a few more tricks. This part gives you all the exercises you'll ever need.

Chapter 4 shows you some of the basic elements of counting, tablature, chord diagrams and strumming, followed by a few simple songs. Chapter 5 explores the world of right-hand technique, such as holding the pick, right-hand support, pick direction, tone development, dynamics and tremolo, as well as some exercises to strengthen and loosen your right hand and wrist.

Chapter 6 focuses on the left hand and describes fingerings for both open (easy) and closed (a little tougher) positions. I also discuss left-hand techniques (for example, slides, hammer-ons, pull-offs and muting) and loads more great chords. Chapter 7 is all about a specific way of playing chords that was a favourite of the great mandolin virtuoso Jethro Burns: three-string chords. Chapter 8 describes a few common scales and some basic tunes, as well as more sophisticated ways to play accompaniment. I also show you how to use various left- and right-hand techniques to turn a plain melody into something very special.

Part III: Putting Playing Styles into Practice

This part is all about playing different musical styles from around the world. I take a look at the defining techniques used in loads of different genres, including how to play old-time fiddle tunes, dances and blues (Chapter 9), American mountain bluegrass (Chapter 10) and Irish reels and jigs (in Chapter 11). For those of you with itchy feet or who want to check out some truly exotic styles, try Chapter 12 with its sections on traditional Italian folk, European classical and Brazilian choro. If toe-tapping swing and jazz is more your thing, Chapter 13 is for you, and for something that incorporates many of these styles, plus a smidgen of Latin and gypsy to boot, turn to Chapter 14, where I discuss something called new acoustic (or Dawg) music.

Part IV: Purchasing and Caring for Your Mandolin

In Chapter 15, I describe the never-ending quest for a more expensive mandolin; no, not really! In fact, this chapter deals with buying your first mandolin or upgrading to a better model. I take a look at many different styles of mandolin and discuss where (and where not) to look for a good new or used mandolin. Chapter 16 is about building an accessories kit, from picks to metronomes and recording devices. Chapter 17 gives you a step-by-step guide to changing strings, and Chapter 18 covers care and basic repair of your valued possession, including when to turn to the experts.

Part V: The Part of Tens

This part is a *For Dummies* trademark and is made up of top ten lists: Chapter 19 helps to improve your playing with practice tips, Chapter 20 introduces you to the greatest mandolin players of all time, and Chapter 21 offers ways to tap into the thriving mandolin subculture.

Part VI: Appendixes

The appendixes contain a wealth of information that you're sure to find useful for years to come. Appendix A shows you how to make 96 chords, including many that draw a blank stare even from seasoned players. Appendix B is all about reading standard music notation including sharps, flats, key signatures, time signatures and much more. Appendix C lists all the audio tracks.

Icons Used in This Book

I use the following icons to call your attention to information that you may find helpful. These icons are placed in the page margins.

This icon lets you know that I demonstrate a technique or tune on an accompanying audio track. Listening to these tracks as you work on a specific skill or tune helps enormously.

Paragraphs that I mark with this icon contain important info that people tend to forget. Think of them as the little sticky notes that your spouse or partner leaves on the refrigerator, such as 'turn the oven off at 5!'. They may not seem that big, but remembering them sets you up well for the future.

These icons are more about the whys and how things work than simply what to do. They can prove helpful but aren't essential, and so you can skip over them if you prefer, with no damage done.

These icons provide expert advice that helps you avoid common pitfalls and so speed up your progress.

Danger! Danger! This icon indicates something that can cause harm to your playing or to your mandolin.

Accessing the Audio Tracks

Mandolin For Dummies comes with 91 audio tracks – each one an essential aid to mastering the songs, techniques, and exercises that I cover in the book. If you've purchased the paper or e-book version of *Mandolin For Dummies,* just go to www.dummies.com/go/mandolin to access and download these tracks. (If you don't have internet access, call 877-762-2974 within the U.S. or 317-572-3993 outside the U.S.) If you have the enhanced e-book version, you'll find the audio tracks right there in the chapters – just where you need them.

Where to Go from Here

I've written the chapters in *Mandolin For Dummies* so that they're as self-contained as possible. This approach allows you to devise your own personal course through the book, depending on your interests and skill level:

- ✔ If you haven't yet bought a mandolin, jump straight to Chapter 15 to get advice before splashing any cash.
- ✔ If you're a beginner staring at a shiny new instrument, check out the chapters in Part I to start a mandolin journey that can last a lifetime.
- ✔ If you're already an intermediate mandolin player, flip to Part III and discover some of the finer points of different musical styles; for example, check out Chapter 10 for exciting rural bluegrass, and Chapter 13 for sophisticated urban jazz.

However you decide to use this book, now that you've been well and truly bitten by the mandolin bug the thing to do is relax, read on, and enjoy the ride with the greatest little instrument in the world — the mandolin.

Part I
Being Bitten By the Mandolin Bug

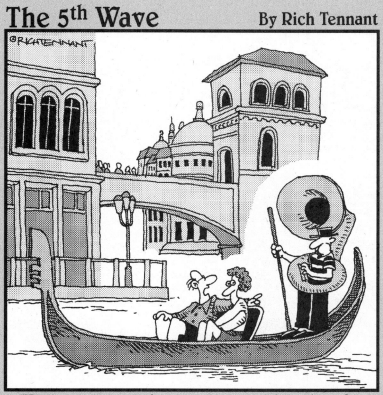

The 5th Wave   By Rich Tennant

"Excuse me, but have you ever thought of playing the mandolin?"

In this part . . .

I introduce you to the family of mandolin instruments, describe the different anatomical parts of the mandolin and preview what lies ahead in this book. I show you how to tune your mandolin and how to hold it, whether you choose to stand or sit while playing.

Chapter 1

Becoming Acquainted with Your Mandolin

In This Chapter
▶ Discovering the mandolin
▶ Bringing the family
▶ Exploring the mandolin's anatomy

*I*n March 1979, I was fresh out of high school — wondering what my future would be — when I met my first mandolin. The event changed my life and sent me on an amazing mandolin journey. Since then I've been playing, composing, travelling, teaching, recording and now writing about mandolins – because the mandolin is such a wonderful instrument.

In this chapter, I show you just why the mandolin is such a wonderful instrument (as if you didn't already know), describing among other things its great sound, sexy looks (steady, Don!), friendly extended family and musical flexibility.

Riding the Mandolin Wave

In today's world of synthesised pop music, smartphone apps and video games, the mandolin is an oasis of low-tech, organic simplicity. Made of wood and strung with steel strings, the mandolin can bring players and listeners enjoyment without the use of the Internet or even electricity. The mandolin is the perfect desert-island instrument as well as one that city-dwellers can use to (re)discover a simpler time with simpler pleasures.

Mandolins have some great advantages, not least of which is that they're small enough to fit in an overhead compartment in a plane. What better way to unwind after a stressful business meeting than to go back to your hotel room and play some mandolin music (quietly, of course, unless you're sure the adjoining rooms are also occupied by mandolin fans!). Try doing that with your piano or cello.

Loving the mandolin sound

For one small instrument, the mandolin can certainly create a number of different but beautiful sounds across a wealth of musical genres:

- **Old world:** Rapid back-and-forth picking (called *tremolo*) is the signature sound of the mandolin. This romantic sound dates back to nineteenth-century Italy, where mandolin players serenaded wealthy Venetians as they travelled by gondola (check out Chapter 12).

- **Country:** Some people associate the mandolin with the high lonesome sound of bluegrass. In the 1940s, Bill Monroe and the Bluegrass Boys came out of the hills of Kentucky playing a new form of country music featuring mandolin that helped to shape the course of American music. I describe bluegrass in Chapter 10 and take you on a pre-bluegrass American mandolin adventure of old-time tunes, ragtime and blues in Chapter 9.

- **Rock:** Many people (including me) were drawn to the amazing mandolin sound through its use in pop or rock settings via tracks by Led Zeppelin, Rod Stewart or R.E.M.

But, however you got here and wherever you want to take your playing — such as to an Irish pub session (see Chapter 11) or a New York jazz club (check out Chapter 13), or deep into the hybrid style of modern-day master David Grisman and his 'Dawg' music (see Chapter 14) — the important thing to know is you're welcome to hang out as long as you like in the wonderful world of mandolins.

To help you on your musical journey, you need to get to grips with the basics of mandolin playing (see Chapter 4). After all, you need to lay the foundations before you can start to build your repertoire! Mastering the essential right- and left-hand playing techniques is also a key milestone (Chapters 5 and 6 enable you to get there) to aim for before you start to tackle chording methods (see Chapter 7), scales and more advanced techniques (see Chapter 8).

Joining a vibrant community

When you begin to look around, you find that you aren't alone and that more mandolin players are out there than you may have thought. Look around your own town or city for mandolin activity, whether it's a local bluegrass band performance, or a mandolin club or orchestra.

If you live somewhere that has little or no mandolin activity, you can become part of the growing online mandolin community. Websites such as www. mandolincafe.com offer lessons, stories and links to just about anything to do with the mandolin. YouTube is another way to see some great performances, get some free lessons or just discover who's who in the mandolin world. You can't possibly feel alone amid the huge number of people posting videos of themselves playing the mandolin.

I designed *Mandolin For Dummies* to get you playing the instrument, so that you too can become part of a worldwide community of mandolin players. To gain some inspiration, flip to Chapter 20 to read about a few mandolin greats, and check out Chapter 21 for tips on entering the buzzing mandolin subculture.

Enjoying a great choice of mandolins

Purchasing a mandolin today is easier than ever before. Gone are the days when the only way to get a mandolin was for you to travel great distances to get to a music shop only to discover that it had only two mandolins to choose from. Along with old-school bricks and mortar shops, today you have lots of online dealers of mandolins with great selections and reputations of having many satisfied customers.

Pacific-rim manufacturing costs have made new high-quality mandolins more affordable than ever before. A quality solid-wood mandolin can cost far less today than a similar instrument did when I was looking for my first mandolin in 1979.

If a well-worn vintage mandolin is your preference, loads of dealers display their inventories online and are willing to ship (properly) a mandolin to you wherever you live. If you're a bit braver, you may even want to find the vintage mandolin of your dreams on eBay.

Today is truly a renaissance period of mandolin builders, with hundreds and even thousands of independent one-person shops turning out both traditional and daring new designs of mandolins of all price ranges. If knowing the person who built your mandolin is something that appeals to you, you're in luck today with lots of options.

Turn to Chapter 15 for loads more on buying mandolins.

Meeting the Mandolin Family

Every relationship comes to the point where you need to meet the family. The mandolin family is very friendly, and unlike your in-laws, mandolins don't whisper behind your back while you're in the other room.

The mandolin family is related to the violin family with basically the same assortment of various-sized instruments intended to be played together to form a single harmonious sound. Figure 1-1 shows a family portrait including the mandolin, the mandola and the mando-cello.

Figure 1-1:
The
Mandolin
family: two
mandolins,
a mandola
and a
mando-cello.

Reproduced by permission of Elderly Instruments.

Reaching the highest notes: Mandolin

Mandolins come in many varieties, but in all cases they're the soprano voice of the mandolin family. The strings are tuned to the notes G, D, A and E (the same as a violin), and mandolins have pairs of strings for each note. The mandolin is primarily responsible for melody and can be thought of as the child in the family. Mandolins like to play in harmony with other mandolins, like children (well, like some children) like to play in harmony with other children. Figure 1-2 shows two mandolins.

Playing with an alto voice: Mandola

The *mandola* (see Figure 1-3) is a sister to the viola from the violin family. Think of the mandola as the mother of the family in that it can play melody but chooses to shine the spotlight on the children, supplying support and at times going unnoticed. It has a rich voice and is tuned to the notes C, G, D and A, placing it in the alto range of the ensemble.

Figure 1-2:
Two man-
dolins: (a)
Gibson F4
model; (b)
Gibson A4
model.

a   b

Reproduced by permission of Elderly Instruments.

Figure 1-3:
A Gibson H4
mandola.

Reproduced by permission of Elderly Instruments.

Lowering the tone: Mando-cello

The *mando-cello* (see Figure 1-4), much like its cousin the violin-cello, can provide rich low notes to fill out the bottom register of the family. You can think of the mando-cello like the deep-voiced father of the family, providing a strong foundation for other mandolins and rarely needing to be in the spotlight. The mando-cello is tuned to C, G, D and A like the mandola, but one complete octave lower.

Figure 1-4: A Gibson K4 mando-cello.

Reproduced by permission of Elderly Instruments.

Spotting the rarely seen mando-bass

Every once in a while at family gatherings, a strange old gent turns up whom you're supposed to call Uncle George. As far as you can figure out, he's not really part of the family, but everyone still seems to get along. This strange old man is the mando-bass (see Figure 1-5) and isn't included in many of the family photos.

These instruments are very rare and for the most part have gone the way of the dinosaur. The role of the *mando-bass* is like other bass instruments, although most people today use a string bass or even an electric bass guitar for this role. The mando-bass has only four strings and is tuned E, A, D and G (like a stand-up or electric bass).

Reproduced by permission of Elderly Instruments.

Accompanying the family: Octave mandolin

You can think of the octave mandolin in Figure 1-6 as the stepchild or adopted child. Although octave mandolins fit into the family, they don't share the genetic lineage that the other members of the family enjoy. The *octave mandolin* (or the octave mandola as it's sometimes called) is tuned G, D, A and E, one full octave lower than the mandolin, placing it somewhere between the mandola and the mando-cello.

These instruments are popular in Irish music and are used primarily to provide accompaniment, although some large-handed individuals may explore them as a melody instrument.

Figure 1-6:
A Trinity
College (flat
top) octave
mandolin.

Reproduced by permission of Elderly Instruments.

Getting to Know Your Mandolin's Anatomy

Mandolins come in many shapes and sizes but share enough anatomical similarities to be considered mandolins. Here, I look at a modern F5-style mandolin because it's the most popular mandolin around today.

The F5 has some cosmetic features that other models don't have, making it more decorative. Check out the photo in Figure 1-7 to see the full anatomy of the mandolin.

Flip to Chapter 3 to discover the proper ways to hold the mandolin.

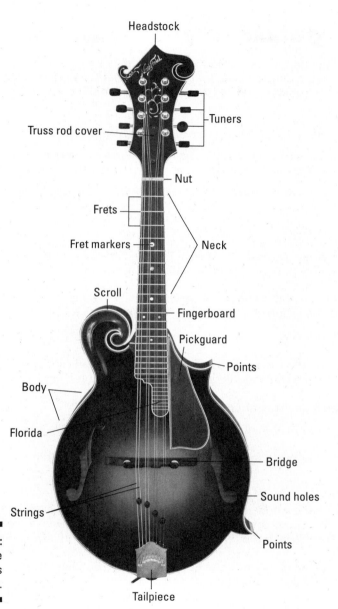

Headstock

Tuners

Truss rod cover

Nut

Frets

Fret markers

Neck

Scroll

Fingerboard

Pickguard

Points

Body

Florida

Bridge

Sound holes

Strings

Points

Figure 1-7:
The
mandolin's
anatomy.

Tailpiece

Looking at the body

The mandolin body is the hollow wooden chamber where the sound is produced. The type of wood used in the body is a determining factor in how a particular instrument is going to sound. The mandolin body is divided into three parts:

- The top (or *soundboard*) is usually made of spruce.

- The back is usually constructed from a harder wood; maple is the most popular, but birch, mahogany or rosewood are also used.

- The sides are also made from a hardwood, with maple being used most often.

Strings

Mandolin strings are made of steel and come in sets of eight. Chapter 2 shows you how to tune up your mandolin's strings.

Many older mandolins need to be strung with light-gauge strings, and bowl-back mandolins should only be strung with ultra-light strings.

Soundholes

The *soundholes* in the top allow the sound to come out (not surprisingly). Mandolins come with two different types of soundholes:

- Round hole, like a soundhole on an acoustic guitar
- F-shaped holes, similar to the soundholes on a violin

Check out Chapter 15 for photographs of different mandolin models.

Bridge

The *bridge* is the wooden piece that sits approximately in the middle of the body and functions as a guide to line up the strings and transfer vibrations from the string to the top. The bridge is only held on with string pressure.

If you take off all the strings, the bridge falls off. Read Chapter 17 for the complete lowdown on changing mandolin strings.

Tailpiece

The *tailpiece* is a stamped or cast piece of metal that serves as a place to anchor or attach the strings. It's attached to the side of the mandolin body and, unlike the bridge, doesn't fall off when you are changing strings. Tailpieces are functional but they can also be decorative, as I describe in Chapter 16 on building your mandolin accessories kit.

Scroll

Not all mandolins have scrolls. In general, if the mandolin has a scroll, the model begins with the letter F, as in F5- or F4-model mandolins. Musicians and manufacturers may argue over whether the scroll makes any sound difference, but what's clear is that these models are harder to build and so more expensive.

Points

Points are another cosmetic appointment that not all mandolins have. The typical F5 mandolin has two points coming off the bottom of the body. The bottom points are handy to rest on your leg when you are playing while seated, to keep the instrument from moving. Some mandolins have two points: one where the scroll would be and one opposite that location.

Pick guard

A *pick guard* (sometimes called a finger rest) is a protective piece made of wood or plastic that can serve as a place to rest your third and fourth fingers as a reference guide or to keep the mandolin from getting scratched up.

Not all mandolins have pick guards, and some people (including myself) remove them to allow more sound to come out of the soundhole.

Introducing the neck

The neck is the long, slender part attached to the body and runs parallel to the strings. Your left hand is going to spend a lot of time on the neck, and so get familiar with the different parts.

Fingerboard

The fingerboard, or *fretboard,* is a thin piece of hardwood with very precise grooves or channels cut in it, into which the frets (see the next section) are hammered or pressed. The fingerboard is glued to the neck.

Frets

Frets are the strips of metal that are vertical on the fingerboard. In effect, these metal strips shorten the length of the string when you hold them down with your finger, adjusting the pitch of the string. As you fret closer to the mandolin's body, the pitches or notes get higher. Each of these pitches has a letter name, and together the letters make up the musical alphabet. For a complete fingering chart, see Chapter 6.

Fret markers

The *fret markers* are little pearl dots placed in the fingerboard at frets 5, 7, 10 and 12. Often, these markers are also placed on the side of the neck facing up, so the player can see the dots too.

If you're coming to mandolin from playing guitar, the fret markers are a little different. The guitar fingerboard is marked at the ninth instead of the tenth fret.

Florida

A *Florida* is the fingerboard extension, named because of its resemblance to the shape of the state of Florida. The extra frets it provides were added to the mandolin to give the player access to notes that are even higher, as if the mandolin notes aren't high enough already. Very few mandolin players ever play these notes.

Headstock

The *headstock* is the piece at the end of the neck that supplies a place to fasten the tuners. The mandolin maker usually puts the brand name on the headstock.

Nut

The *nut* is the slotted piece located at the end of the fingerboard that acts as a guide for the strings. They pass over the nut on the way to the tuners.

Tuners

Since you asked, the *tuners* are the gear-driven pegs to which the strings are attached. The tuning of each string is achieved by turning the knob on the end of each tuner.

Truss-rod cover

The *truss-rod cover* is a plate mounted on the headstock that's removed when you want to adjust the truss rod. The truss rod itself is a steel rod that runs the length of the mandolin's neck and which you can use to straighten a bowed neck. Not all mandolins have this feature.

Some of the aforementioned parts of your mandolin are repairable, and so if you're 'handy' and want to solve a problem yourself, Chapter 18 may well be able to help.

Using string vibrations to produce sound

When the mandolin is strung and tuned up, the strings create a downward pressure on the top. When you pluck the strings, they vibrate at specific pitches, transferring these vibrations to the top. In turn the top vibrates, turning the vibrations into sound.

Chapter 2

Getting to Grips with Tuning and Terminology

In This Chapter
▶ Meeting some musical terms
▶ Discovering the need for tuning
▶ Tuning up your mandolin

Much of the fun of being a musician is playing in groups and 'talking shop' with other instrumentalists. To do so, you need to be in tune musically and with the correct lingo, which is where this chapter comes in.

By the way, I'll never forget the first time I heard 100 mandolin-family instruments being tuned simultaneously. I was attending my first Classical Mandolin Society of America conference and planned to participate in the En Masse Orchestra (made up of over 100 stringed instruments such as mandolins, mandolas, mando-cellos, guitars and basses). At the first rehearsal, the sound was like I'd stepped inside the world's biggest beehive! The sound of over 800 strings being tuned at the same time is certainly intoxicating, but you need to know what you're doing to tune your mandolin accurately in such situations. (I suggest an electronic tuner!)

In this chapter, I explain a few common musical terms that you need to know when tuning and when talking with other musicians. I also describe why you have to tune up, and show you several ways to get the job done.

Coming to Terms with Musical Terminology

When you learn to play a musical instrument, you're going to come across musical jargon. You see symbols written down and hear players using differ-ent terms. For example, music is made up of *pitches* (different notes), *rests* (empty spaces) and *rhythms* (specific timing). In this section, I define a few musical terms that make up the language people use when speaking about and playing music. (Appendix B has much more on musical notation.)

You can fill a whole book on musical terminology, and many people have. If you want to go deeper into the subject, check out *Music Theory For Dummies* by Michael Pilhofer and Holly Day (Wiley).

Identifying musical notes with letters

Musical notes are known by letters. The musical alphabet goes from the letter A to the letter G, before starting again at A. Just to confuse you, in fact the sequence starts at C and follows the alphabet around to C again (C, D, E, F, G, A, B, C). The sound of this sequence of notes (the white notes on a keyboard) is the very familiar 'do, re, mi, fa, so, la, ti, do' and is called a *C major* scale. In addition to these eight notes, between most of these letters are other notes called *sharps* and *flats* (the black keys on a keyboard; see Figure 2-1 and the next section).

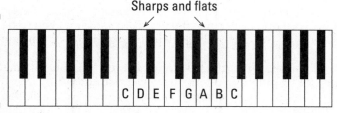

Sharps and flats

Figure 2-1: The white and black keys on a keyboard.

C D E F G A B C

Make the effort to remember the names (the letters) of the notes on the mandolin (although don't worry about remembering every sharp and flat at this stage, because you're sure to pick them up as you go along). Just like people, notes feel more important when you remember their names!

Sharpening up and flatting down your notes

In music, a *sharp* note indicates that it's a little higher in pitch and *flat* means that the note is a little lower in pitch:

- A sharp is represented by an italic hash sign: ♯.
- A flat is represented by an italic lowercase letter 'b': ♭.

When reading music to play on the mandolin, a sharp symbol immediately before a note name indicates that you need to play one fret higher than the named note, and a flat means to play one fret lower. For example, you can find C♯ one fret higher than C and B♭ one fret lower than B.

Stepping up to the mark: Distances between notes

You may hear musicians use the words *half step* and *whole step*, terms that refer to the distance between two notes. On the mandolin, one fret is the distance of a half step, and two frets equal a whole step.

In more formal musical language, a half step is called a *semitone* and a whole step is called a *tone*.

Scaling the heights with chords and scales

A *chord* is the term for when you play a group of notes at the same time. Basic chords consist of three notes (sometimes called *triads*), and more complex chords can be made up of four or more notes.

Scales consist of a series of notes, such as the C major scale that I describe in the earlier section 'Identifying musical notes with letters'. You create melodies by picking notes out of a scale. Scales are also where chords, harmony parts, bass lines and all other melodic parts come from. The terms *scale* and *key* mean the same thing, so when someone asks 'what key are you in?', they are asking you what scale is being used in this song.

Western music has 12 possible notes (including sharps and flats), so you can write music in 12 possible keys. Scales and chords are broadly categorised into two types:

- **Major** chords and scales, which are usually thought of as having a happy sound. 'Happy Birthday', the Beatles' 'Here Comes the Sun', and 'Happy Together' by the Turtles are all happy songs using major chords in a major key.

- **Minor** chords and scales, which have a darker, somewhat mysterious sound and can even be downright sad. Some examples include 'Poor Wayfaring Stranger', 'What Child is This?' ('Greensleeves') and Led Zeppelin's 'Stairway to Heaven'.

So, in essence, western music has 24 keys: 12 major and 12 minor.

Each instrument has certain keys that are easier than others for players to master. Mandolins tend to be happy in C, D, G, and A major. A minor and E minor are also popular and easy on the mandolin. (I demonstrate most of these scales and use them in songs in Chapter 8.)

Grasping the Tuning Basics

All instruments need to be tuned, with some being easier to tune than others. Tuning your mandolin can be a frustrating experience – because of its pairs of strings (called *unison* strings) that are tuned to the same note – but discovering how to do so is necessary for you to be able to make beautiful mandolin music. Although a properly tuned mandolin makes one of the most beautiful sounds around, an out-of-tune mandolin is quite simply annoying.

When you tune your mandolin, you're adjusting the pitch of the strings to achieve three aims:

✔ All the strings are in tune with each other. For example, if you play an open or unfretted D note on the d-string it sounds the same as a D played on the g-string.

✔ The unison strings are tuned together. (Mandolins have eight strings played as if they were four: two g-strings, two d-strings, two a-strings and two e-strings.) If, say, one of your d-strings is slightly higher or lower than the other d-string, you get an out-of-tune or sour sound.

✔ The mandolin as a whole is in tune with other instruments.

To tune the strings of a mandolin, you simply turn the button or key that is attached to the tuning peg located on the headstock of the mandolin (see Chapter 1 for the lowdown on mandolin anatomy). Mandolins have eight tuning pegs – one for each string – and by turning the button one way the string gets tighter, making the pitch higher. By turning the button the other way the string gets looser, making it lower in pitch.

Be sure you turn the button that is attached to the string you're trying to tune.

When you're tuning, the terms *sharp* and *flat*, which I define in the earlier section 'Sharpening up and flatting down your notes', refer to small adjustments that you need to make to get the string in tune. For example, 'your d is still a bit flat' means that your d-string is a bit lower than it should be and you need to tune it a smidgen higher.

Sounding Tuneful: Methods for Tuning your Mandolin

You can tune your mandolin in a number of different ways, depending on what equipment you have available. If you're playing alone, you only need to be in tune with yourself, but when you play with other musicians, you all need to be in tune with each other.

In this section, I go over a few common ways of tuning your mandolin. Getting the mandolin in tune can be tricky, but modern digital technology has made the job much easier and more reliable than in years gone by.

Here's a piece of reassuring mandolin wisdom from master player Jethro Burns: 'I spend half of my time tuning this mandolin and the other half playing out of tune.' If a great player like Jethro feels this way, you don't need to worry when you do too!

Using an electronic tuner

If you ever have a chance to play with a group, and the other players are all tuning up simultaneously, you soon discover that tuning by ear (for example, as I describe in the later section 'Tuning your mandolin to itself') in such cases can be very difficult.

For this type of situation, most seasoned players tune their mandolins with a small clip-on electronic digital tuner. These little wonders may have been partly responsible for the recent popularity of the mandolin because, for the first time in history, tuning a mandolin is relatively easy. You can buy these tuners for under £20 (in the UK) or from $15 to $30 (in the US) from just about any music shop or online musical instrument seller. Tuners are available in a variety of price ranges depending on options, quality and accuracy. Some tuners feature a display that lights up, others don't; some are smaller and lightweight, whereas others are bulkier, and so on.

Look for a *chromatic tuner* which reads any note, so that you can use it to tune most instruments. Chromatic tuners have the bonus feature of not only reading the notes you require to tune your mandolin but of being able to read any note you play on it, so they can be useful for finding out where the various notes are located on the fingerboard.

Electronic tuners, which attach to the headstock (see Chapter 1), measure vibrations caused by string movement when you pluck a string. These vibrations transfer from the string through the bridge to the body, and all the way along the neck to the headstock of the mandolin, where the tuner converts them into musical notes.

Tuners vary, but they all work in basically the same way. Here's how to use one:

1. **Clip the tuner onto the mandolin headstock.**

   Ensure that the display is right side up, and position it so that you can see the display clearly (see Figure 2-2).

2. **Turn on the tuner and pluck your g-string, remembering to pluck only one of the unison strings at a time.**

   You want the tuner to read each individual string, not pairs. Make sure the display is indicating G as the note (not F♯ or G♯) and adjust the string until the arrow or LED display is centred. Some displays also use colour to indicate the note being sharp (♯), flat (♭) or in tune.

Figure 2-2:
Electronic
clip-on
tuner.

Tuning your mandolin to itself

Tuning the mandolin to itself is known as *relative* tuning, a technique useful on mandolins and other stringed instruments but not advised for improving the sound of your relatives! (Certain mothers-in-law can make a miserable squawking noise that sounds like a cat being stepped on, but unfortunately none of the tuning techniques in this chapter are effective in this case.)

You tune your mandolin to itself by matching a fretted note on one string to an open note of the next string. Here's how to do it (see Figure 2-3):

1. **Start by making sure both of your g-strings (fourth pair) are tuned together in unison by plucking them both at the same time. While the note is ringing, adjust one of the g-string tuner buttons until both strings sound alike.**

2. **Pluck the g- (the fourth pair of) strings at the seventh fret to produce a D note.** Check out Chapter 6 for more on how to fret strings.

3. **Play the top string of the open d- (third pair of) strings, which is also a D note, and compare the two sounds.** When you're in tune, these notes sound the same. If the d-string is too low, tune it up a little (or if it's too high, tune down), and then try again. Repeat the process until both strings sound the same. When the top d-string matches the g-string at the seventh fret, move to the bottom d-string and do the same.

Always tune one string of each pair at a time. Pick down on the top string of a pair first, letting your pick or *plectrum* rest on the bottom string so that string doesn't vibrate and interfere with you tuning the top string. For tuning the bottom string, do the same in reverse: pick upwards through the string, with your plectrum then resting on the top string to keep it from vibrating. When you've tuned each string individually, try playing them in unison, as you may need to make micro-adjustments for the pair to ring in unison.

4. **Repeat for the other strings. Pluck the d- (third pair of) strings at the seventh fret to produce an A, which needs to match the a- (second) string open.** Adjust that string until it's in tune.

5. **Play the a- (second pair of) strings at the seventh fret and tune the open e- (first pair of) strings to that note (an E).**

Figure 2-3:
Relative tuning using the seventh fret.

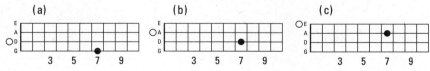

Another way to double-check your relative tuning is to use the octaves. *Octave* is a word used to describe the distance or interval between a low g-note (or any note) and a higher g-note (or any note of the same name). These octaves sound very much like each other, and you can use them for tuning. For example, the fifth fret of the d-string is a G note, and so you can still use this g-note from the d-string to tune the open g-string (see Figure 2-4).

Figure 2-4:
Relative
tuning using
the octave
and the fifth
fret.

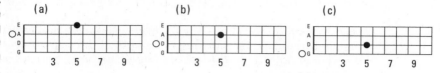

Tuning to another instrument

When playing with other musicians, you need to be in tune with each other. Because only professionals can tune instruments such as piano or accordion (and not very often), the rest of the musical world needs to adapt to these instruments by tuning to them. Figure 2-5 indicates where the open strings of a mandolin are located on a piano.

Track 1 contains the sound of a mandolin's four open strings, which you can use for tuning.

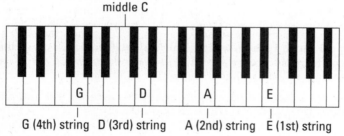

Figure 2-5:
Tuning open
mandolin
strings to a
piano.

Chapter 3

Getting a Handle on Your Mandolin

*I*f you're thinking to yourself, 'Come on, Don, I know how to hold a mandolin!', please hold onto your horses instead for just a moment. Whenever you're learning to play any musical instrument, getting the fundamentals sorted out straightaway is going to save you a lot of heartache and effort, because you don't have to waste time later unlearning what you learnt wrongly in the first place.

The fact is that how you place your fingers, hands, arms and body can all affect how easy or difficult you find playing your mandolin; even very small changes can alter the sound you produce.

So in this chapter, I show you how to hold your mandolin, and more precisely I demonstrate the modern American style of holding the instrument. This technique works well for carved-back and flat-back mandolins of both A and F body styles (check out Chapter 15 for details on the different types of mandolins), and is appropriate for playing old-time, Irish, bluegrass, swing and most styles of music performed on the mandolin. Classical mandolin players who play bowl-back mandolins use a different technique that involves sitting with one leg crossed over the other.

Sitting Down on the Job

Sitting down is the most popular position for playing the mandolin. A straight-backed chair without arms is perfect.

The best position is to sit upright and not lean back in your chair. And I suggest using a strap even when you're sitting down, because the strap helps to support the mandolin as you play. I use a long strap (in part due to my big belly!) which allows the mandolin to rest in my lap when I sit.

The worst possible position for playing while sitting would be to slouch back in your chair with your mandolin resting on your belly, with your left hand clutching the neck as if it were a hammer or a shovel.

The guidelines I offer here are commonly used with good results by most people, but how people sit when playing the mandolin varies based on individuals' body shapes and mandolin shapes. The key thing is to find something that is comfortable for you, but do try these steps for size:

1. **While leaning forward just a bit, place your mandolin in your lap, and rest it on your thighs.**

   Many mandolin players lean forward a bit, hunching slightly over the mandolin (see Figure 3-1).

2. **Position your mandolin so that the neck is angled slightly upward.**

   If you're playing an F5-style mandolin, the lower point should sit comfortably on your left thigh. Some players use a foot stool (similar to those that classical guitar players use) to elevate the left leg a bit here. By elevating the left leg, you achieve the desired neck angle due to the fact that the lower body point of the mandolin is resting on the left leg. (However, F5 mandolins are the only body style that have this lower body point.) The edge where the back and rim meet will be touching your mid-section somewhere around your ribcage.

3. **Try to position the mandolin so that the instrument is not muted or muffled by the back being pressed against your clothing.**

   Your right arm should be touching where the rim meets the top about 3–4 inches (7–10 centimetres) above the tailpiece (see Figure 3-1). Your right forearm actually helps support the mandolin and prevents it from swinging around.

4. **Position your right hand so that your pick is about 1 inch (2½ centimetres) from the end of the fingerboard (see Figure 3-1).**

   You should now have four points of contact, not counting your left hand): left thigh, right thigh, ribcage and underside of right forearm.

5. **Place your left hand on the neck with your fingertips pointing straight down at the fingerboard.**

6. **Support the back of the neck with your thumb (not the palm of your hand) and try to keep your left wrist straight. You may have to push the mandolin neck out away from your body until you can straighten out your wrist.**

If you play a bowl-back mandolin, the technique for sitting as you play is a bit different. For starters, you don't use a strap with bowl-back mandolins. There's nowhere to attach a strap on a bowl-back mandolin, even if you really wanted to! Instead, set the body of the bowl-back mandolin on your right leg, which you may need to elevate to prevent the mandolin from slipping around. You can do this simply by crossing your right leg over your left or by using a foot stool to slightly elevate your right leg. Another useful device that keeps the mandolin from sliding around against your clothing and out of your lap is a napkin-sized chamois or any non-slip type of material placed on your leg beneath your mandolin. You can then use the same right- and left-arm positioning tips as I give in the preceding steps.

You can find more information about proper left- and right-hand specifics in Chapters 5 and 6. If you're a left-handed mandolin player, just reverse my directions, making left into right and right into left. Simple!

Figure 3-1:
Playing the
mandolin
while sitting.

Your left wrist needs to remain stress-free and straight in order to have the strength and reach to fret notes correctly with the fingers of your left hand. You may need to push the neck of the mandolin slightly away from your body until your wrist is relaxed and straight. Figure 3-2(a) shows a relaxed and straight wrist; try to avoid your wrist resembling the one in Figure 3-2(b).

Figure 3-2:
The left arm:
(a) correct
wrist posi-
tion; (b) poor
wrist
position.

Playing While Standing Up

Although most mandolin players sit down to play (as I describe in the preceding section), sometimes you may find yourself wanting to play the mandolin while standing, just like bluegrass musicians do. This convention developed because bluegrass music is concert music, originally performed around one microphone, in which singers or soloists step up to the microphone when their turn comes to be featured. Also, many car park jam sessions are held standing.

You need a strap in order to play standing up. Start by standing up straight and placing the strap over your left shoulder, as I describe in the following section. With the neck at a slightly upward angle, position your right hand by bringing your right forearm to rest were the rim meets the body just above the tailpiece and place your right hand so that the pick is about an inch from the end of the fingerboard (see Figure 3-3).

Figure 3-3:
The standing-up position for playing the mandolin.

As with playing when sitting, place your left hand on the neck with your fingertips pointed straight down at the fingerboard. Support the back of the neck with your thumb (not the palm of your hand) and try to keep your left wrist straight. This may involve pushing the mandolin neck out away from your body until you can straighten out your wrist.

When standing, the mandolin tends to get muffled because you're holding the back against your clothes. One solution for this problem is a device called a *toneguard*, which holds the mandolin away from your clothes and enables the mandolin back to resonate fully.

Strapping Yourself in to Play

I suggest using a strap, whether you plan to sit or stand while playing your mandolin. Feel free to buy whatever type of strap you like, but my favourite is a rawhide boot lace.

Manufacturers make mandolin straps specifically for F-model mandolins that have a loop sewn into one end that easily goes over the scroll. This type of strap will not work on an A-model mandolin, because the mandolin has no scroll, so remember to specify which type of mandolin you're putting your strap onto to make sure you get the correct style.

Here are the two common ways of using a mandolin strap (see Figure 3-4):

- ✔ **Method one,** the one I recommend, involves running the mandolin strap over your head and around your back in the same way that many guitar players use a strap. The strap runs from the mandolin headstock, over your left shoulder, around your back and meets the mandolin at roughly the bottom of the right side of your ribcage.

- ✔ **Method two** was made famous by the father of bluegrass, Bill Monroe. Bill used a short strap that went only over his right shoulder. Many bluegrass mandolin players use this approach.

There's more than one way to wear a strap!

Most mandolin players buy a mandolin strap from a music shop or a specialist online dealer when they've decided on the colour, style (A model or F model), material and length they like. However, three of the greatest mandolin players the world has ever seen (who I look at in Chapter 20) took their own very individual approaches when they came to strap on their mandolins. David Grisman uses a strap very similar in design to a saxophone neck strap that hangs around his neck and attaches to the mandolin at the scroll. Bill Monroe used a rawhide strip that looked a lot like a leather boot lace. (I'm not sure if it was really a boot lace but it certainly looked like it could have been one.) And Dave Apollon played a Gibson F5 mandolin standing up but without a strap at all!

Figure 3-4: Wearing the mandolin strap: (a) traditional method; (b) Bill Monroe's strap position.

The mandolin strap attaches to your mandolin at the strap button located at the endpin of the mandolin (I run through the different mandolin parts in Chapter 1). You can attach the other end in a variety of ways depending on your preference or the style of mandolin. In the following list, I describe three common ways of attaching the strap to the neck side of the mandolin (see Figure 3-5):

- ✔ **Tie the strap to the headstock.** Run the strap or a small piece of leather shoelace attached to the strap around the headstock. Most people thread the strap under the strings just past the nut.

- ✔ **Loop the strap around the scroll.** If you have an F5-style mandolin, you can loop the strap around the scroll. Some straps are made specifically for this method; they have a loop included in their design.

- ✔ **Using a strap button at the heel of the neck.** Many players feel that the mandolin balances better if you attach the strap to the heel of the neck. In most cases, you need to have a strap button installed in order to attach a strap in this way.

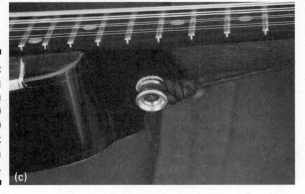

Figure 3-5:
Attaching
a mandolin
strap: (a)
tying; (b)
looping;
(c) using a
strap button.

Part II
Starting to Play the Mandolin

The 5th Wave   By Rich Tennant

ROBBY MAKES HIS FIRST SOUND ON A MANDOLIN

©RICHTENNANT

MUSIC STORE
MANDOLIN SALE

MUSIC STORE
OPEN

In this part . . .

You discover the basic building blocks of music, including counting and naming the notes, strumming a few chords and playing your first few easy tunes on the mandolin. I also take a comprehensive look at left- and right-hand techniques when playing mandolin, including a way of making chords that opens up a whole new world. You also pull all your newly acquired skills together to make mandolin music.

Chapter 4

Making Music on the Mandolin

*I*n this chapter, I introduce you to the necessary basics that allow you to make your mandolin sing. I show you how to read tablature, understand chord diagrams, and play by ear so that you can get playing quickly without knowing how to read music. Also, I cover rhythm and counting, strumming patterns, a few simple chord progressions and a brief overview of the working parts of a song. I also talk you through your first few simple melodies, and bring everything together so that you can start playing some tunes!

Playing Without Having to Read Music

You can discover how to play music in a variety of ways. Most folk, blues, bluegrass, rock and country musicians play by ear (see the 'Developing a musical ear' section later in this chapter) and don't read standard musical notation – you don't see high-energy blues bands or bluegrass groups reading music on stage. Instead, these musicians learn by ear, or some even use tablature (which I explain in the later section 'Understanding tablature' and Figure 4-1), and many professional musicians get all they need to know about a song from a chord progression (check out the later section 'Moving on to chord progressions' and Figure 4-23).

Throughout this book, I present concepts and songs in both standard notation and tablature, along with chord symbols and suggested strumming patterns.

Listen to all the audio tracks, because knowing what you want to sound like is important. As an old saying goes: 'If you can't say it, you can't play it.'

Understanding tablature

Tablature (or tab) is a way of communicating musical ideas by showing you where to put your hands and fingers instead of assigning each note a musical name (see Figure 4-1 below for a tab example). Tab is a popular way of learning to play the string instruments used in folk and rock genres.

Here's how tablature works:

✔ Four horizontal lines represent the four strings, with the thickest string (g) being the lowest.

✔ Numbers on the lines indicate the frets (not your fingers).

✔ Standard notation stems (check out the later Figure 4-4 to see these) attached to the tablature note heads indicate the rhythm.

Even though mandolins have eight strings, they're set up in such a way that really you have four pairs of strings, with each pair being tuned in *unison* or to the same note. As a result, I talk about each pair of strings as if they're one.

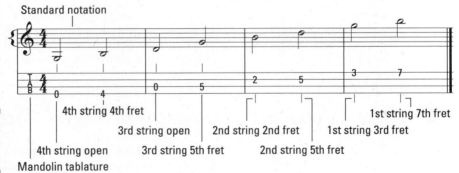

Figure 4-1:
Tablature
example.

Reading chord diagrams

As I describe in Chapter 2, *chords* are groups of notes that you play simultaneously. They function as the song's background, against which you sing or play the melody. Almost every song has a set of chords played in sequence.

Chord diagrams (or chord boxes) are illustrations of the instrument's fingerboard, showing you where to put your fingers to form chords. Take a look at Figures 4-2 and 4-3 to see how the mandolin fretboard is represented.

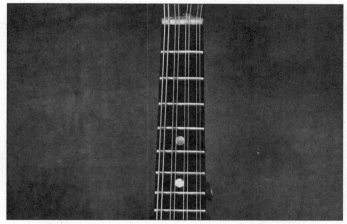

Figure 4-2:
First five
frets.

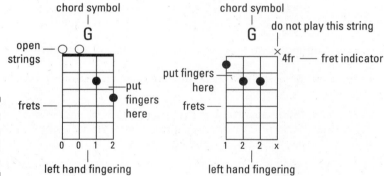

Figure 4-3:
Sample
chord
diagram.

Here are the parts of a chord diagram (for the different parts of the mandolin, such as the nut and frets, check out Chapter 1):

✔ The vertical lines represent the strings of the mandolin, with the g-string (thickest) being on the left and the e-string (thinnest) being on the far right.

✔ The thick horizontal line at the top represents the nut of the mandolin.

✔ Thin horizontal lines represent the frets.

✔ The dots show you where to place your fingers.

✔ The Os at the top of a string indicate to play that string open.

✔ The Xs at the top of a string indicate not to play that string.

✔ A small number to the side of the illustration indicates the fret, telling you how far up the neck to play the chord.

Developing a musical ear

All the best musicians have the ability to hear a piece of music once or twice and identify elements of rhythm chords and melody in the music that they've just heard. Very few people, if any, are born with this skill, and developing your ear is an essential skill that all musicians need to work at. At first, hearing subtle changes in rhythm or pitch is very difficult, but don't give up; developing the skill takes time. Ear-training courses are available on CDs or via online courses, but most musicians learn to play by ear simply by spending a lot of time trying to imitate what they hear on recordings.

Slowing recordings down is a time-honoured tradition that yields very good results. The Amazing Slow Downer is available for purchase for around $50 from www.ronimusic.com and is a popular computer program that works quite well.

Basic ear-training is often broken down into three categories:

✔ **Interval:** Being able to hear the distance (up or down) from one note to the next.

✔ **Rhythm:** Being able to hear rhythm patterns or sequences (see the later sections 'Strumming chords: Getting some rhythm patterns together' and 'Finding the beat: Rhythm' for more.

✔ **Chords:** Being able to hear a chord progression (see the later section 'Moving on to chord progressions' for more).

Keeping the Musical Beat by Counting

Counting is one of the most important elements of music, and the toughest to pick up for the beginner musician. In general, music is usually counted in repeating patterns. The rhythm for playing a piece of music is called the *time signature*, and for western music the most common rhythm is *4/4 time* (also called, appropriately enough, *common time*), which contains four strong beats in a repeating pattern (check out the later section 'Counting to four').

In this section, I discuss counting the beats in various ways.

As you pick up more about counting in the following section, try to identify the beat in all the music you hear throughout the day, whether it's from your car radio, 'I'm placing you on hold' telephone music or your iPod.

Feeling the beat

Feeling the rhythm and moving some part or parts of your body in sync with a steady beat is a skill that develops over time as you practise it. On a very basic level, most people can clap along with a large group of concert goers when the singer leads by clapping and the drummer pounds out a steady beat on the drums. Many people move their entire body to the beat by dancing, more shy types prefer to tap their feet to the beat, while the intellectual beatnik jazzers snap their fingers.

Developing to a very high level this skill of feeling the beat is vital to playing music. An easy way to practise is to put on some recorded music and tap your foot or your fingers to the music.

Counting to four

Try counting four beats out loud while keeping the count as steady as possible: '1, 2, 3, 4, 1, 2, 3, 4, 1, 2, 3, 4, 1, 2, 3, 4'. Listen to Track 1, which contains an example.

While tapping your foot to recorded music, try to count '1, 2, 3, 4, 1, 2, 3, 4' and so on. At first this may seem difficult, but it gets easier with practice. If you have difficulty moving your feet and your mouth at the same time, just do one at a time. Don't give up; you can do this!

Dividing up beats

When you can hear and count four beats confidently as I describe in the preceding section, start sub-dividing the beats.

Splitting four large beats into eight small beats

To create shorter beats, cut each strong beat in half, changing '1, 2, 3, 4, 1, 2, 3, 4' into '1 and 2 and 3 and 4 and 1 and 2 and 3 and 4 and'. Keep in mind that the speed of the beat hasn't increased or decreased; you're just saying 'and' between each number (see Figure 4-4 and listen to Track 2 for an example).

US and UK musical terms

I use US terms to indicate note length throughout this book, with the UK term afterwards. As I explain in the Introduction, each US term seems clearer, more logical and easier to understand. In the following table, I list the terms side by side:

US term	UK term
Whole note	Semibreve (pronounced 'semi-breeve')
Half note	Minim
Quarter note	Crotchet (pronounced 'crotch-it')
Eighth note	Quaver
Sixteenth note	Semiquaver

one   two   three   four   one   two   three   four

Figure 4-4:
Eighth notes
(quavers).

one and two and three and four and   one and two and three and four and

The technical names for notes on the strong beat that last until the next strong beat (that is, '1, 2, 3, 4') are *quarter* notes, and the quicker notes followed by 'ands' (that is, '1 and 2 and 3 and 4 and') are *eighth* notes. (These are *crotchets* and *quavers* in British musical parlance; see the nearby sidebar 'US and UK musical terms' for more explanation.)

Splitting four large beats into 16 smaller beats

In this sub-division, divide each strong beat in four equal parts, called *sixteenth* notes in the US and *semiquavers* in the UK. Thus, '1, 2, 3, 4' becomes '1 e and a 2 e and a 3 e and a 4 e' and so on. The speed of the beat doesn't increase or decrease, you just say '1 e and a' (pronounced one eeh and ah) in the same space that you were using to just say '1'.

Take a look at Figure 4-5 and listen to Track 3 for a demonstration of sixteenth note (semiquaver) rhythm notation.

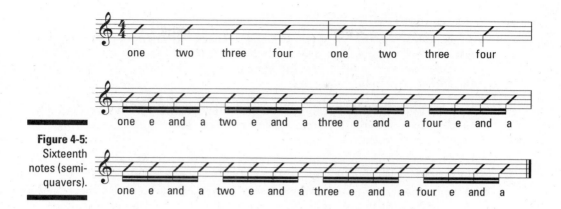

Figure 4-5:
Sixteenth
notes (semi-
quavers).

Extending notes: Half notes and whole notes

Half notes (*minims*) last twice as long as quarter notes (*crotchets*) and are shown as a stem with a hollow note head (see the first two bars of Figure 4-6). (*Bars* are musical slang for measures – a *measure* is the distance between the vertical lines of the musical staff or tab. A measure also is determined by the time signature. For example, in 4/4 time, four quarter notes equal one measure or bar.) Half notes last for two full beats each. In this example, you'd play on beats 1 and 3.

Whole notes (*semibreves*) are worth four beats, or are twice as long as a half note, filling up an entire measure. Whole notes are indicated by a hollow note head without a stem (see measures 3 and 4 of Figure 4-6). Listen to Track 4 Part 1 for a demonstration.

Figure 4-6:
Whole
notes (semi-
breves) and
half notes
(minims).

Dotting and tying notes

Dots and ties in notation or tablature perform essentially the same job. They make the notes longer, but in slightly different ways.

Dotted notes

A dot after a note, tab or rhythm slash increases the length of the note by one half. For example, a dot after a half note (minim) increases the length by a quarter note (crotchet), resulting in a note with the duration of three quarter notes (crotchets).

In measure 1 of Figure 4-7, the dots appear next to quarter notes (crotchets), making the length equal to one quarter note and one eighth note, or three eighth notes (quavers).

Tied notes

When notes are tied, you add their length together. The sign to indicate ties is an arch between the notes. In measure 2 of Figure 4-7, the quarter notes (crotchets) tied to eighth notes (quavers) equal a sum of three eighth notes (quavers).

Figure 4-7:
Dots and
ties.

Compare measure 1 and measure 2 in Figure 4-7 to see how dots and ties are used to accomplish the same sound. Listen to Track 4 Part 2 to hear how they sound identical even though they're written differently. Just as, in simple arithmetic, two plus one equals three, or one plus two equals three, a dotted quarter note (a crotchet), a quarter note tied to an eighth (a crotchet tied to a quaver) or an eighth tied to a quarter (a quaver tied to a crotchet) are all the same length of three eighth notes (quavers).

Resting: Playing the silence

The combination of notes and rests results in what people lovingly refer to as melody. Rests come in all the standard lengths (whole notes, half notes, quarter notes and so on), as shown in Figure 4-8, and are counted just like standard notes. Standard notation and tab in *Mandolin For Dummies* use a set of musical signs called *rests* to indicate silence. When you see a rest, make sure you stop any notes that are ringing, by taking pressure off the string or by gently resting your finger on the string, known as *muting* (see Chapter 6 for more on muting strings).

Figure 4-8:
Rest
notation.

Repeating sections of a song

Many songs have sections that repeat. A thick double bar line with two dots to the left is telling you to repeat a section. When you see this repeat sign, go back to the beginning of the piece or to the thick double bar line with two dots to the right. Figure 4-9 shows repeat signs (also see Appendix B on reading standard notation).

Listen to Track 5 as you read Figure 4-9 for a demonstration of how repeat signs work. In example 1, you play the first two bars, repeat back to the beginning, play the first two bars again and continue on. In example 2, you start at bar 1 and play to bar 3. At the repeat sign, you go back to measure 2, play measures 2 and 3 and continue on.

(a)

(b)

Figure 4-9:
Repeat
signs.

Here's a short exercise using many of the elements I discuss in this section. Watch out for rests, dots, ties and repeat signs. Play along with Figure 4-10 and Track 6, making sure to mute the ringing string right where the rest starts.

Figure 4-10: Playing the rests.

Simplifying time signatures

The time signature of a piece of music gives you a good idea about the basic pulse or beat of a tune. It doesn't, however, provide any indication of *tempo* (speed).

When written, a time signature looks a bit like a fraction. Common time is written as 4/4 and pronounced as 'four four' time. This fraction or time signature is telling you to expect to feel four strong beats in a repeating pattern and to consider each strong beat as one quarter note (quaver).

Another common time signature is 3/4, often referred to as waltz time. In waltz time, you have a repeating pattern of three strong beats, where each strong beat is considered to be a quarter note (a quaver).

Figure 4-11 and Track 7 contain eight separate counting exercises. Practise each line a few times in succession, saying it out loud as you do so.

Introducing Your First Five Chords

A good way to start playing music is to get to know a few common chords. After you have down the five chords that I describe in this section – G, C, D, A and E – you can strum along with hundreds of songs. Even though the mandolin is a beautiful melody instrument, it can also be very useful playing rhythm. Strumming along to recorded music gives you a wealth of musical knowledge regarding how songs are put together and the importance of good rhythm.

When you strum a chord, listen carefully and ask yourself: how does it sound; can you hear all the strings; do they create a pleasing harmony and sound right together? Try playing each string independently to hear how clear each note is. If the note doesn't ring out clearly or you hear a buzzing sound, check that you're pressing down hard enough with your fingertips until the notes sound good. You don't want to press down with a 'death grip', but just hard enough to play the notes cleanly without buzzing. Doing this may hurt a bit at first, but you won't take long to build up callouses on your fingertips.

To help you with fingering chords, I call the fretting hand the left hand, which is the case for right-handed players (who strum with their right hands). If you're a left-handed player, you fret notes with your right hand and strum with your left.

Getting to grips with the G chord

In this section, I show you how to produce a two-finger open G chord. *Open* refers to the fact that some of the strings are left open or unfretted (check out Figures 4-12 and 4-13):

1. **Put the index finger of your left hand on the second fret of the second string.**

2. **Put the second finger of your left hand on the third fret of the first string.**

3. **Strum all four pairs of strings with your right hand.**

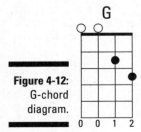

Figure 4-12: G-chord diagram.

Figure 4-13:
G-chord
photo.

Choosing the C chord

Here, I demonstrate the steps for making a two-finger, open C chord (as Figures 4-14 and 4-15 display):

1. **Put the index finger of your left hand on the second fret of the third string.**

2. **Put the second finger of your left hand on the third fret of the second string.**

3. **Strum all four pairs of strings with your right hand.**

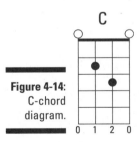

Figure 4-14:
C-chord
diagram.

Figure 4-15:
C-chord
photo.

Discovering the D chord

You finger an open D chord on the mandolin as follows (check out Figures 4-16 and 4-17):

1. **Put the index finger of your left hand on the second fret of the fourth string.**

2. **Put the second finger of your left hand on the second fret of the first string.**

3. **Strum all four pairs of strings with your right hand.**

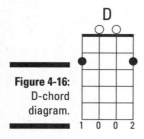

Figure 4-16:
D-chord
diagram.

Figure 4-17:
D-chord
photo.

Adding the A chord

In this section, I show you the open A chord (see Figures 4-18 and 4-19). This chord can be a bit tricky because you need to hold down two strings at the same fret, but don't worry. You do so by using one finger if your fingertip is wide enough or two fingers if you have thinner fingers.

Consider this fingering as an all-purpose A chord, in that it works for A major as well as A minor. I tell you more about these types of chords in Chapter 6.

To make the A chord:

1. **Put the index finger of your left hand on the second fret of the third and fourth strings.** If your index finger can't hold down both strings, go ahead and use two fingers.

2. **Strum all four pairs of strings with your right hand.**

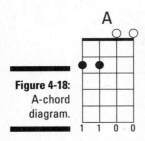

Figure 4-18:
A-chord
diagram.

Figure 4-19:
A-chord
photo.

Examining the E chord

Here's how to produce an open E chord (check out Figures 4-20 and 4-21). As with the A chord in the preceding section, you need to hold down two strings at the same fret: this time, the middle two strings. Again, as with the A chord, this E fingering is also an all-purpose chord suitable for both E major and E minor. (Chapter 6 has more on major and minor chords.)

If your index finger isn't wide enough, use two fingers to fret the chord.

To make the E chord:

1. **Put the index finger of your left hand on the second fret of the second and third strings.**

2. **Put the second finger of your left hand on the fourth fret of the fourth string.**

3. **Strum all four pairs of strings with your right hand.**

E

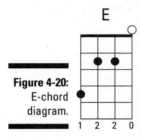

Figure 4-20:
E-chord
diagram.

1 2 2 0

Figure 4-21:
E-chord
photo.

Strumming chords: Getting some rhythm patterns together

When you combine chords with a few strumming patterns, you have the musical foundation for playing many great songs. Thousands of different strumming patterns (sometimes called rhythm patterns) are available. Musical styles have their own rhythmic characteristics that determine which strumming pattern is most appropriate.

Strumming patterns follow rhythmic notation. Rhythmic notation is written on the musical staff, but doesn't show the individual notes the way that standard musical notation does. Instead, the addition of slashes represents strumming or counting, and symbols indicate whether to strum upwards or down.

Take a look at Figure 4-22 for a few simple strumming patterns and listen to the demonstrations on Track 8. Be sure to follow the pick direction (up and down) markings.

Notice in Figure 4-22 that the up strokes land on the 'and' part of the beat. This technique is very important and also holds true for picking individual notes. I cover picking in detail in Chapter 5.

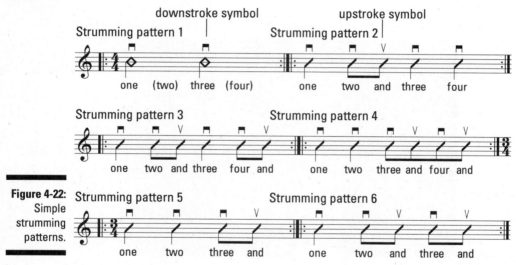

Figure 4-22:
Simple
strumming
patterns.

Breaking Down the Parts of a Song

In this section, I identify a few basic elements of a song, including taking a look at the beat or rhythm and the chord progression. You can then combine these two elements to create some strumming patterns (as I describe in the preceding section). Of course, I also examine everyone's favourite song part: the melody.

Finding the beat: Rhythm

In the beginning was rhythm. And it was good. As time passed, melody and *counterpoint* (a second melody that complements the main melody) were added to rhythm to make music, which all starts with a beat or a sequence of beats.

Try to identify the basic timing of a piece of music (check out the earlier section 'Keeping the Musical Beat by Counting' for an introduction to this skill). Count 1, 2, 1, 2 or 1, 2, 3, 1, 2, 3 or 1, 2, 3, 4, 1, 2, 3, 4 to determine the beat pattern or time signature of the music (which I define in the earlier section 'Simplifying time signatures'). Most popular music can be counted in sets of 2s, 3s or 4s.

Moving on to chord progressions

A *chord progression* is a series of chords, played in a specific order with measured amounts of time for each chord (see Figure 4-23 for some examples). Each song has its own chord progression, but many songs share common ones. Chord progressions can be played by a single mandolin or a complete rhythm section.

Memorising a few chord progressions to songs is a great way to get up and play your mandolin quickly.

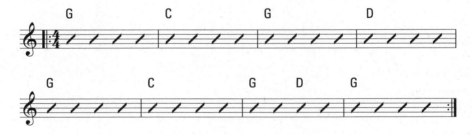

Figure 4-23: Two sample chord progressions.

Strumming the chords

Strumming is the act of lightly brushing all the strings with a pick held in your right hand, while holding the chords down with your left hand. A strumming pattern is a sequence of up and down strums played in repetition (loads of common strumming patterns exist), and your right hand is the time-keeper. You therefore need to keep it moving in time with the beat. The part that requires coordination is keeping the strumming pattern steady with the right hand, while changing chords with the left hand. This action is a bit like rubbing your tummy and patting your head at the same time, but louder!

Check out Figure 4-24 and Track 9 for a few strumming patterns applied to chord progressions.

Figure 4-24: Strumming patterns with chords.

Performing the melody

The melody of a song is the part the vocalist normally sings. In instrumental music, often one instrument is responsible for the melody while the other instruments take responsibility for supplying a solid rhythm, which can include strumming a rhythm while following a chord progression.

Sections of a song

Simple songs contain one section that's repeated many times with different lyrics each time (the *verse*). Many forms of music contain two or more sections of a song, perhaps including the verse, chorus, *bridge* (a third part used to connect one part to another; the Beatles called this the *middle eight*), intro and ending. In traditional fiddle tunes, these sections are called the A part and B part. In Chapters 9–14, I look at songs with more than one part.

You can pick up melody by ear (see the earlier section 'Developing a musical ear') or from reading music (I present the music in this book in standard musical notation and tablature with lyrics when applicable). I also demonstrate all melodies instrumentally on the audio tracks.

Figure 4-25 demonstrates the presentation of melodies with lyrics in this book.

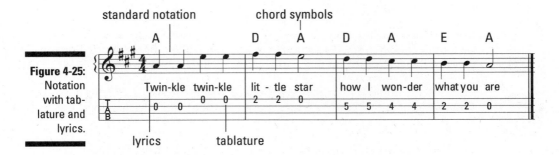

Figure 4-25: Notation with tablature and lyrics.

Playing along with other people

Playing with others is one of the most valuable experiences you can have as a budding musician. You simply can't achieve the same magic that happens when making music with other people while playing solo or with play-along tracks. Playing with other musicians requires you to use many of the skills that I discuss in this section, including finding the beat, following a chord progression while maintaining a solid strumming pattern, and playing the melody.

Listening becomes very important when playing music with other people. You need to listen to the timing to make sure that you're playing in sync. You also need to start thinking about volume. Are you playing so loudly when strumming that you're covering up the melody? Do yourself a favour and find some other people to come along on this musical adventure with you.

If you're struggling to stay in time with other musicians, the metronome or a play-along audio track, remember the golden rule and divide your attention as follows: listen 70 per cent and play 30 per cent.

Playing Your First Songs

In this section, I help you pull together your new skills from the preceding sections and start making music. These first few songs are likely to be familiar to you; you may even have sung some of them as a young child.

The object of these songs is to get you playing simple melodies. After you learn the melodies, be sure to play the suggested strumming patterns while following the chords.

In a real musical situation (in a band), you need to be able to play not only melody, but also to supply a good solid rhythm while others play or sing the melody. Suggested strumming patterns are included in Figure 4-22.

Listen to the audio tracks before you try to play these songs. Playing something without knowing what it's supposed to sound like is very difficult. Listen first!

The five songs in this section are included in the audio tracks with the melody part in the right speaker and the suggested strumming pattern in the left speaker. Instead of relying on a guitar player or software to be the backing track, I have recorded a rhythm mandolin track for each song. I suggest you learn to play rhythm on the songs so you can play the melody and the rhythm. The melodies are played first with a metronome and then with the strumming accompaniment.

'Ode To Joy' theme

This well-known simple theme comes from Beethoven's Ninth Symphony. Pay attention to the pick direction in the third line of this piece. Use strumming pattern 1 from Figure 4-22.

The 'Ode To Joy' theme is on Track 10 (see also Figure 4-26).

Figure 4-26:
'Ode to Joy'
theme.

'Down in the Valley'

'Down in the Valley' is a traditional American folk song that most people have heard many times. This song is in 3/4 time (which I describe earlier in the

'Simplifying time signatures' section), and so be sure to count it with a repeating series of three strong beats (see Figure 4-27 and Track 11). I suggest using all down strokes when playing the melody. Use strumming pattern 5 (see Figure 4-22) for the rhythm.

Figure 4-27: 'Down in the Valley'.

'Go Tell Aunt Rhodie'

Many people sang this song at a very young age (see Figure 4-28 and Track 12). I suggest using all down strokes when playing the melody, and strumming pattern 3 (see Figure 4-22) for the rhythm.

Go Tell Aunt Rhodie

'Skip to My Lou'

'Skip to My Lou' is sung by many people as young children. Follow the pick direction closely (see Figure 4-29 and Track 13). Strumming pattern 2 (see Figure 4-22) works nicely with this song.

Figure 4-28: 'Go Tell Aunt Rhodie'.

Skip to My Lou

Figure 4-29: 'Skip to My Lou'.

'Red River Valley'

'Red River Valley' (also known as 'Cowboy Love Song') is an old cowboy song dating back to the late 1800s. It starts with two *pickup* notes (notes that fall before the first 'one' of the first measure); the first two notes are on beats 3 and 4 (see Figure 4-30 and Track 14). Play this song using all down strokes when playing the melody and use strumming pattern 3 (see Figure 4-22) for the rhythm.

Figure 4-30: 'Red River Valley'.

Chapter 5

Picking with the Right Hand

• •

In This Chapter

▶ Picking up the pick

▶ Discovering up and down styles

▶ Sounding out with volume and tremolo

▶ Trying out some picking exercises

• •

The right hand is responsible for the majority of the heavy lifting involved in playing the mandolin. After all, this hand picks and strums the strings and so controls much of what makes your mandolin playing great (or not). When I first started playing, I didn't pay attention to pick grip, pick direction or many of the things I describe in this chapter. Only years later did I realise the vital importance of gaining a good right-hand technique. Don't make the same mistake!

To help you out, this chapter describes the proper right-hand technique, including holding the pick, up and down picking, developing good tone and using volume and note length effectively. I also include some right-hand exercises that help develop your strength, skills and dexterity even further.

Holding the Pick

Holding the pick may seem so simple that you're tempted to skip right over this section, but please don't!

Good pick grip is essential to getting great tone, volume and speed:

1. **With your thumb pointing up, make a loose fist with your right hand.**

2. **Place the pick on the side of your index finger near your top knuckle and fingernail (see Figure 5-1(a)).**

3. Place the pad of your thumb over the pick (see Figure 5-1(b)).

4. Hold the pick very loosely; allow it to move or wobble around a little bit (flick to the later section 'Keeping a loose grip' for more).

Figure 5-1:
Holding the
pick.

Supporting and Guiding Your Right Hand

Opinions vary among mandolin players about whether to touch the top of the mandolin with your right hand while picking melodies. Some people claim that anything touching the mandolin top restricts the sound, but most players do lightly touch the top in one way or another. I like to do so because touching the mandolin or lightly planting your right hand on it gives a guide or reference, which results in more accuracy when you're moving from one string to another.

Feel free to experiment. You can provide a guide for your right hand in a couple of ways, as the next two sections 'Touching the bridge' and 'Brushing the pinky' describe. If you have trouble picking accurately, read the information a few times before trying again.

Touching the bridge

Lightly touch the heel of your hand near or behind the bridge (check out Chapter 1 for a discussion of the different parts of the mandolin) and pivot at your wrist; many of today's top mandolin pros use this technique. The object is lightly to brush against the bridge or slightly behind it (see Figure 5-2).

Be careful not to mute the strings or apply very much pressure to the top.

Figure 5-2:
Touching
the bridge.

Brushing the pinky

Another way of achieving a guide for the right hand is lightly to brush the top of the instrument with the little finger (the pinky) of your right hand. Some mandolins have pick guards or finger rests installed, making this technique a bit easier.

Don't use your little finger as a straight, rigid post. Keep it loose and lightly brush against the top or pick guard (see Figure 5-3).

Resting on the rib

Most mandolin players touch the underside of their forearm against the mandolin for support where the top meets the rib (or side), 5–8 centimetres (around 2–3 inches) above the end pin (see Figure 5-4). Some players add an armrest for support as an accessory (see Chapter 16). An armrest attaches to the ribs of the instrument so as not to touch the top, which would possibly damp the sound. Armrests also function to protect the finish on the top of the instrument.

Figure 5-3:
Brushing
with your
little finger.

Figure 5-4:
Right arm
touching the
mandolin
rib.

Arching your wrist while strumming

The earlier two sections 'Touching the bridge' and 'Brushing the pinky' describe picking positions, but when strumming you *don't* want to support your right wrist or brush your little finger. Arching the wrist, using more forearm and supporting at the rib (with the underside of your forearm) gives you a wider stroke, which is better for strumming (I describe strumming in more detail in Chapter 4).

Imagine that you have a match burning between the finger and thumb of your right hand. As the flame gets closer, you start to feel the heat. Soon it's getting very hot, and you flick your wrist with such force that the flame is blown out. This movement is what your wrist needs to feel like when strumming or playing rhythm.

Picking Up and Down

Getting a handle on pick direction is one of the most important elements of playing mandolin. You can use a variety of pick patterns to achieve different rhythmic feels and tempos, such as alternate picking, down picking, jig picking, cross picking and tremolo picking. I discuss all these patterns in this section, except for tremolo, which I cover in its own later section 'Sustaining a Note: Tremolo'.

Whatever pattern you're using, the key to mandolin playing is having a strong, well-organised right hand.

Picking alternate strong and weak beats

In *alternate picking*, you play the down-beats (strong) with a down-stroke, and up-beats (weak) with an up-stroke (flip to Chapter 4 for all about beats and up- and down-strokes). This technique sounds fairly simple, but not all music starts right on the beat or consists of even up- and down-strokes.

Alternate picking isn't just down-up, down-up, alternating pick strokes. Don't make the mistake of thinking that the first note of a song is always down, and so the next note must be up, and so on.

Learning to count eighth notes (quavers) as I describe in Chapter 4 is a valuable skill when studying alternate picking. Just remember that numbered beats (or on beats) are down and 'ands' (or off beats) are up.

See Figure 5-5 and listen to Track 15 Part 1 for a simple exercise in alternate picking.

On the audio tracks for Figures 5-5 through to 5-12 I demonstrate each track slowly (at half speed) first, followed by an up-to-tempo version. Remember that the main purpose in developing a good alternate-picking technique is to be able to play fast when needed.

Figure 5-5:
Basic
alternate
picking.

Crossing strings (or moving from one string to another) while alternate picking can cause some trouble. Many melodies require moving from one string to another in order to play. To help you do this, play through Figure 5-6 – Track 15 Part 2 – a few times, making sure that you follow the proper picking direction.

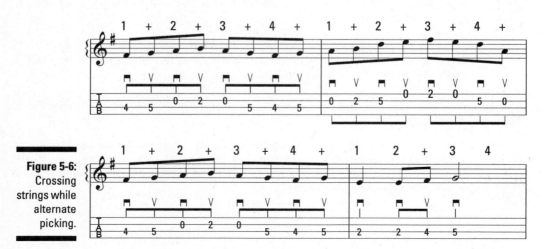

Figure 5-6:
Crossing
strings while
alternate
picking.

A syncopated (not even) phrase creates some challenges as well. *Syncopation* is a placement of rhythmic accents on off-beats, and is a major element in musical styles such as swing, ragtime and most forms of dance music. Check out Figure 5-7 and Track 15 Part 3 for an example of a syncopated phrase with alternate picking. Pay very close attention to pick direction.

Some phrases start on the off-beat or up-beat. When you tap your foot to the beat, the tap (foot hitting the floor) is the *down-beat*. The part of the beat where you pick your foot up is called the *up-beat* or the *off-beat*. In fact, your picking hand should be in sync with your foot if you're tapping your foot in time with the beat. In this case, you need to be able to start a phrase on an up-stroke. Figure 5-8 and Track 15 Part 4 show you how to play a phrase starting on the off-beat, using the proper alternate-picking technique.

Figure 5-7:
Alternate
picking a
syncopated
phrase.

Figure 5-8:
Alternate
picking an
off-beat
phrase.

Getting down with down-strokes

Down-strokes are by nature stronger than up-strokes and provide a full, rich tone with good volume. They work really well for melodies in which the notes aren't extremely fast. Blues, bluegrass, jazz and even classical mandolin players benefit from being able to play melodies using all down-strokes.

Figure 5-9 and Track 16 demonstrate the down-stroke technique.

Down-strokes also really shine in a shuffle rhythm, which I go into detail about in Chapter 9 on the blues. The shuffle rhythm requires being able to subdivide each strong beat into three beats (see the later section 'Keeping-time exercises').

Figure 5-9:
Down-
stroke
technique.

Visiting Ireland: Jig picking

Jig picking describes a picking pattern used in Irish jigs. The *jig* is a dance with two strong beats to the measure (see Chapter 4 for more on beats per measure). The interesting thing about this rhythm is that each strong beat is divided into three beats, and therefore is commonly written as 6/8 time (flip to Chapter 4 for all about time signatures). In reality, jigs should be written as 2/2 time with a triplet being played for each beat, but those people who scribe music from sound to standard notation decided to write jigs in 6/8 time. The pattern widely used by most Irish players is that of down-up-down, down-up-down, which puts the emphasis on the first beat of each set of three and makes the rhythm suitable for dancing. This is also the picking pattern used for triplets in Irish music. I describe Irish-style playing in more detail in Chapter 11.

Check out Figure 5-10 and Track 17 for an example of jig picking.

Figure 5-10: Jig picking pattern.

Rolling out the notes: Cross picking

The great bluegrass mandolin player Jesse McReynolds is given credit for developing this unique style of playing, where banjo-style *rolls* (patterns) are played on the mandolin while using a traditional, flat, regular guitar-style pick. Guitar and banjo players perform similar rolls or patterns by picking strings with their fingertips or with picks attached to their fingers. The origins of this style date back to classical mandolin music, but Jesse, influenced by the five-string banjo rolls of Earl Scruggs, created a unique way to use this technique in a bluegrass setting.

As Figures 5-11 and 5-12 show, two basic rolls exist. These unique rolls create a rhythmic feel that you can't replicate with alternate picking (check the earlier section 'Picking alternate strong and weak beats'). Cross picking's unique sound is also due in part to the continuous ringing of open strings while melodic parts are played on the fretted strings.

I demonstrate a cross-picking *forward* (in other words, down-down-up, down-down-up, down-up) roll in Figure 5-11 and Track 18 Part 1, and a cross-picking *reverse* (or down-up-up, down-up-up, down-up) roll in Figure 5-12 and Track 18 Part 2.

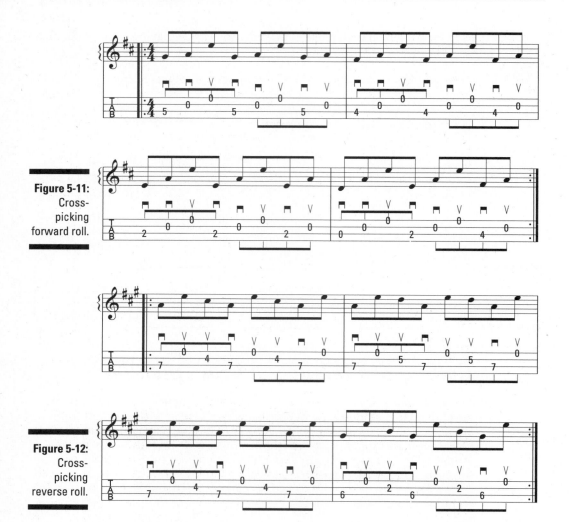

Figure 5-11:
Cross-
picking
forward roll.

Figure 5-12:
Cross-
picking
reverse roll.

Developing Good Tone

In this section, I show you the most important elements in getting a full, rich tone. Producing a good tone from a mandolin is a long-term project that most mandolin players chase for years. The mandolin is capable of making the most beautiful sound, but you can also create a sound somewhere between an out-of-tune piano and stepping on a tone-deaf cat!

Listening to a variety of mandolin players is the best way to form an opinion on what sound you like. Some mandolin players known for their great tone are: David Grisman, Tim O'Brien, John Reischman, Mike Compton, Butch Baldassari and Peter Ostroushko.

Finding the sweet spot

Every mandolin is different, but most pro players agree that picking near the end of the fretboard produces the most pleasing tone (Chapter 1 describes the different parts of the mandolin). Playing closer to the bridge produces a very bright tone that may be desirable in certain situations but is too bright for general use, and playing too far over the fretboard yields a tone that's reminiscent of a harp. Near the end of the fretboard gives you the best of both worlds (see Figure 5-13).

Figure 5-13: A mando-lin's sweet spot.

Having your Florida removed!

Many mandolins are made with a fingerboard extension (commonly called a *Florida* because of its shape) that allows access to up to 29 frets. Not only are these very high extra frets difficult to play, but also they can cause an annoying clicking sound when touched by the pick when playing in the sweet spot. Because of this problem, many mandolin players have their Florida surgically removed by a qualified instrument builder or repair person. Another option is to have the last few frets removed by a qualified luthier and have the fretboard *scooped* (in other words, have some wood removed) so the pick doesn't hit these tiny frets when you play.

Picking the right pick

Mandolin players are very fussy about the pick they use. Picks vary in shape, material, thickness and price (see Figure 5-14). The choice of pick can make a dramatic difference to tone and volume.

Picks have different feels in your hand, create different kinds of tone, and feel different in the way they interact with the strings. Pick selection, just like the type of strings you choose to use, becomes a personal decision based on getting the tone you're looking for out of your particular instrument.

Most seasoned mandolin players use quite stiff picks, but beginners with a less-developed right hand may do better with a more flexible pick. The increased flex of a pick can have a forgiving quality at first.

Figure 5-14:
A selection
of mandolin
picks.

Exploring the world of boutique picks can get quite expensive. A handmade pick of some mystery material can cost as much as £40, which is about 100 times the cost of a basic model.

Keeping a loose grip

Holding the pick loosely is one of the most difficult and most beneficial things you can do to improve your tone. In a mandolin teaching video, a very young Chris Thile tells about holding the pick so loosely that while competing in mandolin contests he occasionally dropped it during his performances. Apparently contest rules allow you to start again if this happens.

Getting your pick angle right

The angle of the pick as it comes across the strings can make a big difference in your playing tone and in the instrument's overall response to how the pick glides across the strings. The most common pick position is to have the front or leading edge (the part closest to the neck) angled slightly forward (in other words, tipped slightly towards the ground). (Some great players play with their picks flat and parallel to the strings, and a few even hold the pick with the front edge tipped up, leaving the back edge of the pick to contact the string.)

Like locating your mandolin's sweet spot (see the earlier section 'Finding the sweet spot'), you need to experiment and see what works best for you. Figure 5-15 shows the generally accepted pick angle.

Figure 5-15: The accepted pick angle.

(a)　　(b)

Following through: The rest stroke

I find that using a rest stroke helps my tone when playing down-strokes. The *rest stroke* is similar to what golfers do after making initial contact with the ball. They don't let the club stop at the point of impact but continue the swing.

Play the fourth string (g) with a down-stroke and let the pick follow through, resting on the third string. This technique guarantees that both of the fourth strings are vibrating, giving your sound much more potential. Doing so gives an extra 20–30 per cent in volume and makes the notes sound more even.

Keeping things loose: It's all in the wrist

One thing that all good mandolin players have in common is a very loose wrist. Most of the motion when picking notes on the mandolin should come from the wrist – not from the forearm or the right hand fingers that hold the pick. Many of the best mandolin players keep an even down-up motion (with the wrist) when playing melodies, regardless of what melody they are playing. The key is to be able to relax while playing music. The patterns and exercises in this chapter are a good measuring stick; if you can play them without trouble, you're going to be able to make music without much trouble, too.

Loosening up your wrist takes time, and so don't expect to be able to do this overnight.

Try to avoid moving your thumb when picking. One of my favourite ways to monitor wrist movement is to watch myself play in front of a mirror. If you watch yourself play, it allows you to tell quite easily whether you're relaxed or not. Keep making adjustments until you look relaxed.

Playing Louder Isn't Always Better

If loud is good, surely louder must be better, right? Well, no! Sometimes mandolin players seem to be searching constantly for the loudest mandolin on the planet. But in the hands of a good mandolin player, even the loudest mandolin can (and should) be played at a variety of levels.

One of the challenges with playing f-soundhole mandolins (which I describe in Chapter 15) is that the sound projects in a very focused way, and sometimes the player isn't hearing the mandolin the same way as other people in the room are.

In this section, I lead you through mandolin *dynamics* (volume) and some basic guidelines when playing music with others.

Understanding dynamics

Playing dynamically is something that develops over time and with practice. Dynamic levels in music fall under six basic headings ranging from very soft to very loud. You can use the legitimate musical terms (in Italian) or standard (English) words to describe and communicate dynamics. Here is a list of the Italian musical terms, the dynamic symbols and their translations:

- **Pianissimo: pp** – very soft
- **Piano: p** – soft
- **Mezzo-piano: mp** – medium soft
- **Mezzo-forte: mf** – medium loud
- **Forte: f** – loud
- **Fortissimo: ff** – very loud

Knowing when not to play loudly

In classical music, the volume to play at is written into the score, but in more casual forms of music you need to decide the volume on your own.

In general, playing very loudly when a singer is singing or another player is soloing is considered poor taste. In such situations, your job becomes a supporting role, and you need to focus on strumming chords or playing background parts without overpowering the soloist. Music is like a team sport. Aim to make the other players sound better with the addition of your part.

As I write in Chapter 4, a great rule to follow is to listen 70 per cent and play 30 per cent. The object is to make the entire group sound its best, not to make you stand out.

Choosing when to play loudly

The old saying 'There's a time and place for everything' is true as regards playing loudly.

When you're playing in a bluegrass jam session and are called upon to play an instrumental break, you need all the horsepower you can find in order to cut over the sound of the banjo and the other instruments that tend to be naturally louder than the mandolin. If your fellow band members are experienced players, they may bring their volume down in order to make room for you, but don't count on it.

You may find that playing your licks or solos at full volume is difficult and requires coordination and strength. Work at the exercises that I provide in the later section 'Becoming dynamic with volume exercises' to help build up your skill and confidence.

Balancing act: Four strings are louder than one

When you strum chords, more strings are ringing and more sound is produced than when you play single-note melodies. This fact creates a problem, because when you're strumming chords your role is to give slightly quieter support, and yet when you're playing melody your role is to be featured! Therefore, you need to be able to play at a variety of dynamic levels. To help, I suggest strumming chords very lightly while keeping a steady beat. When playing melody or a solo you need to dig in a little more, which can cause some issues at first. Avoid the common tendencies to play faster and grip the pick harder when playing louder, and stay relaxed. Also try to get a feel for how hard you can pick the strings before they fret out or buzz against the frets. This buzzing sound is something to avoid if possible.

When you start to play with other musicians, try to record your sessions for your personal review. For more information about inexpensive portable recorders, turn to Chapter 16.

Sustaining a Note: Tremolo

Tremolo is a musical term for when you rapidly repeat a single note. Mandolin players accomplish this effect by picking the same note many times in a series of down-up, down-up strokes. When done properly, the effect is like the note becoming one long sustained (constant) note. Tremolo is one of the most beautiful sounds possible on the mandolin, but also one of the most difficult to achieve. In this section, I present you with a variety of tremolo techniques.

Staying in time: Measured tremolo

Measured tremolo refers to a tremolo that's in time with the music. The actual tremolo speed depends on the tempo of the music and the desired tremolo effect. I describe several combinations of tremolo strokes per beat in this section.

I strongly suggest that you get a good handle on the timing exercises in the later section 'Keeping-time exercises' before you attempt measured tremolo.

When playing tremolo, half the notes are down-strokes and the other half are up-strokes. Therefore, your overall tremolo needs to be exactly twice as fast as your down-stroke. When working on a new tremolo part, try playing it with repeated down-strokes first, adding in the up-strokes when you feel confident.

Four strokes per beat

This type of tremolo is most useful for songs played at medium to fast tempos. For a four strokes per beat tremolo (see Figure 5-16), set your metronome to 100–130 beats per minute (bpm) and practise two down-strokes per click of your metronome (check out Chapter 16 for more on metronomes).

At first you may need to go more slowly, which is no problem. When you can stay even with the metronome, add the up-stroke to complete the four-stroke tremolo.

You can hear an example on Track 19 Part 1.

Figure 5-16:
Four-stroke
tremolo.

Six strokes per beat

This tremolo is used often in medium-tempo music. For a six strokes per beat tremolo (see Figure 5-17), set your metronome to 80–100 bpm and start by practising three down-strokes per click. When you're confident of staying even with the metronome, add the up-stroke to create the six-stroke tremolo.

Listen to Track 19 Part 2 for an example.

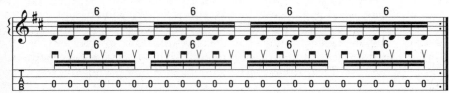

Figure 5-17:
Six-stroke
tremolo.

Eight strokes per beat

The eight-stroke tremolo speed works well for medium-slow tempos. To play this tremolo (see Figure 5-18), set your metronome to 64–74 bpm and first practise four down-strokes per click, before adding the up-strokes when you can stay even with the metronome to complete the eight-stroke tremolo.

You can hear an example of eight-stroke tremolo on Track 19 Part 3.

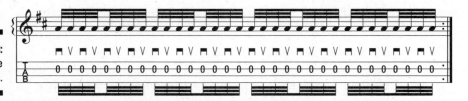

Figure 5-18:
Eight-stroke
tremolo.

Twelve strokes per beat

This type of tremolo is normally used in very slow tempos. Set your metronome to 40–54 bpm for a 12 strokes per beat tremolo (see Figure 5-19), first practising six down-strokes per click. When you're able to stay even with the metronome, try adding the up-stroke to complete the 12-stroke tremolo.

Listen to the example on Track 19 Part 4 for what a 12-stroke tremolo sounds like.

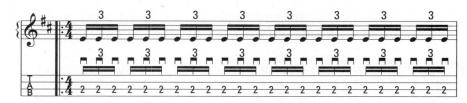

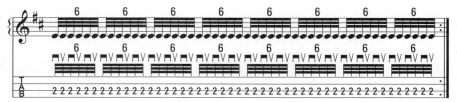

Figure 5-19: Twelve-stroke tremolo.

Varying the pace: Free tremolo

Free tremolo (also called *expressive tremolo*) isn't timed (as measured tremolo is in the preceding section); it can speed up and slow down for your desired feel. Free tremolo can be a very nice effect for a ballad, or in classical music (or any music) without a strong beat.

I demonstrate this technique on Track 20 Part 1.

Playing melody with slow tremolo

Although not really tremolo in the purest sense of the word, slow tremolo is a great way of creating a sustaining sound while maintaining a rhythmic drive. The idea is to play steady eighth or sixteenth notes (quavers and semiquavers) when playing a melody made up of longer notes. This technique works well when playing a melody (a song) that's normally sung by a vocalist.

You can hear an example of slow tremolo on Track 20 Part 2.

Practising Your Skills

The picking exercises in this section help you to improve your technique, dexterity, tone, timing, dynamics and tremolo. Remember to use your metronome and take things slowly at first.

Practice may not make perfect, but it does make permanent; in other words, each time you play something, your memory holds a picture of the performance, including the mistakes. If you make the same mistake over and over again, you remember it that way, which doesn't help you improve. Get things right at a slow tempo and then speed up.

Trying out alternate-picking exercises

I designed the picking exercises in this section so that they help you move from any string to any other string on any beat while maintaining proper alternate picking (which I discuss in the earlier section 'Picking alternate strong and weak beats').

Check out Figure 5-20 – a fairly easy four notes per string exercise, provided you just keep your wrist moving and play the down-up pattern twice on each string – and listen to Track 21 Part 1 for the exercise.

The exercise in Figure 5-21 (on Track 21 Part 2) is tricky due to the fact that in some cases you move from one string to the other on an up-stroke. The exercise in Figure 5-22 (on Track 21 Part 3) features two notes per string, or one cycle of down-up picking per string. Remember that some melodies require you to change strings on an up-stroke, and others require you to change on a down-stroke, so you need to get comfortable with both of these movements.

Many mandolin players keep their right hands moving through an entire song to maintain proper pick direction, and I think this is a great idea. Don't stop moving your hand, and keep an even down-up motion going when playing.

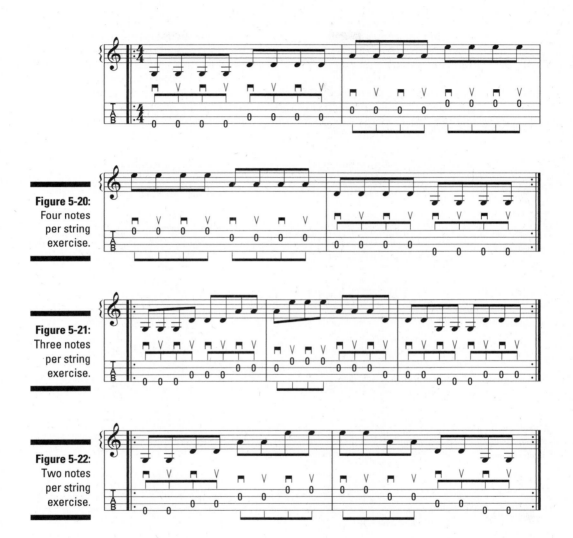

Figure 5-20:
Four notes
per string
exercise.

Figure 5-21:
Three notes
per string
exercise.

Figure 5-22:
Two notes
per string
exercise.

I've designed the next four exercises to reinforce good alternate-picking technique. The time when pick direction consistently gets turned around is when you need to change from one string to another, and this, combined with the fact that up-strokes tend to be harder to control than down-strokes, makes this set of exercises very valuable.

The idea in each of the following exercises is to be able to get from each string to the other three strings while keeping your wrist moving and following good alternate-picking technique. Don't be fooled by playing Figure 5-23 one time and saying to yourself 'These are easy, so I don't need to practise these!' Play these exercises with your metronome set at 74 bpm, making sure to play a down-stroke (repeating string) on each metronome click, leaving the up-stroke (other strings) to land between the clicks. Play each exercise two or three times in succession without stopping, before moving on to the next one. These exercises get tougher as you progress through them, but as soon as you can execute all of these at 74 bpm, start increasing your speed while making sure to keep your wrist moving in a down-up alternate-picking pattern.

Try out the exercises in Figures 5-23 to 5-26 and on Track 22 Parts 1–4.

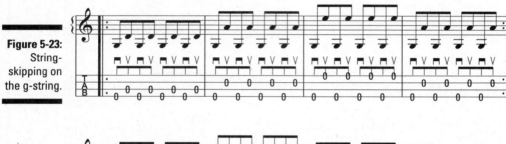

Figure 5-23: String-skipping on the g-string.

Figure 5-24: String-skipping on the d-string.

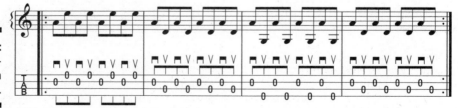

Figure 5-25: String-skipping on the a-string.

Seeking out more picking patterns

The alternate-picking patterns that I present in this book are common among many mandolin teachers. If you enjoy this type of thing, check out *Mike Marshall's Mandolin Method: The* *Great Book of Finger Busters* (published by Adventure Music Publishing), which contains an exhausting combination of such exercises.

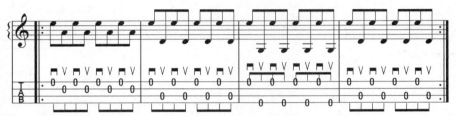

Figure 5-26: String-skipping on the e-string.

The final exercise in this section is a pattern that takes two measures to complete and uses only two strings. Although I show it using the fourth and third strings, also repeat the pattern on the second and third strings, followed by the first and second strings. You may even want to try this picking pattern while holding down some basic chords with your left hand. If you listen closely to Chris Thile, you'll hear him playing patterns like this (and more complex ones) at blistering speeds on his mandolin.

I demonstrate the exercise in Figure 5-27 and on Track 23.

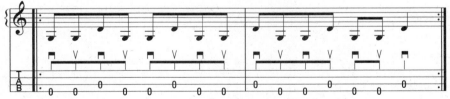

Figure 5-27: Two-measure patterns.

Keeping-time exercises

These exercises are all about simple division. The magic numbers are 2, 3, 4 and 6. You need to be able to divide beats into equal parts using down-strokes or alternate picking.

Using your metronome set to 84 bpm (quarter note), play through the exercises in Figures 5-28 to 5-31 (which I demonstrate on Track 24 Parts 1–4) following the pick direction indicated by the markings above the tablature numbers. You may need to slow the metronome down for Figures 5-30 and 5-31, because the divided notes get moving pretty fast. Be sure to repeat these exercises many times in succession, without stopping.

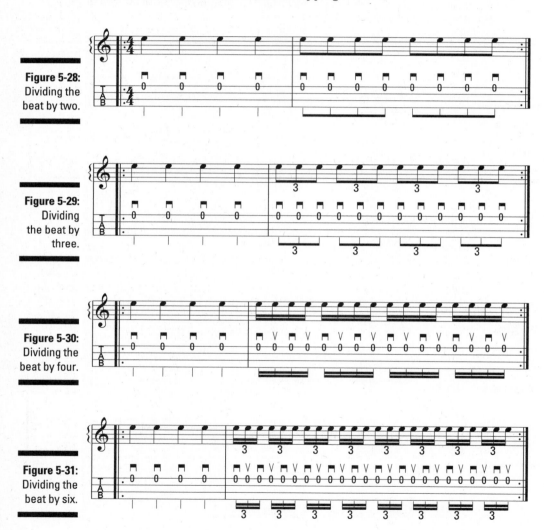

Figure 5-28: Dividing the beat by two.

Figure 5-29: Dividing the beat by three.

Figure 5-30: Dividing the beat by four.

Figure 5-31: Dividing the beat by six.

Chilling out with rest exercises

Ah, finally the type of workout I enjoy, the rest exercise! This one is all about counting when you're between notes. Play each exercise in Figures 5-32, 5-33 and 5-34, being very careful to follow the suggested pick direction. Practise with your metronome set at around 72 bpm. Be sure to play each exercise at least three times in succession, without stopping, before moving on to the next one.

Be sure to count, and try to hear the part in your head before you play it on your mandolin.

You can hear these three examples on Track 25 Parts 1, 2 and 3.

Figure 5-32: Rest exercise one.

Figure 5-33: Rest exercise two.

Figure 5-34: Rest exercise three.

Becoming dynamic with volume exercises

Play this first dynamics exercise six times, once for each of the six dynamic levels that I describe in the earlier section 'Understanding dynamics'.

I demonstrate this exercise in Figure 5-35 and on Track 26 Part 1.

Figure 5-35:
Dynamics
exercise
one.

Follow the printed dynamics markings in this second dynamics exercise. These markings are indicated above the tablature with musical dynamic marks, and above the standard notation in laymen's terms.

See Figure 5-36 and listen to Track 26 Part 2.

Figure 5-36:
Dynamics
exercise
two.

Stretching out with tremolo exercises

Remember that you should play tremolo only where indicated in Figure 5-37 by hash marks on the stem of the note or tab. For this exercise, use a six strokes per beat tremolo (thus you need to play three down-strokes per beat (per quarter note or crochet); flip to the earlier section 'Staying in time: Measured tremolo' for more.

When dividing one beat into three equal parts, use the word 'tri-pl-et' broken into three syllables as a guide. The down-strokes in the first two measures are 1, 2, 3, 4 (tri-pl-et, tri-pl-et, tri-pl-et, tri-pl-et). When you can play that, add the up-stroke to the tremolo notes.

I demonstrate this exercise in Figure 5-37 and on Track 27 Part 1.

Figure 5-37: Tremolo exercise.

The next exercise is an excerpt from 'Waves of the Danube', an old tune written in 1880 by Romanian composer Iosef Ivanovici. Play a four strokes per beat tremolo on this one. The tune is in 3/4 time (which I describe in Chapter 4), and so the down-stroke rhythm is 1 and 2 and 3 and 1 and 2 and 3 and. After you can play the melody using all eighth note (quavers) down-strokes, try adding the up-strokes. Because the entire piece is to be played with tremolo, you don't need to put individual tremolo marks on certain notes.

Check out Figure 5-38 and listen to Track 27 Part 2.

Figure 5-38:
Trying out
tremolo on a
song.

Chapter 6

Fretting Notes and Chords with the Left Hand

In This Chapter

▶ Using your left hand effectively

▶ Playing more chords

▶ Picking up a few left-hand techniques

*U*nless you have extraordinarily long, particularly bendy fingers (and I mean alien-shaped digits!), you need two hands to play the mandolin. I discuss in Chapter 5 what your right hand does when playing, and in this chapter I focus on your left-hand technique.

I describe the correct left-hand position and fingerings when fretting single notes and forming chords. I also show you some left-hand skills such as slides, pull-offs, hammer-ons and double stops, along with some common major, minor (m) and seventh (7) chords. I also discuss moving your left hand up and down the mandolin neck, and what this technique helps you do.

So this chapter allows you to discover all about fretting with (but not worrying about!) your left hand.

Positioning and Working with Your Left Hand

A mandolin player's left hand is responsible for the sexy part of playing – the notes. You can see this even from just watching someone playing air guitar – or air mandolin in this case! The mandolin hero wannabe moves the fingers of his left hand as fast as he can, but just kinda holds his right hand somewhere near where the strings would be.

In this section, I show the basics of how to position your left hand on the mandolin, and I explain which finger goes on which fret. I throw in some finger-strengthening exercises for good measure along with some left-hand effects that you can employ in your playing, such as hammer-ons, pull-offs and slides. Moving from one note to another or one chord to another (in time), though, is where having a strong, well-positioned left hand with all four fingers ready to play on command makes all the difference.

Positioning your left hand

Getting the correct left-hand position is vital because it enables you to reach all the frets required to play in a variety of musical keys and styles (see Chapter 2 for more on keys). In this section, I point you in the right direction (read Chapter 3 for some suggested ways of holding the mandolin). To position your left hand:

1. **Place the pad of your left thumb on the neck where it's fastened to the fingerboard, as I show in Figure 6-1(a).** Make sure that your wrist is straight and relaxed. Let gravity pull your hand and fingers towards the ground, while relaxing your entire arm from your fingertips all the way to your neck.

2. **Bring your fingers up to the fingerboard by rotating your wrist in a clockwise direction.** This movement should feel like opening a door by turning the handle with your left hand. The only points of contact with the neck need to be the pad of your thumb and the side of your first finger, somewhere between the first and second joints.

3. **Curl your fingertips down towards the fingerboard while pointing your fingers in the direction of your torso.** Some guitarists are taught to place the fingers parallel to the frets, but mandolin players angle their fingers more like the left-hand position used by violin players.

4. **Make sure that you have a space between your palm and the back of the mandolin neck, as in Figure 6-1(b).** I've seen many students mistakenly clutching the mandolin neck as if it's a hammer or a baseball or cricket bat. Unless you intend to hit someone with your mandolin, this isn't recommended (mandolins don't work very well as hammers and usually splinter into many pieces upon the first solid blow).

The left hand doesn't support the mandolin. The mandolin needs to be supported by the strap, your right forearm on the rib of the mandolin and your legs if you're sitting down.

If you choose to sit while playing, leaning slightly forward puts you in a good position while keeping the back of the mandolin off your stomach. You can use your shirt or stomach to act as a damping or muting device resulting in a choked sound, if you're after that effect. Alternatively, by allowing the back of the mandolin to resonate, you can produce the full sound of your mandolin.

Figure 6-1: (a) Left-hand thumb position; (b) back of neck to show the left-hand position; (c) the proper angle for left-hand fingers.

Tying your fingers to the frets

Not tying them literally, of course; I mean to start with your fingers positioned so that certain fingers play certain frets. The position I show you in this section is called *first position* (see Figure 6-2).

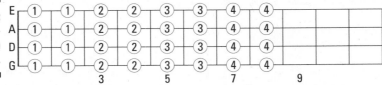

Figure 6-2: First-position fingering.

In mandolin fingering, each finger is responsible for two frets, and in first position these are as follows:

- The first (the index) finger covers frets one and two.

- The second finger covers frets three and four.

- The third finger covers frets five and six.

- The fourth finger (your little finger) covers frets seven and eight. (Also read the nearby sidebar 'Deciding how to use your little finger'.)

Deciding how to use your little finger

On the fretboard, the seventh fret of every string is the same note as the adjacent string played open (for example, the seventh fret of the g-string is a D note, the same as the open third string). If you use your little finger only for the seventh and eighth frets, you may be asking yourself 'Why don't I just play those notes on the next string and avoid using my fourth finger?' Good question. The answer is that in some musical keys, you can indeed use the open string and do not really need your fourth finger at all.

However, a fretted note sounds different and is more expressive than an open note, and many musicians choose to use the fourth finger instead of the adjacent string open (although I choose the open strings more often and enjoy the sound of the open string on the mandolin).

When playing further up the neck, or when playing in certain keys (Ab, Eb, Db), you have no option but to use all your fingers, and so getting the strength and coordination working on all four fingers is a great idea.

Also, when playing scales or melodies, play each note with a separate finger (although in certain situations you'll want to play two or more notes in succession with the same finger, called *embellishments*, when performing the slides, hammer-ons and pull-offs that I cover later in the 'Creating effects with your left hand' section).

Rules are meant to be broken, of course, but only when you know and understand the rules first!

Exercising the left hand

In this section, I present an exercise to build the strength and coordination in your left-hand fingers.

In this exercise (Track 28 and Figure 6-3), I indicate the proper finger number above each note. Although I show the pattern only on the g-string, each string feels slightly different, and so therefore make sure that you practise the exercise on all four strings.

Go slowly and take things easy to ensure you don't hurt your finger muscles. This exercise is difficult at first, but you gain finger strength and coordination over time.

Keep your fingers close to the fingerboard. Flying fingers may look impressive, but keeping them as close to the fingerboard as possible is more efficient and improves tone and speed.

Figure 6-3:
A left-hand finger exercise.

Creating effects with your left hand

In this section, I describe some embellishments that you can perfect via a few left-hand *articulations* that add creativity and shape to melodies. You can use slides (*glissando*), hammer-ons and pull-offs as *slurs* (denoted by curved lines connecting two notes) connecting two or more notes together, as well as employ muting techniques to separate the notes intentionally with a silence or space.

Sliding notes to embellish your playing

A *slide* is a left-hand technique that involves moving your fretting finger while holding down a string. Getting the right amount of pressure takes a bit of practice: too much pressure and you have difficulty moving your finger (and may peel the skin off your fingertip); too little pressure results in a deadened or muted note.

Slides can be thought of as two distinctly different techniques. In both cases, the slide can go up or down in pitch:

✔ **Note-to-note slide:** Sliding from one note to another as a way of connecting the two notes.

Play a note and, without picking the note a second time, slide your finger to the next note while maintaining the notated rhythm. With a little practice, you can do this movement and still have enough note ringing to clearly make out the new note. Note-to-note slides are indicated with a line connecting the two notes (see Figure 6-4(a) and Track 29 Part 1).

✔ **A single-note slide:** Sliding into a single note from an undetermined spot.

Start from somewhere above or below the note (anywhere from one to a few frets) and quickly slide into the targeted note. This type of slide is indicated by an angled line placed just before the targeted note and is played so it doesn't add or subtract any time value to the targeted note. This type of slide is shown in Figure 6-4(b) and can be heard on Track 29 Part 1.

Figure 6-4:
(a) A note-
to-note slide
and (b) a
single-note
slide.

Adding hammer-ons

A *hammer-on* is a way of moving from a lower note to a higher note by fretting the higher note with a brisk hammering motion. You can perform a hammer-on from an *open* (that is, unfretted) string to a fretted note, or from one fretted note to a higher note on the same string.

The word 'hammer' is appropriate because you need to bring your finger down quickly and firmly to get this technique to work, which can take a bit of practice to get good results.

You can use hammer-ons in two basic ways. The first type is as a *legato* technique, which means that the musical notes are played smoothly and connected. This type of hammer-on is accomplished by picking a note and then hammering the next note (without picking it) with a finger on your left hand. The end result is that you've played two notes with only one pick-stroke.

I show this type of hammer-on in Figure 6-5(a), indicated by a slur with the letter 'h' near the line. Listen to Track 29 Part 2.

Be sure to keep your fingertips curled and fret the note with the tips (not the pads) of your fingers. Eventually you build up a callous on the tip of each finger, making this technique a bit easier.

The second type of hammer-on is an embellishment to a single note and not a way of connecting two notes. This type of hammer-on happens immediately before the written note and doesn't have any effect on the length of the targeted note. I show this type of hammer-on in Figure 6-5(b), indicated by a *grace note* (a small note) just prior to the targeted note. Hear this technique on Track 29 Part 2.

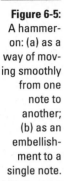

Figure 6-5: A hammer-on: (a) as a way of moving smoothly from one note to another; (b) as an embellishment to a single note.

Performing pull-offs

Pull-offs are another way for the left hand to slur one note into another. In some ways, they're the opposite of hammer-ons (which I describe in the preceding section): pull-offs are a way of transitioning from a higher note to a lower note on the same string without re-picking the note.

You perform a pull-off by pulling across the string and lightly plucking it with your fretting finger as you release it. You can pull off to an open string or to another fretted note. You can even pull off two or three notes in a row with some practice. Remember to try to keep these notes in time, because they tend to speed up on you if you aren't careful! I show this type of pull-off in Figure 6-6(a) and on Track 29 Part 3.

Figure 6-6: A pull-off: (a) as a way of moving from note to note; (b) as an embellishment to a single note.

As with the other left-hand articulations that I cover in this section, pull-offs can also be used to articulate one note instead of transitioning from one note to another. When used in this manner, they're written as grace notes just prior to the targeted note. In this type of pull-off, the rhythmic value of the target note doesn't change; the pull-off is merely an approach to the targeted note. I show this type of pull-off in Figure 6-6(b) and on Track 29 Part 3.

The great Kenneth (Jethro) Burns used a four-fingered pull-off where he fretted the note with his fourth finger, followed by pulling off with all four fingers down to an open string.

This technique is indicated by a quarter note (crotchet) followed by three grace notes attached to the next note, which needs to be an open string because you've just used all your fingers to make this super pull-off work (see Figure 6-7 and Track 30 Part 1).

Figure 6-7:
Jethro-style super pull-off.

Combining hammer-ons and pull-offs

This technique combines the legato techniques from the two previous sections, resulting in a very smooth-sounding transition of notes. For this effect, you need to: pick a note (fretted or not); be sure to let it sustain the proper amount of time; follow it by a hammer-on of a specific time; and end with a pull-off.

In most cases, all three of these notes are the same length. This embellishment is indicated by a slur covering all three notes, with the letters 'hp' placed near the curved line. This type of articulation is used quite often for playing triplets (which I describe for you in Chapter 11), but can also be used for a legato eighth-note (quaver) effect.

Check out Figure 6-8, and Track 30 Part 2 for examples of this combination using eighth notes (quavers) and as a triplet.

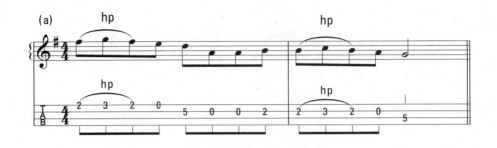

Figure 6-8: Hammer-on pull-off combination.

Muting

Muting is a left-hand technique used to stop a note from ringing, creating a short silence between the muted note and the next note. This silence in music is very important and often overlooked by beginners. The classical term for it is *staccato*.

To indicate a *muted* (or shortened) note, the note has a small dot placed above or below it (see Figure 6-9 and Track 30 Part 3). Muting is accomplished in two basic ways:

✔ **Muting an open-string note:** Accomplished by lightly touching one of your left-hand fingers to the string that you intend to stop or mute. Be careful not to push the string down to the fret, or another note may begin to sound.

✔ **Muting a fretted note:** Accomplished by the fretting finger releasing just enough pressure to stop the note. Be careful not to pull your finger away from the string, or another note may begin to ring.

Figure 6-9:
Muting
fretted and
open notes.

Discovering More Essential Chords

Along with playing beautiful melodies, mandolin players are also expected to be able to play chords and form part of the rhythm section during singing or banjo, fiddle or guitar breaks. In fact, mandolin chords can be very simple to play. I describe five easy ones (G, C, D, E and A) in Chapter 4 to start you off, and by learning the additional chords that I show you in this section, you can strum along to hundreds of songs.

With the exception of barré chords in the later section 'Focusing on barré chords', the chords I feature in this section are *open chords*, meaning that at least one of the strings is open (not fretted).

When changing chords, look for notes that stay the same, and keep as many fingers in the same place as possible, only moving the ones you need to.

Trying out a few major chords

As I mention in Chapter 2, major chords tend to have an optimistic 'up' type of sound. See Figure 6-10 for open-string versions of F and B♭ major chords. (Turn to Chapter 2 for all about ♭ (flat) notes.)

Becoming sadder with some minor chords

Minor (m) chords have a darker or more mysterious type of sound, although you can also use them in major or happy-sounding songs. (Many of The Beatles' love songs, for example, contained minor as well as major chords.) European gypsy music, Spanish flamenco music, 'Dawg' music (see Chapter 14) and heavy metal music all use minor chords. The science part about minor chords is that the third of the chord (see Figure 6-27) is one half-step (or one fret) lower than in a major chord.

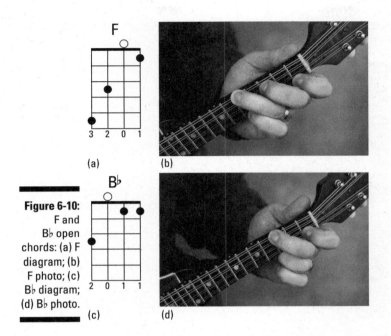

Figure 6-10:
F and
B♭ open
chords: (a) F
diagram; (b)
F photo; (c)
B♭ diagram;
(d) B♭ photo.

Figure 6-11 shows you the open-string versions of Gm and Cm chords.

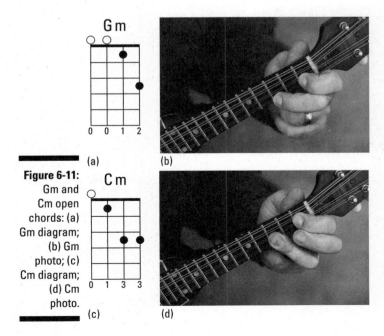

Figure 6-11:
Gm and
Cm open
chords: (a)
Gm diagram;
(b) Gm
photo; (c)
Cm diagram;
(d) Cm
photo.

Figure 6-12 demonstrates the open-string versions of Em, Am and Dm chords.

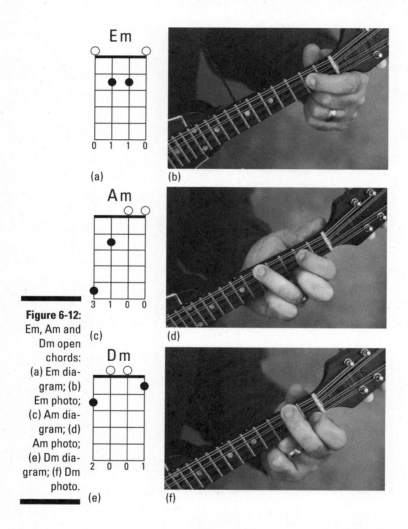

Figure 6-12:
Em, Am and Dm open chords: (a) Em diagram; (b) Em photo; (c) Am diagram; (d) Am photo; (e) Dm diagram; (f) Dm photo.

When you have the above minor chords down pat, take a look at Figure 6-13 for open-string F♯m and Bm chords. Flip to Chapter 2 for more on ♯ (sharp) notes.

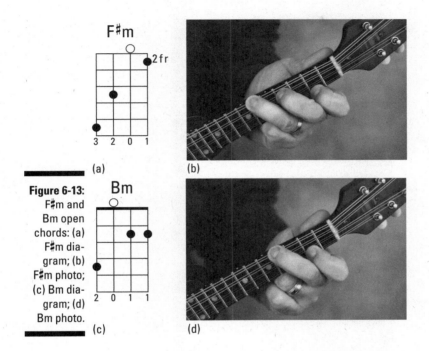

Figure 6-13: F♯m and Bm open chords: (a) F♯m diagram; (b) F♯m photo; (c) Bm diagram; (d) Bm photo.

Opening up to seventh chords

Seventh chords (7) tend to have a sound suggestive of anticipation or motion. Figure 6-14 shows the open-string versions of G7, C7 and D7 chords.

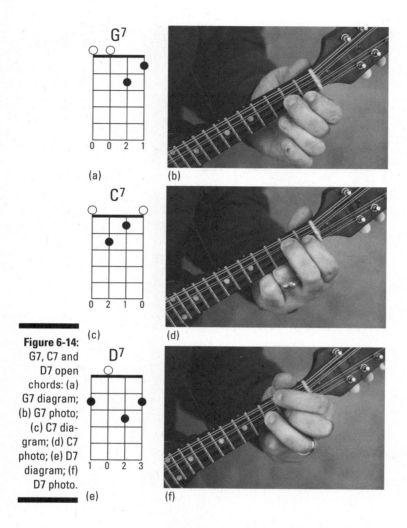

Figure 6-14:
G7, C7 and
D7 open
chords: (a)
G7 diagram;
(b) G7 photo;
(c) C7 dia-
gram; (d) C7
photo; (e) D7
diagram; (f)
D7 photo.

See Figure 6-15 for open-string versions of E7 and A7 chords.

Focusing on barré chords

Unfortunately, these chords aren't ones to play in the pub (although they work there as well as anywhere else). If you're coming to mandolin from a guitar background, the concept of barré chords won't be new to you. The mandolin barré chords shown in this section are four-string closed chords in which you lay your left-hand index finger rigidly across the g and d strings (like a bar), leaving your other three fingers available to fret notes on the a and e strings. By moving your left hand up the fretboard, this barré chord becomes another chord by raising the pitch of each string an equal amount.

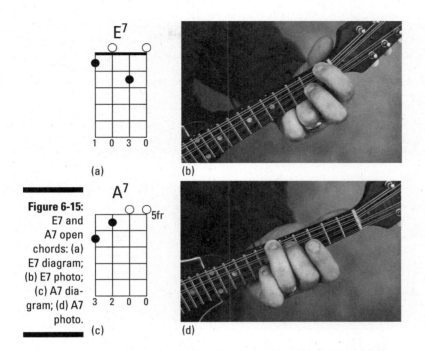

Figure 6-15: E7 and A7 open chords: (a) E7 diagram; (b) E7 photo; (c) A7 diagram; (d) A7 photo.

The idea is that you start with one of the simple open chord shapes and move it up the mandolin neck. But first you need to change the fingering so that your index finger can take the place of the nut (see Figure 6-16). The most commonly used form of barré chord for the mandolin starts out as a G chord (which I show you in Chapter 4).

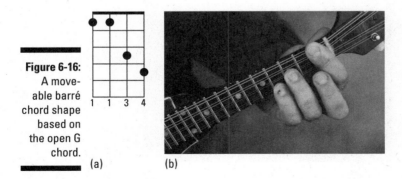

Figure 6-16: A move-able barré chord shape based on the open G chord.

You're trying to keep the 'shape' of the chord while removing any open strings. When you hold that chord shape, the *root note* (the name of chord) is the lowest note and is played by your index finger on the g-string. If you know the notes of the g-string, you're in luck! Just move your index finger to the chord you want and voilà, you have a new chord! If you don't know the notes on the g-string yet, just take a look at Figure 6-26 (later in this chapter).

You don't need to barré all four strings when making this chord. The barré is really only on the g- and d-strings.

When forming a barré, the lowest note on the g-string is always the letter name of the chord. For example, the second fret of the g-string is the note A. By making this barré chord at the second fret, you're making an A chord (see Figure 6-17).

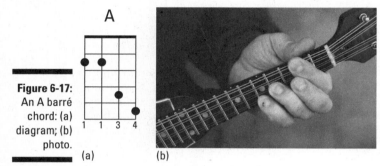

Figure 6-17:
An A barré chord: (a) diagram; (b) photo.

(a)   (b)

When you're comfortable with this shape and can move it up and down the neck with ease, you're ready to move one of the other notes in the chord one or two frets and so make a minor and a seventh chord based on this barré shape. Figure 6-18 shows the Am version, and Figure 6-19 shows the A7 version of this barré chord.

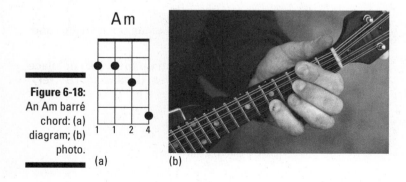

Figure 6-18:
An Am barré chord: (a) diagram; (b) photo.

(a)   (b)

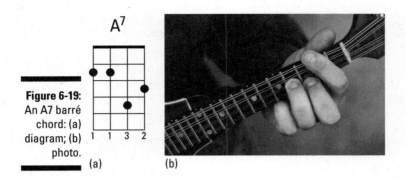

A⁷

Figure 6-19:
An A7 barré
chord: (a)
diagram; (b)
photo.

1 1 3 2

(a)   (b)

Trying out Left-Hand Techniques

In this section, you get to stretch out a bit as I lead you through several left-hand techniques, including changing the position of your left hand so that you can access all of the wonderful high notes of the mandolin that live beyond the seventh fret. When you leave first position (in other words, the seventh fret and below), you need to know some basic scale patterns that you can play higher on the fretboard.

Changing your left-hand position

The first position that I describe in the earlier section 'Tying your fingers to the frets' isn't the only place to put your left hand, and here I show you how to alter it and how to move up the neck (the mandolin's, not your own).

Position playing refers to playing in a specific region of the fingerboard:

- ✔ **First position** or **open position** is when you play using open strings and only fret notes up to the first six or seven frets.

- ✔ **Second position** is when you move your left hand up the neck and place your left hand so that your index finger is on a fret (third or fourth fret) that you'd normally play with your second finger.

- ✔ **Third position** is when you move your left hand further up the neck and place your hand so that your index finger is on a fret (fifth or sixth fret) that you'd normally play with your third finger.

TIP

Try to learn one position of the mandolin at a time. I suggest that you may be most comfortable playing tunes in a few keys in first position before moving up the neck.

Moving up the mandolin's neck

Trying to contemplate the possibility of 12 major and 12 minor scales (I explain scales in Chapter 2) multiplied by the number of up-the-neck positions available on the mandolin can easily give you a headache. Instead, just remember that no matter how many scales or positions exist, you only have four fingers and, as a result, only four shapes or patterns for each scale.

In this section, I show the G major, A major and D major scales in each of the four shapes. This concept is called FFcP (Four Finger closed Position) and is demonstrated in depth on the following website: www.jazzmando.com.

First finger

Play the scale, starting with your first finger on the *root note* (first note of the scale). Check out Figure 6-20, noticing the specific pattern or shape on the fingerboard. Because all the notes are *closed* (fretted), you can move this pattern or shape to another location (up, down or across strings) on the fingerboard, and it becomes another key.

Although the pattern starts with the first finger playing the root note, it ends with the fourth finger playing the octave (I define octaves in Chapter 2). You can continue the scale into the next octave using the fourth-finger pattern.

Figure 6-20: Root note on the first finger (fingerboard).

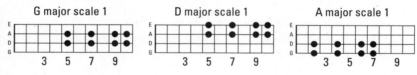

Second finger

Try the same scale again, but this time play the root note of the scale with your second finger. Notice that this fingering of the same scale makes a new pattern (see Figure 6-21). You can move this scale pattern up, down or across the strings, and the root note is the one under the second finger.

Although the pattern starts with the second finger playing the root note, it ends with the first finger playing the octave, and so you can continue the scale into the next octave using the first-finger pattern.

Third finger

Play the same scale again but this time play the root note with your third finger. Once more, this fingering of the same scale makes a new pattern (see Figure 6-22). This scale pattern can also be moved up, down or across the strings, and the root note is the one under the third finger.

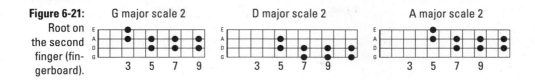

Figure 6-21:
Root on the second finger (fingerboard).

Although the pattern starts with the third finger playing the root note, it ends with the second finger playing the octave. You can continue the scale into the next octave using the second-finger pattern.

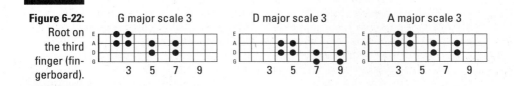

Figure 6-22:
Root on the third finger (fingerboard).

Fourth finger

Last but not least, play the same scale but this time play the root note with your fourth finger. Notice that this fourth-finger root fingering makes a new pattern (see Figure 6-23). This scale pattern can also be moved up, down or across the strings, and the root note is the one under the fourth finger.

The pattern starts with the fourth finger playing the root note, but ends with the third finger playing the octave. You can continue the scale into the next octave using the third-finger pattern.

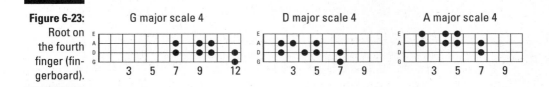

Figure 6-23:
Root on the fourth finger (fingerboard).

Playing two notes simultaneously: Double stops

Double stop is a term that describes the technique of fretting two strings at the same time. Double stops can be tough to understand at first but are an essential part of mandolin playing. The technique enables you to add extra colour and harmony to your mandolin playing. In order to understand double stops, you need a basic understanding of *chord tones* (as shown in Figure 6-27), which are the notes included in a chord, and a good understanding of the fingerboard (as shown in Figure 6-26).

Major and minor chords have three notes (see Figure 6-27); double stops are simply two notes from a chord, played simultaneously. In use, a double stop often includes the *melody* note (the top note of the double stop) and another chord *tone* (the bottom note of the double stop) played simultaneously.

In Figures 6-24 and 6-25, I show a variety of A major and A minor double stops. In each case, the double stop is named by the highest chord tone (root, third, fifth – see Chapter 7 for more on these terms). In all cases, the named chord tone is the highest note and is played on the higher of the two strings being used. I've organised the double stops in Figure 6-24 according to chord tones. Measure 1 shows two double-stop shapes for an A major chord featuring the fifth of the chord as the highest or top note. In the first example, the double stop contains the notes A and E, which are the root and the fifth of the A major chord. In the next example, the double stop contains the notes C♯ and E, which are the third and the fifth of the A major chord.

The idea here is to memorise these double-stop shapes and combine the shapes with your growing knowledge of the fretboard and chord tones, enabling you to play double stops up and down the neck for a variety of chords. This won't happen overnight, but over time you'll begin to see where these double stops are located.

As you get to grips with double stops, you'll find some overlap or similarity to chords that you may already know. For example, the all-purpose A chord shown in Chapter 4 is a double stop with two additional open strings added to it. This double stop appears as the first double stop position in Figures 6-24 and 6-25 due to the fact that both A major (A, C♯ and E) and A minor (A, C and E) contain the notes A and E. Figures 6-26 and 6-27 (later on in this chapter) may be useful in finding double stops for any chord or song.

Don't forget to memorise the chords to every song that you learn to play. Many embellishments are based around expanding the melody to include additional notes of a chord, which can be tricky because you need to understand where the chords change in relation to the melody. This type of playing takes years to develop, and so don't expect to be very good at it overnight. Be patient and keep working at it; eventually it becomes a natural part of your playing.

A major double stops

The double-stop shapes in Figure 6-24 apply to the A major chord, but by looking up the chord tones in Figure 6-27, finding the location of the chord tones in Figure 6-26, and applying the double-stop shapes in Figure 6-24, you can play double stops in all keys and positions of the mandolin.

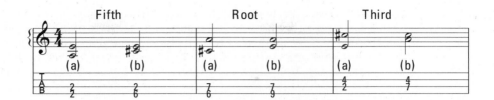

Figure 6-24: A chord double stops.

To find double stops for any chord, follow these steps:

1. **Determine what notes are in the chord (use Figure 6-26).**

2. **Find the notes on the mandolin neck (using Figure 6-27).**

3. **Refer to Figures 6-24 and 6-25 for the double-stop shapes for each chord.**

4. **Apply double stops to the melody, remembering to follow the chord progression of the song.**

A minor double stops

Figure 6-25 demonstrates double stops for the Am chord. Notice that the only difference between Am and A (major) is that the third of the chord is one fret (half step) lower, as shown in Table 6-27. This means that the double-stop shapes for minor chords are slightly different from their major chord partners when the double stop contains the third of the chord.

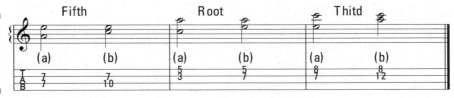

Figure 6-25: Am chord double stops.

Figure 6-26 shows you where all the notes on the mandolin are located. Notice that only the *natural* notes (that is, not sharps or flats) have letter names. Also notice that, like a piano, the sharps and flats are in black, where the natural notes are in white. When locating a C♯, first find a C note, and then move up one fret (half step) to the next note that appears in black. This note is C♯. Note that this pitch (C♯) can also be called D♭ by starting at D and moving down one fret (half step).

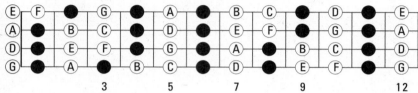

Figure 6-26:
The mandolin fingerboard.

The fancy musical term for the fact that C♯ sounds exactly like Db, and actually is the same pitch, is *enharmonic equivalent*, meaning two names for the same pitch. As you learn more about scales (see Chapter 8) you'll be able to see why this is done.

Figure 6-27 shows all 12 major and minor chords and the notes that each chord contains.

Chord	Root	Third	Fifth	Chord	Root	Third	Fifth
C	C	E	G	**Cm**	C	E♭	G
D♭	D♭	F	A♭	**D♭m**	D♭	F♭ (E)	A♭
D	D	F♯	A	**Dm**	D	F	A
E♭	E♭	G	B♭	**E♭m**	E♭	G♭	B♭
E	E	G♯	B	**Em**	E	G	B
F	F .	A	C	**Fm**	F	A♭	C
F♯	F♯	A♯	C♯	**F♯m**	F♯	A	C♯
G	G	B	D	**Gm**	G	B♭	D
A♭	A♭	C	E♭	**A♭m**	A♭	C♭ (B)	E♭
A	A	C♯	E	**Am**	A	C	E
B♭	B♭	D	F	**B♭m**	B♭	D♭	F
B	B	D♯	F♯	**Bm**	B	D	F♯

Figure 6-27:
Chord tones.

Chapter 7

Playing 'Jethro'-Style Three-String Chords

- -

In This Chapter

▶ Discovering Jethro Burns's chords

▶ Working with major and minor three-string chords

▶ Trying out seventh three-string chords

▶ Getting all jazzy

- -

Although many chords that you play on the mandolin use all four strings (as I describe in Chapter 6), this approach is by no means the only way to form chords. The great mandolin virtuoso and innovator Jethro Burns, for example, preferred to use three-string chords.

Three-string chords take full advantage of the symmetry of the mandolin fretboard, meaning that unlike a guitar, ukulele or banjo, the relationship of each string to the next string on the mandolin fretboard is always the same. What this means in plain English is that not only can you move chord shapes up and down the neck to arrive at different chords, as demonstrated by barré chords in Chapter 6, you also can move the same chord shape across the strings to arrive at yet more chords. Multiply this concept by just a few easy-to-play shapes and you suddenly unlock hundreds of chords!

But wait, there's more! In jazz, a common practice is to use good voice leading when switching from one chord to the next. *Good voice leading* means moving from chord to chord as efficiently as possible (that is, moving only the notes that need to move, and by as short a distance as possible). So if you're playing a G7 around the fifth fret and your next chord is C, you look for a C chord around the fifth fret with as many common *tones* (notes belonging to both chords) as possible. Three-string chords make this easy.

So, because three-string chords are such a great weapon to have in your mandolin arsenal, I use this chapter to describe three-string chords in major, minor and seventh forms. And because Jethro was a great player of jazz mandolin, I take a look at some jazzy chords as well. Three-string chords work well in jazz, and also in blues or pop songs with more complex chord progressions. Jethro used these three-string chords (which I use throughout Chapter 13) to create chord–melody arrangements, or melody and chords played simultaneously.

Don't let all the chord shapes and terms that I describe in this chapter scare you. Simply expand your chord vocabulary naturally as your musical repertoire grows. For example, you don't need to learn an E♭7 chord if you don't know any songs that use it. As you discover and practise more pop and jazz songs, these at-first-strange-looking chords are sure to become more familiar.

Introducing Jethro Burns's Three-String Chord Style

A chord is the sound of three or more notes being played at the same time; you can build chords from any of the seven notes in a scale. The specific note with which you start building each chord is called the *root*. A *triad* (three-note chord) consists of a root, a note that's an interval of a *third* (two scale steps) above the root, and a note that's an interval of a *fifth* (four scale steps) above the root. You can arrange these notes in any order: the root note doesn't need to be the lowest note; the lowest note can be the root, the third or the fifth. Chapter 6 lists the major and minor triads.

Great as three-string chords are, you need to pay attention when playing them, because the mandolin has four (pairs of) strings, which leaves one string unused when playing three-string chords. This can create a bit of a problem when strumming all four strings. If the chord only uses the d-, a- and e-strings, for example, you need a bit of practice to avoid hitting the unused g-string with your pick, whereas if the chord only uses the g-, d- and a-strings, you can mute the unused e-string with the side of your third or fourth finger.

Overall, three-string chords work best in styles like jazz, blues, choro or pop music, where accompaniment styles don't make much use of up-and-down strumming. And if you're playing folk music such as old-time fiddle tunes and waltzes, the traditional open four-string chords shown in Chapters 4 and 6 work best.

Perfecting Three-String Major Chords

In this section, I demonstrate the three-string major chords that form the core of the Jethro-style chording technique. These chords consist of three different easy-to-make shapes that you'll be able to play – no matter what size hands you have! In later sections of this chapter, I explain how you can transform these major chords into minor chords or seventh chords by moving one of the *chord tones* (the notes in chord) up or down a few frets.

Root-on-top major chords

Figure 7-1 contains multiple chord diagrams that show how this root-on-top chord form can function as many different chords, depending on where you place your hands on the fretboard, along with a photo of a three-string D major chord with the root on top. You can make this chord shape using your first, second and fourth fingers, or your first, second and third if you have big hands!

In these root-on-top major chords, the chord letter name is the highest note.

Figure 7-1: Root-on-top major chords: (a) chord diagrams; (b) photo.

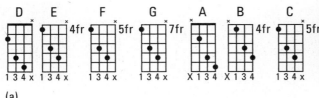

(a) (b)

Third-on-top major chords

This chord shape requires you to use only two fingers: your index finger to barré the two lowest strings, and your third finger for the next string. You make the chords A, B, C and D by placing this shape on various frets using the three lowest strings (g, d and a), and to make the chords E, F and G you move the same shape over to the higher strings (d, a and e). Check out Figure 7-2 to see the chord diagrams and a photo of an A major chord with the third on top.

The third of the chord is the highest note, and the letter name (root note) is the lowest note in this chord form.

Figure 7-2: Third-on-top major chords: (a) chord diagrams; (b) photo.

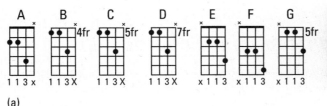

(a) (b)

Fifth-on-top major chords

To master this easy-to-play chord, you need to use just two fingers. However, you have to make a slight adjustment to the way your fingers touch the fretboard, because you need your second finger to cover two strings. Lay your first and second fingers flat as opposed to standing them on their tips. You can think of this as a mini-barré (not to be confused with the mini-bar you'd find in a hotel room!) that is performed by your second finger. For the fifth-on-top major chord diagrams and a photo of an E major chord with the fifth on top (and to see how your fingers should look while laid flat), take a look at Figure 7-3.

In this chord form, the fifth is the highest note, and the letter name (root note) is the middle note.

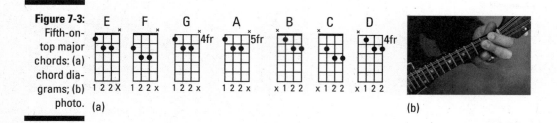

Figure 7-3: Fifth-on-top major chords: (a) chord diagrams; (b) photo.

(a)   (b)

Mastering Three-String Minor Chords

The beauty and simplicity of the three-string chording method becomes apparent when you look at minor chords. These minor forms are nothing but slight variations on the three major chord forms I look at in the preceding section. The only difference between a major chord and a minor chord is that you play one note – the third of the chord – one half step or one fret lower in the minor chord. The other two notes remain the same. Minor chords have a darker or sadder sound than major chords, but are used in many songs in combination with major chords to create a more colourful sound.

To find out more on minor chords, flip to Chapters 2 and 6. And remember: there's nothing trivial (or under-age) about these minor chords!

Root-on-top minor chords

The root-on-top three-string minor chord is only a small variation on the root-on-top major chord. You hold your first and fourth fingers in exactly the same shape as in the root-on-top major chord form, but move the note you play with your third finger down one fret and play it with your second finger. Just remember that your third finger is major and your second finger is minor, and you'll be fine. I show you the moveable chord diagrams and a photo of my hand making the three-string root-on-top D minor chord form in Figure 7-4.

In these minor chords, the chord letter name (the root note) is the highest note in this form.

Figure 7-4:
Root-on-top minor chords: (a) chord diagrams; (b) photo.

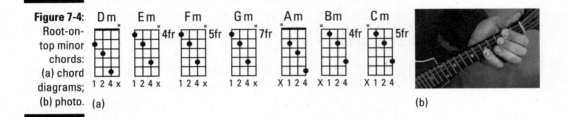

(a)   (b)

Third-on-top minor chords

The third-on-top three-string minor chord is only a small variation on the third-on-top major chord. You hold your first finger in exactly the same position as in the third-on-top major chord form, but you move the note you play with your third finger down by one fret and play it with your second finger. The same rule applies as with the root-on-top three-string chords, in that the third finger is major and second finger is minor. Figure 7-5 shows you the chord diagrams (remember these chords are moveable) and a photo of an Am three-string minor chord with the third on top.

The third of the chord is the highest note, and the chord's letter name (root note) is the lowest note in this form.

Figure 7-5:
Third-on-top minor chords: (a) chord diagrams; (b) photo.

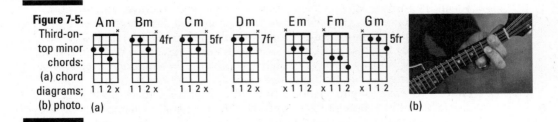

(a)   (b)

Fifth-on-top minor chords

The fifth-on-top three-string minor chord form varies only slightly from the fifth-on-top major chord form. In this form, the note that needs to be moved down one fret to become minor is the lowest note in the chord, which you play with your first finger. This transition, although still quite easy to do, isn't as simple as the other two chord forms in this section.

To show the difference between the major and minor chords in this form, first make the fifth-on-top major chord (see Figure 7-3). Next, move your first finger down one fret and replace your second finger with your third finger, creating a mini-barré with your third finger. Remember to keep your third finger flat – not on its fingertip – to make the barré.

Check out Figure 7-6 for the chord diagrams and a photo of the fifth-on-top three-string moveable chord, played between the second and fourth frets to make an F♯m chord.

In this form, the fifth of the chord is the highest note, and the letter name (root note) is the middle note.

Figure 7-6:
Fifth-on-top minor chords: (a) chord diagrams; (b) photo.

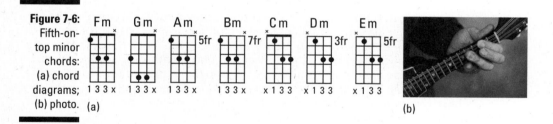

Trying on a few Seventh Chords for Size

Seventh chords suggest a feeling of movement or un-resolve, and are commonly used in many types of music, including blues, jazz, ragtime and pop. In this section I demonstrate four variations on the seventh chord instead of three, simply because seventh chords technically have four notes in them. I do, however, show you ways to play seventh chords with only three strings, by eliminating one of the four notes – either the root or the fifth of each chord – to leave only three notes (including the third and seventh). Jazz musicians often delete notes from their chord playing, focusing only on the most colourful notes of each chord. They agree that the two most important or colourful notes in seventh chords are the third and the seventh.

The three-string seventh chords here derive from the three-string major chord forms shown earlier in this chapter. Technically these chords have four notes in them – the *root* (or name of the chord), the *third* (the note that determines whether the chord is major or minor), the *fifth* (the note that is the least important) and the seventh. The *seventh* is the seventh note in the scale, counting from the root but with one interesting twist: you flat the note by one half step or one fret. So, to make a G7 chord, for example, you count up the G scale (G, A, B, C, D, E, F#) to the seventh step to determine that F# is the seventh note. You flat it by one half step (that is, one fret) to arrive at F (sometimes called F natural). This is the formula for the common seventh chord that is also referred to as a *dominant seventh*.

Root-on-top seventh chords

The root-on-top seventh chord form is very common among blues and jazz mandolin players (and is used in the blues and ragtime tunes in Chapter 9).

 You can see how this chord is derived from one of the three-string major chords shown earlier in this chapter, by comparing the D7 chord diagram in Figure 7-7 to the D chord diagram in Figure 7-1. Two of the three notes are included in both chords, meaning that one of the D chord notes was sacrificed in order to include the seventh note, therefore making this a three-string seventh chord. This is achieved by moving the fifth of the D chord (A) up three frets, or one and one half steps, to the flatted seventh (C) turning the D chord into a D7.

Take a look a Figure 7-7, which shows the chord diagrams and a photo of my hands playing a B7 with the root on top. In these moveable seventh chords, the letter name or root of the chord is the highest note in this form.

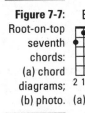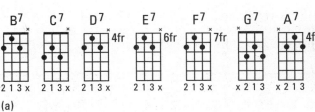

Figure 7-7: Root-on-top seventh chords: (a) chord diagrams; (b) photo.

Third-on-top seventh chords

The third-on-top seventh chord form is nothing more than the third-on-top major chord (see the earlier 'Third-on-top major chords' section) with the lowest note (played by the first finger) moved down two frets or one whole step. The lowest note in the major chord form is the root note of the chord. By moving the root note down two frets, you replace the root with the flatted seventh, making this a three-note seventh chord with the third on top.

Figure 7-8 contains the moveable chord diagrams and a photo of a three-string chord with the third on top played in the position of B7. Compare it with Figure 7-7, which was also a B7 but shown as a different chord form.

The third of the chord is the highest note, and the root note is in fact missing from this form. Some seventh chords sacrifice the root of the chord, leaving just the third, fifth and seventh notes.

Figure 7-8:
Third-on-top seventh chords: (a) chord diagrams; (b) photo.

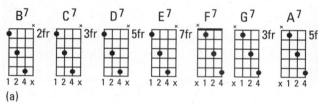

(a)

(b)

Fifth-on-top seventh chords

Make this chord by starting with a fifth-on-top major chord (see the 'Fifth-on-top major chords' section earlier in this chapter) and moving the root note (here, that is the middle note) down two frets. Compare the F chord in Figure 7-3 with the F7 chord in Figure 7-9 and you'll see that the only difference is one note being two frets lower in the F7 than in the F.

I show you the moveable chord diagrams and a photo of an F7 chord with the fifth on top in Figure 7-9. The fifth of the chord is the highest note, and the root is also missing from this form (as I explain in the preceding section).

Grasping the magic of three-string chords

You aren't going to get to grips with all these three-string chords overnight, but stick with it and these little three-note wonders are sure to prove well worth the trouble. I have a video at www.youtube.com/donjulinlessons where I demonstrate 324 three-string chords in less than four minutes. All these chords are alterations of the basic three inversions (chord shapes) that I cover in this chapter.

Another jazzy tip

Chord melodies (ways to play the melody and chords at the same time by yourself), which I describe in more detail in Chapters 8 and 13, are fairly common in the jazz world and require you to know many extended chords based around the three-note chord inversions that I describe in this section. To hear what I'm talking about, listen to some of Burns's albums on the Acoustic Disc label, such as *Swing Low, Sweet Mandolin, Bye Bye Blues* and *Tea For One*.

Figure 7-9:
Fifth-on-top seventh chords: (a) chord diagrams; (b) photo.

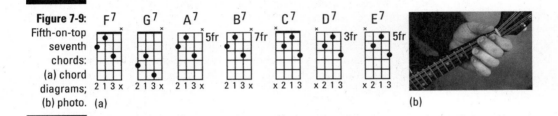

(a) (b)

Seventh-on-top seventh chords

This form is simply the root-on-top major chord form (shown in the 'Root-on-top major chords' section earlier in the chapter) with the root or top note moved down two frets. To illustrate this, compare the D chords in Figure 7-1 with the D7 chord in Figure 7-10.

Figure 7-10 contains the seventh-on-top seventh chord diagrams and a photo of a D7 chord with the seventh (C) on top. The seventh of the chord is the highest note, and the letter name is missing from this form (as I describe in the earlier section 'Third-on-top seventh chords').

Figure 7-10:
Seventh-on-top seventh chords: (a) chord diagrams; (b) photo.

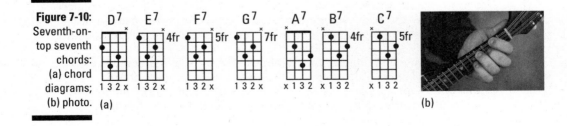

(a) (b)

Revving up for Jazzy Chords: Nice!

In this section I introduce you to a few great, easy-to-play, jazzy-sounding three-string chords that really spice up your playing. If jazz and/or swing is your groovy thing, also check out Chapter 13, which contains more information on playing jazz styles on the mandolin.

Listening to jazz musicians talk about chords can be a bit like maths nerds discussing some arcane form of trigonometry; such discussions can get very philosophical and obscure. Loads of books already exist on the theory and mind-bending equations (with *The Jazz Theory Book,* written by Mark Levine and published by Sher Music, being highly regarded, if you're so inclined) so I don't cover much of that here.

Don't think too hard about technical issues (such as 'demolished' and 'argumentative' chords), because you'll give yourself a headache. Just learn a few songs that use such unusual chords, and digest the sound a bit before trying to understand the theory.

Learning the notes on the mandolin fretboard (whether you plan on reading music or not) makes your life much easier when tackling these jazzy chords. Refer to Chapter 6 for an illustration of a mandolin fretboard that includes the note names.

Sounding unresolved with diminished chords

Diminished chords are chords with flatted thirds (see the earlier 'Mastering Three-String Minor Chords' section) and flatted fifths (and even double flatted sevenths) that sound like minor chords on steroids, in that they sound even sadder than minor chords (yes, that is possible!). These diminished chords (which you can also call *diminished seventh chords*) are used in swing, classical, ragtime, bossa nova, choro and other styles, and they have a tense, very unresolved sound. You can use them as transitional chords – as a way of connecting one chord to the next – but only for short durations of one measure or less. This chord shape is used for both diminished and diminished seventh chord forms.

One of the coolest things about diminished chords is that you can use one shape (see Figure 7-11) to make any number of diminished chords. By using this one shape, all you need to do is make sure that the note name of the chord (the root note) is one (any one) of the notes in the chord.

Notice in Figure 7-11 that the first three chords are all G diminished and that they are all the same shape. Now, see that the root note (G) is in a different spot in each chord. In the first example, G is on top; in the second one, G is in the middle; and in the third chord, G is on the bottom. The same holds true for the three A diminished chords that follow. All in one easy-to-use chord shape! This shape is the same one as used for the fifth-on-top seventh chord. It may seem strange, but one three-string chord shape really can have this variety of names.

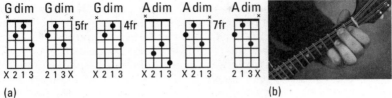

Figure 7-11: Diminished chords: (a) diagrams; (b) photo.

Adding augmented chords to your mandolin armoury

Augmented chords (sometimes called *augmented seventh chords*) are unique in that the fifth of the chord is raised one half step or one fret higher. They function in a similar way to seventh chords (see the earlier section 'Trying on a few Seventh Chords for Size') and supply a similar function of leading or pulling the song to the next chord. You can't really stop a song on an augmented chord. Well, I guess you can, but it would sound very strange. As with the diminished chords from the preceding section, augmented chords are presented in one moveable shape.

Figure 7-12 shows that the first three chords are all G augmented and that, like the diminished chords, they're all the same shape. And like diminished chords, the root note (G) is in a different spot in each chord: first on top, then in the middle, and finally on the bottom. The same holds true for the three A diminished chords too.

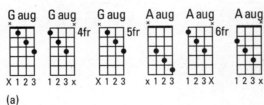

Figure 7-12: Augmented chords: (a) diagrams; (b) photo.

Dressing up some minor chords: Minor sevenths

Minor seventh chords are minor chords with a flatted seventh added. Just think of them as dolled-up minor chords. I talk a bit more about their function in jazz in Chapter 13. (Check out Chapter 6 for more on minor and seventh chords.)

Figure 7-13 shows four common minor seventh chord shapes. As with the seventh chords shown earlier in this chapter, there are four moveable shapes named by which *chord tone* (the notes in a chord) is on top. The Gm7 in Figure 7-13 has the root on top or as the highest note; the Bm7 features the third on top; the Em7 has the seventh on top, and the F#m7 contains the fifth on top. Notice that the F#m7 is the same shape as the A chord shown in Figure 7-2 – a case of two chords named differently that require you to place your hand in the exact same shape. Remember that all four of these minor seventh chord forms are moveable both up and down the neck as well as sideways over one string.

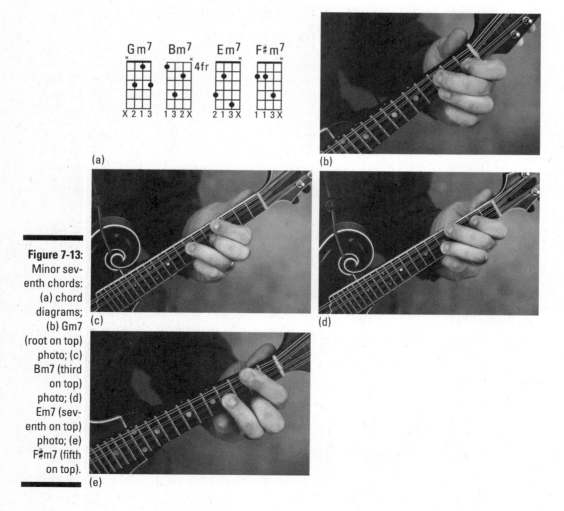

Figure 7-13: Minor seventh chords: (a) chord diagrams; (b) Gm7 (root on top) photo; (c) Bm7 (third on top) photo; (d) Em7 (seventh on top) photo; (e) F#m7 (fifth on top).

All minor seventh chords like the seventh chord earlier in this chapter techni-cally contain four notes and so, in order to make a three-note version, one note (and hence one string) is eliminated. (After all, the title of this chapter is 'Playing Jethro-style Three-String Chords'!). I present a few four-note minor seventh chords in Chapter 14.

Here is your chance to put many of the chords used in this chapter to use. Figure 7-14 is a common jazz chord progression using major, minor, seventh, diminished, augmented and minor seventh Jethro Burns style three-note chords. You can hear this tune on Track 31.

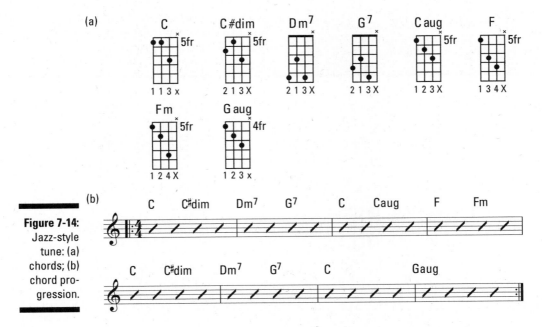

Figure 7-14: Jazz-style tune: (a) chords; (b) chord pro-gression.

Figure 7-15 is a jazzy, Jethro-style, blues-based progression using major, sev-enth, augmented and diminished three-string chords, which you can hear on Track 32.

Homer and Jethro

Homer and Jethro were American superstars! Jethro's real name was Kenneth C. Burns (1920–1989) and Homer's was Henry D. Haynes (1920–1971). They were best known for their satirical versions of popular songs.

Homer and Jethro were not only funny, but also could play with the best. You may want to find a copy of their records *Playing it Straight* and *It Ain't Necessarily Square*, both on RCA. These recordings impacted a generation of mandolin players such as Sam Bush, David Grisman,

Jimmy Gaudreau, Barry Mitterhoff, Peter Ostroushko, Don Stiernberg and many others. According to Don Stiernberg, 'One theory is that the modern mandolin style is a combination of the Jethro school and the Bill Monroe (bluegrass) school. Without those two players, and the synthesis of their work by David Grisman, Sam Bush and all the rest, you wouldn't be able to enjoy the work of Chris Thile and the other virtuosi of today.' (See Chapter 20 for brief biographies of some of these great musicians.)

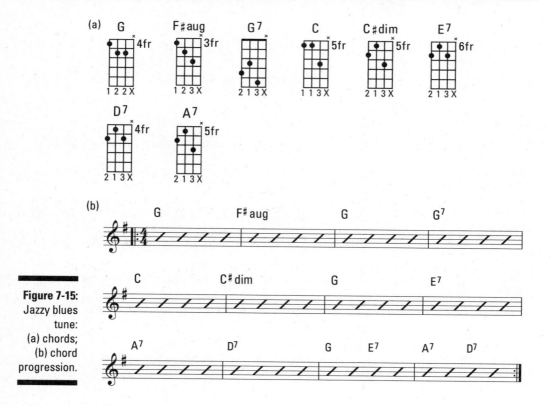

Figure 7-15: Jazzy blues tune: (a) chords; (b) chord progression.

Chapter 8

Playing Mandolin Music: Scales and Melody

The point of practising the chords and various left- and right-hand techniques that I describe in Chapters 4–7 is to play tunes and songs, perhaps in front of an audience (no one wants to hear you practising a new chord!). So if you're confident in those aspects, you're reading the right chapter, because here you begin to make melodic mandolin music.

Scales are integral to playing melodies, so I present a few common ones along with several songs composed from these scales. These pieces range in style from old time to light classical and even a rockin' skiffle tune. Each of these tunes requires you to use specific left- and right-hand techniques (check out Chapters 5, 6 and 7) with fairly simple melodies to make them come alive on the mandolin. I also show you a few mandolin rhythm styles to spice up your rhythmic playing.

I recorded the audio tracks for this chapter using a Flatiron Cadet 'pancake' mandolin (which you can see in Figure 15-4(a) in Chapter 15).

Understanding How to Play Melody

First and foremost the mandolin is a melody instrument. In this section I want to impress on you a couple of invaluable tips for getting to grips with playing melodies, as well as the central importance of scales.

Listening to the great players

Being able to hear what you want to play is essential. My mantra is 'Hear it, learn it, memorise it!'

All the great mandolin players discovered how to play in this way. Although learning by ear can be frustrating at first, going very slowly and tackling just one phrase at a time helps a lot.

Don't try to take on 30 seconds of music at a time; instead, break it down into 3- to 5-second phrases. When you can play a phrase many times without making mistakes, go on to the next one; and when you have a few phrases down, start stringing them together.

In this way, you can eventually make it through the entire melody. Then put on a recording of the piece and try to play along with it.

Speaking a tune

Music is sound, and imitation is the most successful form of learning. I urge you to listen to a recording at least a few times before you try playing the tune because you need to be able to sing, hum or at the very least hear the melody in your head before you attempt to play it. As I say, 'If you can't say it, you can't play it!'

One of the best tools for learning music from a recording is via the Amazing Slow Downer at www.ronimusic.com. This software allows you to adjust the speed of a recording without affecting the pitch, and also has some other features that make learning by ear much easier.

Rising to the challenge of scales

The *major scale* is the cornerstone of music in western or European culture (as opposed to Asian, African or Martian culture). The major scale consists of a pattern of *whole steps* (two frets) and *half steps* (one fret) – the pattern for the major scale being whole, whole, half, whole, whole, whole, half. Other scales such as modes (see Chapter 11) and different types of minor scale (which I look at later in this chapter) are *alterations* (flatting or sharping certain notes) or *variations* (starting the note sequence on a different note from usual) on this major scale.

Scales: What's the big deal?

Scales are nowhere as scary as they may seem at first. Think of a scale as no more than a group of notes that sound good together. Musicians then use this group of notes to create melodies and chords. *Scale* and *key* mean the same thing, and so a musician who asks 'What key are we in?' wants to know what scale to use to find the melody notes or the chords.

Music from different locations around the world may use different types of scales. For example, most traditional gospel hymns and ragtime tunes written in the early years of America are in major keys, while Irish tunes can be major, minor or modal (see Chapter 11). Eastern European music, meanwhile, is known for its use of the harmonic minor scales (see the 'Mining the A minor scale for two different approaches' section later in this chapter).

The melodies (and chords) that you play on the mandolin consist primarily of notes within a scale. For example, tunes in the key of G are made up of melody notes from the G scale played along with chords that contain notes from the G scale. Memorising the G scale – including

- ✔ knowing the note names
- ✔ being able to sing or hum the scale, and
- ✔ knowing where to place your fingers on the fretboard to play the notes of the scale

– makes learning any song in the key of G much easier. Being able to read standard notation and tablature and being able to play by ear are all great skills to possess, but you can benefit greatly by knowing the scales used in the music you choose to play.

When you learn scales, a good tip to remember is to do what some people call *noodling* – that is, just playing random patterns of notes from a scale or trying to find familiar melodies by ear that contain the notes of the scale you're working on. Time spent exploring the sound and fingerings of a G scale, for example, turns out to be time well spent when you set out to learn a new tune in the key of G from a book or by ear.

Exploring some Major Scales

In all, 12 major scales exist, but mandolin players tend to like scales that have sharps in the key signature more than scales that have flats in the key signature (see Appendix B).

Mandolins are commonly used in the major keys of D, A, G and C. These scales are easy to play – in part, because they all contain open strings, which takes advantage of the ringing open-string sound and makes left-hand fingering much easier. You can play hundreds of melodies by using these scales without even using your fourth finger!

Discovering the D major scale

The key of D major contains two sharps (C♯ and F♯). The *primary* or most common major chords in the key of D are D, G and A (or A7). The *secondary* but still important minor chords in the key of D are Bm, Em and F♯m.

Figure 8-1 shows a D major scale in first (that is, open) position (check out Chapter 6 for all about playing positions). Notice that the root note (D) is larger and bolder than the other notes in the figure (Chapter 7 describes root notes). Practise the scale from D to D first, and then try to memorise all the notes below and above the basic range of the D scale.

Figure 8-1: The D major scale.

Adding scale runs

Scale runs (which are sometimes called *passing tones*) are the extra notes that aren't essential to the melody.

One way to think about scale runs is as if you're singing the song. In such a case, you'd normally sing only the melody, but when you hear a melody played as an instrumental, the musician usually uses more notes from the scale from which the song is derived. The melody notes are still included, but additional notes are played to make the melody more interesting and to create more melodic variation.

Following 'The Flop-Eared Mule'

In this section, I show you a mandolin arrangement of 'The Flop-Eared Mule' featuring scale runs to fill out the melody.

The melody of this tune is in the key of D; Figure 8-2 shows how someone may sing this song using the basic melody. An old-time strum pattern (such as I provide in Chapter 9) would sound great with a tune like this one. I show the chords in Figure 8-3.

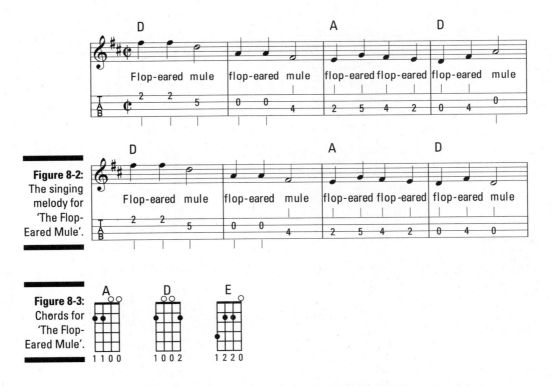

Figure 8-2: The singing melody for 'The Flop-Eared Mule'.

Figure 8-3: Chords for 'The Flop-Eared Mule'.

Adding scale runs, drone strings (see the following section for how to drone!) and some eighth notes (quavers) makes 'The Flop-Eared Mule' really sound like mandolin music (see Figure 8-4 and Track 33).

Listen to 'The Flop-Eared Mule' on Track 33 a few times and then try to play along with it. I suggest playing the chords using the strumming pattern from Figure 9-1 (see Chapter 9) along with the recording before trying to learn the melody.

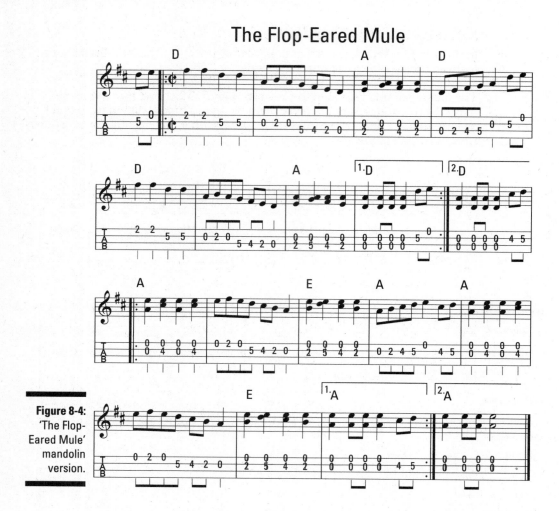

The Flop-Eared Mule

Figure 8-4:
'The Flop-
Eared Mule'
mandolin
version.

Notice the two parts to 'The Flop-Eared Mule' and the *repeat signs*, the latter being indicated by double-bar lines and two dots at the end of each part, creating the form *AABB*. (The first section is the A part, and the second section the B part. By following the repeat signs or just by listening, you can see that you play the A part twice followed by the B part played twice – hence the AABB form.)

Pay attention to your pick direction (see Chapter 5) and remember that, in alternate picking: numbered beats are down; ands are up.

Accessing the A major scale

The key of A major contains three sharps (C♯, F♯ and G♯). The *primary* or major chords for the key of A major are A, D and E (or E7), with the *secondary* or minor chords being F♯m, Bm and C♯m. Figure 8-5 shows an A major scale in first (open) position with the root note (A) larger and bolder than the other notes (Chapter 7 covers root notes for you). The A scale has two full octaves in first position.

Before I get onto a tune in A major ('Simple Gifts'), I want to introduce a couple of extra techniques to spice things up a little and allow you to play the chords using an interesting arpeggio technique.

Figure 8-5:
The A major scale.

Using drone strings

A *drone* is an adjacent open string that you pick at the same time as you're picking your melody string. The open string harmonises (creating a two-note chord) with the fingered or open note that you're playing on the melody string. This technique works best in keys that contain the open strings needed for the drone effect. Good drone keys for mandolin are G (drone g- and d-strings), D (drone d- and a-strings), and A (drone a- and e-strings).

The drone can be higher or lower than the melody, and usually is the root (first) or the fifth step of the scale you're playing in (which, in this section, is A – so, **A**, B, C♯, D, **E**, F♯, G♯, A). For example, if you're playing in the key of A, the a-string and the e-string can be drones, because they are the first and the fifth steps of the scale (see Figure 8-5) while you play the melody. If the melody is on the a-string, drone the e. If the melody is on the e-string, drone the a. Notice in 'Simple Gifts' how the drone strings create a fuller sound (see the later section 'Playing Simple Gifts' and Figure 8-8).

Providing a non-strumming accompaniment with arpeggios

Strumming isn't always the best option when you're supplying a rhythm accompaniment. Another option is to use a string-crossing arpeggio pattern. *Arpeggios* are also called *broken chords* because they use the notes of the chord, sounded one note at a time. Figure 8-6 illustrates three examples of this type of accompaniment.

Figure 8-6:
Three examples of arpeggio accompaniment picking patterns.

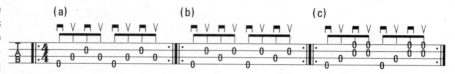

Playing 'Simple Gifts'

This popular song is a Shaker hymn written in 1848 by Elder Joseph Brackett. This arrangement uses drone strings to spice up the melody and give it a uniquely mandolin type of sound. The rhythm mandolin part is demonstrated on Track 34 using the non-strumming accompaniment technique (shown in Figure 8-6(a)) and the simple chords in Figure 8-7.

Figure 8-7:
'Simple Gifts' chords.

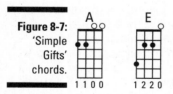

I suggest playing this medium-tempo melody of 'Simple Gifts' using all down-strokes (see Figure 8-8 and Track 34). When you can play the melody, you may want to learn the accompaniment part.

Simple Gifts

Figure 8-8:
'Simple Gifts' melody.

Getting to grips with the G major scale

The key of G major contains one sharp (F♯), and features the *primary or major* chords G, C and D (or D7) and the *secondary* or minor chords Em, Am and Bm. Figure 8-9 shows a G major scale in first (open) position, with the root note (G) larger and bolder than the other notes. The G scale has two full octaves in first position.

Figure 8-9:
The G major
scale.

'Minuet in G' (BMW Ahn. 114), from the *Notebook for Anna Magdalena Bach*, was once thought to be written by JS Bach, but is now universally attributed to Christian Petzold. This piece is surely one of the most played pieces of classical music in the entire world.

Track 35 features the melody for 'Minuet in G' (as shown in Figure 8-11) in the right speaker, and a rhythm mandolin playing the chords (see Figure 8-10) in the left speaker using the waltz strumming pattern shown in Figure 9-1 (turn to Chapter 9 for more on waltzes). This approach blends the two musical styles of classical and folk.

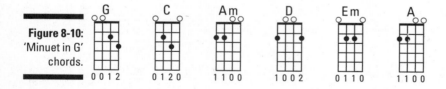

Figure 8-10:
'Minuet in G'
chords.

Notice the *staccato* marks (dots above certain notes) placed over many of the quarter notes (crotchets) (see Figure 6-9 in Chapter 6). Staccato markings indicate that you need to shorten the note a bit to put a small amount of silence between the notes. To do so on the mandolin, you use left-hand muting techniques (which you can read up on in Chapter 6).

A fretted note is easier to mute than an open note, and so I choose to play some of the staccato notes with my little finger at the seventh fret instead of the open string of the same note.

Minuet in G

Figure 8-11:
'Minuet in G'
melody.

Avoiding sharps and flats with the C major scale

The key of C major contains no sharps or flats. Its *primary* or major chords are C, F and G (or G7), and the *secondary* or minor chords are Am, Dm and Em. Figure 8-12 shows a C major scale in first (open) position with the root note (C) distinguished from the other notes by being larger and bolder.

Two octaves of the C scale almost fit into first position, and so you need to bend the rules a bit and play the highest two notes (B and C) with your fourth finger at the seventh and eighth frets of the e- (first) string.

Figure 8-12: The C major scale.

The tune 'Skiffle Mando' uses double stops and slides (I describe both of these left-hand techniques in Chapter 6) and demonstrates how a mandolin can play a boogie-style rock tune (this piece features a rocking rhythm part similar to a 1950s rhythm guitar riff).

Notice the occasional use of a note that's not in the C major scale. The notes B♭ and E♭ appear in the rhythm and the melody. Rock music originates in the blues, and *blue notes* (out-of-key notes) are quite common. For more information about blues styles, look at Chapter 9.

Figure 8-13 shows the rhythm part for 'Skiffle Mando', and Figure 8-14 the melody part. Listen to Track 36 to hear how these two parts work together.

Skiffle Mando

Skiffle Mando

Figure 8-14:
'Skiffle
Mando'
melody.

Trying Out Minor Scales

Minor scales can be a bit tough to nail down, because many different types exist. In this section, I cover two:

- ✔ **Pure minor scales** are the most common type of minor scale and get used in a variety of musical styles ranging from the melody in the carol 'God Rest Ye Merry Gentlemen' to the heavy metal guitar riff in Ozzy Osbourne's 'Crazy Train'. This scale is also called *relative minor* or *Aeolian* mode (see Chapter 11). The A (pure) minor scale contains the notes A, B, C, D, E, F, G and A.

- ✔ **Harmonic minor scales** are less common in popular music (or at least in my neighbourhood!), but they have a haunting, beautiful sound due to the fact that the seventh step of the scale is one half step higher (one fret) than in the pure minor scale. Players often use this type of scale in Eastern European folk music. The A (harmonic) minor scale contains the notes A, B, C, D, E, F, G♯ and A.

You've most likely heard the anti-feline saying 'There's more than one way to skin a cat' – and that applies to learning scales. The *pure minor scale* (I use Am for this example) can be derived from the two formulas listed below. Not all people remember scales in the same way, so feel free to use the method that makes the most sense to you, being confident that both methods result in the same scale:

✔ Start with an A major scale (see the earlier section 'Accessing the A major scale') and *flatten* (lower by one fret) the third (C♯), the sixth (F♯) and the seventh (G♯) notes in the scale.

✔ Use the exact same notes of a C major scale (see the earlier section 'Avoiding sharps and flats with the C major scale') from A to A (also called the *Aeolian mode*). I provide more information about modes in Chapter 11.

The harmonic minor scale can also be derived from scales you might already know (see Chapter 6). As with the pure minor, I offer two common ways to arrive at the A (harmonic) minor scale:

✔ Start with an A major scale (see the earlier section 'Accessing the A major scale') and *flatten* the third (C♯) and the sixth (F♯) notes in the scale.

✔ Start with the A (pure) minor scale described earlier in this section, and raise the seventh step one half step (one fret).

Mining the A minor scale for two different approaches

Take a look at Figures 8-15 and 8-16, which demonstrate pure and harmonic Am scales.

Notice that the only difference in these two scales is that the harmonic minor has a sharp (raised) seventh step, giving this scale a more Eastern European sound.

Figure 8-15:
Am pure
minor scale.

Figure 8-16: Am harmonic minor scale.

The song in which you're going to use the Am harmonic scale welcomes you to the dark side, where gypsy campfires burn until dawn. The melody of 'Waltz Ukrainian Style' features many *syncopated* phrases (phrases that start on an up-beat – see Chapter 5) and notes that you need to play with up-strokes, and so pay close attention to the timing of this one. Remember to count it out (see Chapter 4) and use the rule 'numbered beats are down-strokes and the ands are up-strokes'. (You won't get the right sound unless you do so.)

'Waltz Ukrainian Style' (see Figure 8-17 for the chords) uses the A (harmonic) minor scale for first two sections. The mood lightens a bit in the third part (that is, the last two lines starting with the G7 chord) with a happy major key change for a few bars and then back to the main theme in the key of A (harmonic) minor.

The rhythm for this piece uses the waltz strumming pattern used in Figure 9-7(a) in Chapter 9, but instead of letting all of the strings ring, try muting beats two and three using the technique demonstrated in the swing rhythms in Chapter 13, to mute the chords with the left hand.

Figure 8-17: 'Waltz Ukrainian Style' chords.

This tune also contains a position shift (which I explain in Chapter 10) as well as the direction marker 'D.C. al Fine' (see Figure 8-18). (Appendix B has a description of this musical notation term and many others.) Watch the tablature at measure 25 (at the Dm chord) and play the D note on the fifth fret with your first finger (third position). Soon after, at measure 27, comes another shift, where your first finger should play the C at the third fret (second position).

Listen to Track 37 to hear the 'Waltz Ukrainian Style' melody as shown in Figure 8-18.

Figure 8-18: 'Waltz Ukrainian Style' melody.

Playing solo with chord melodies

Occasionally, you may want to play solo (without accompaniment) but also want to play more than just the melody. Think of a solo pianist playing left- and right-hand parts at the same time.

One way to achieve this sound on the mandolin is to use what's called a *chord melody*. In the 'Bighorn River Sunset' you can play the melody while adding notes from the chords on the first beat of each new measure. I have arranged this beautiful piece (written by my friend John Goodin) for solo mandolin.

Figure 8-19 and Track 38 illustrate a simple arrangement of 'Bighorn River Sunset' for solo mandolin.

Learning as many ways to play the same chord as possible is a really good idea, and doing so helps you build your own solo chord-melody-style arrangements.

Bighorn River Sunset

Figure 8-19: 'Bighorn River Sunset' arrangement for solo mandolin.

Experiencing the Power of the Pentatonic

Pentatonic scales are five-note major or minor scales with the two most *dissonant* (or sour) notes removed. Composers and players have used pentatonic scales to create some of the most recognisable melodies of all time. They are also used in teaching music to young children in a method where the children improvise on small xylophone-type instruments using these five notes. The idea is that with no dissonant or sour notes in the scale, it is impossible for the child to make a mistake. As it turns out, people of all ages have the ability to understand, sing, play and memorise pentatonic melodies easily.

 Check out an interesting video featuring Bobby McFerrin at `http://youtu.be/ne6tB2KiZuk`, where he demonstrates the universal language of the pentatonic scale on a very non-musical audience.

Taking five with the major pentatonic scale

When you remove the fourth and seventh steps of the major scale, you have what's called a *major pentatonic* scale. The major pentatonic has an easy-going, optimistic, Asian or Oriental sound that sometimes seems a bit directionless due to the missing two notes.

Major pentatonic scales are responsible for some great melodies in time-tested songs such as 'Amazing Grace', the memorable guitar lick in 'My Girl' (a 1965 hit by The Temptations) and most of the lead-guitar work of the blues-rock band The Allman Brothers Band. Figure 8-20 shows the D major pentatonic scale.

Pentatonic scales aren't new!

Cave of Forgotten Dreams, a documentary by Werner Herzog about the Chauvet caves in France, which have been sealed for 30,000 years, reveals charcoal drawings and some very well preserved other remains. One of the things archaeologists found was a flute tuned to . . . guess what? The pentatonic scale!

Figure 8-20:
The D major
pentatonic
scale.

The tune that I show you in this section is 'Angelina Baker', which uses the
D major pentatonic scale (D, E, F♯, A and B). I also demonstrate here how to
play a melody in two octaves or registers. Melodies tend to sound a bit different if you play them in different octaves (high or low). This pentatonic
melody is easy to play in two octaves on the mandolin, and therefore makes a
good tune that you can use to practice this technique.

Playing a melody in more than one octave means being able to play the same
melody in the low range and the high range of your instrument (not always
the same as playing up the neck). In 'Angelina Baker', you can play the
melody high and low without venturing up the mandolin neck. Figure 8-21
shows the chords.

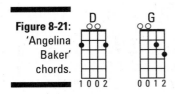

Figure 8-21:
'Angelina
Baker'
chords.

Figure 8-22 shows the lower-octave version of 'Angelina Baker', and Figure 8-23
displays the higher one. Track 39 plays through 'Angelina Baker' twice. First
you hear what matches Figure 8-22, and the second time what matches Figure
8-23. The strumming pattern used on Track 39 is found in Figure 9-1(b) (see
Chapter 9).

The melody as you see it here is much like how someone would sing the
song, and doesn't use any of the mandolin-style embellishments I demonstrate in earlier chapters. I suggest you first learn it as you see it here then
experiment with some drone strings (from the earlier section 'Using drone

strings'), slides, hammer-ons, eighth-note (quaver) runs or any of the other techniques that I explain in Chapter 6.

Angelina Baker (low)

Figure 8-22: 'Angelina Baker' in the low octave.

Angelina Baker (high)

Figure 8-23: 'Angelina Baker' in the high octave.

Moving on to the minor pentatonic scale

By removing the second and sixth steps (the most dissonant or tense-sounding notes) from the pure minor scale (which I define in the earlier section 'Trying Out Minor Scales'), you get the *minor pentatonic*. The sound of the minor pentatonic is indeed minor but isn't too scary or dark, and is used quite often in blues music and blues-influenced music (see Chapter 9). 'E.M.D.' (a mandolin standard by David Grisman) and 'Voodoo Child' by Jimi Hendrix are both great examples of the minor pentatonic scale in action. Figure 8-24 shows the Em pentatonic scale.

Figure 8-24: The Em pentatonic scale.

'Poor Wayfaring Stranger' is a great example of a minor pentatonic melody. This arrangement uses tremolo (see Chapter 5), slides, hammer-ons and position shifts (techniques that I explain in Chapter 6), and scale runs (from the earlier section 'Adding scale runs'). This song is slow, and I suggest using all down-strokes when playing the melody (except for the tremolo parts). The chords I suggest (see Figure 8-25) are stark – both the Em and Am chord shapes are technically incomplete chords in that they don't contain *thirds* (the note in the chord that determines its major or minor quality). The 'minor-ness' of this tune comes through in the pentatonic melody. Check out Figure 8-26 and Track 40 for my mandolin arrangement of 'Poor Wayfaring Stranger'. The chords are played using the strumming pattern in Figure 9-1(a) (see Chapter 9).

Figure 8-25: 'Poor Wayfaring Stranger' chords.

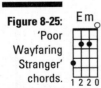

Poor Wayfaring Stranger

Figure 8-26:
'Poor
Wayfaring
Stranger'
mandolin
arrange-
ment.

Part III
Putting Playing Styles into Practice

The 5th Wave   By Rich Tennant

"And that's how you play Rachmaninoff's Concerto Number 2 on the mandolin."

In this part . . .

1 take you on a journey around the world looking at a wide range of mandolin styles. You discover the mandolin styles of Italy, Ireland and Brazil along with American styles including string bands, ragtime and blues, bluegrass, swing and jazz, and even take a quick look into David Grisman's own eclectic blend, called Dawg music. Each chapter contains loads of great songs for you to try out.

Chapter 9

Playing Music from Yesteryear: Old Time, Rags and Blues

North American music of the early twentieth century is fascinating in its own right and because of its amazingly wide influence on many of today's genres. String bands (ensembles made up mainly of string instruments) were popular throughout America in the 1920s and 1930s, and are the roots of country music and bluegrass, just as the blues is widely accepted as the predecessor of jazz, bluegrass and rock and roll.

In this chapter, I take a look at some US music of the early to mid-twentieth century, including fiddle tunes and waltzes, rags and blues. The mandolin played an important role in this musical evolution. For a student of the instrument, knowing about and being able to play some of this music is a great idea and sure to improve your performances enormously.

Searching out the Past: Old-Time Music

Old time is a term that refers to the style of North American folk music that was popular in the 1920s and 1930s. Old-time's roots include folk music styles from Ireland, Scotland, England, most of Europe and even Africa. This type of music was played by ordinary people (not classically trained musicians) at social gatherings that sometimes included dancing. The banjo and fiddle were the primary two instruments, but guitar, accordion, mandolin and jug or washtub bass filled out the sound.

Getting the best tool for the job

Even though the mandolin wasn't always a featured instrument in this music, old-time music fits the instrument quite well. You can play old-time music on any type of mandolin, but most people prefer the sound of vintage A-model mandolins for this style. The Gibson carved-top A models work very well, as do the flat-topped Martins or Washburns from the early 1900s. A favourite among blues and ragtime players is the Strad-O-Lin; these models were made in the 1930s and 1940s. You can still find Strad-O-Lins at a good price if you look around.

That said, I recorded the audio tracks 42–51 on a 1930s Strad-O-Lin mandolin (a favorite of many blues and ragtime players) with a pressed, solid wood top, and f-holes. The chord strumming or accompaniment is in the left speaker, and the melody in the right speaker.

As is true with most musical genres, listening to the music to get the feel of it is vital to playing it well. You can buy recordings dating as far back as the early 1900s. The recording quality is quite poor, but you can hear how the music was authentically played. Check out recordings of Fiddlin' Arthur Smith, Gid Tanner and His Skillet Lickers, the Carter Family, Uncle Dave Macon, and the Dallas String Band, as well as today's Carolina Chocolate Drops.

The best way to learn old-time music is by ear, and so listen to the tracks that come with this book first. You'll perform best if you can get the melody in your head before looking at the written music and trying to play these fiddle tunes and waltzes.

Strumming for old-time fiddle tunes

Fiddle tunes are instrumentals that were originally played on the fiddle for social dancing. They work really well when played on the mandolin though, as you discover in this section. Most fiddle tunes come from the traditional folk music of Ireland and Scotland.

When strumming the chords in old-time fiddle tunes, respecting the melody is very important. Think of the process as building a tune from the top and working down, the top being the melody, and all other parts (strumming, harmony parts, bass lines) needing to fit that melody. In contrast, in some other musical styles, the rhythm player supplies a steady beat and follows the chord changes, giving the melody player or soloist a foundation to work from – that is, building the tune from the bottom up.

Figure 9-1 and Track 41 Part 1 demonstrate some common strumming patterns that fit many old-time fiddle tune melodies.

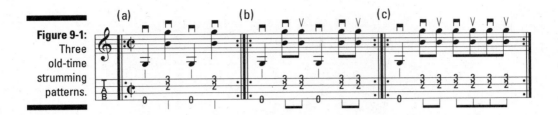

Figure 9-1:
Three old-time strumming patterns.

Another approach is to play the rhythm of the melody with your right hand while your left hand makes the chords (see Figure 9-2 for an example of this type of strumming). In this example, I borrow the melody from the A section of 'The Girl I Left Behind Me' (see Figure 9-5 later in this section), remove the individual *note heads* (the circular parts of the notes that indicate which pitch to play) from the music and replace them with strums. Listen to Track 41 Part 2 for a demonstration of this technique.

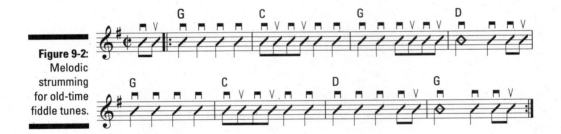

Figure 9-2:
Melodic strumming for old-time fiddle tunes.

The chord structure to most fiddle tunes is fairly simple, usually featuring only two or three major chords. Figure 9-3 shows you the chords used in the following three fiddle tunes. Try using both strumming techniques for each tune and see which you prefer.

Figure 9-3:
Chords for the fiddle tunes in this section.

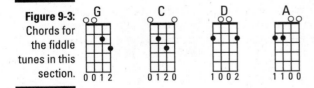

'The Arkansas Traveller' – check out Track 42 and Figure 9-4 – was written in the 1800s by Colonel Sanford Faulkner and was the Arkansas state song from 1949 to 1963. This tune was used in many Merrie Melodies and Looney Tunes cartoons in the 1930s and 1940s. Over the years, many different lyrics have been added to it.

The Arkansas Traveller

Figure 9-4:
'The
Arkansas
Traveller'.

The next tune, 'The Girl I Left Behind Me', appears to have been written in Ireland around 1800 and was adapted by the US army during the war of 1812, after a British prisoner was heard singing it. The army used it as a marching tune for much of the 1800s. Listen to Track 43 and take a look at Figure 9-5 before having a go yourself.

The Girl I Left Behind Me

Figure 9-5:
'The Girl I
Left Behind
Me'.

Check out Track 44 and Figure 9-6 for the tune 'Soldier's Joy', which although considered an American classic, in fact can be traced back to Scotland. The light and happy-sounding melody also has a darker meaning: in the American Civil War, 'soldier's joy' was slang for a mixture of whisky, beer and morphine.

Soldier's Joy

Figure 9-6: 'Soldier's Joy'.

Waltzing on the mandolin

Like the fiddle tunes that I discuss in the preceding section, the roots of the waltz lie in Europe, although waltzes feature in almost all folk music styles. Also, many classical composers including Schubert, Strauss and Chopin wrote waltzes. The waltz is a dance that at one time was considered socially unacceptable because of its sexual energy and body contact between dance partners (the scandal!).

Waltz music is written in 3/4 time and has a beat of um-pa-pa, um-pa-pa. Old-time waltz strumming on the mandolin is usually played using a pattern on the bass note (g-string) on beat 1, followed by two light strums on beats 2 and 3 (see Figure 9-7). A common way to count the waltz is 1, 2, 3, 1, 2, 3.

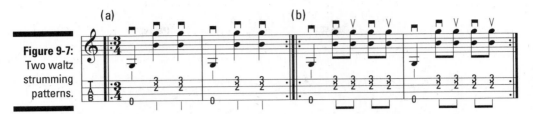

Figure 9-7:
Two waltz strumming patterns.

'Waltz of the Little Girls' (the chords are in Figure 9-8, and the full piece is in Figure 9-9 and on Track 45) is a lovely traditional French tune originally called *La Valse Pour les Petites Jeunes Filles*. It's great fun to play on the mandolin.

Proper pick direction is crucial for this piece, and so bear in mind the golden rule of alternate picking: 'numbered beats are down-strokes and "ands" are up-strokes' (flip to Chapter 5 for more info on picking). Watch for the measures with dotted quarter notes (crotchets) and play the following eighth note (a quaver) with an up-stroke.

Waltzes tend to be a bit more sophisticated harmonically (as regards chords) than the fiddle tunes in the preceding section, using a combination of major and minor chords. Use the strumming pattern in Figure 9-7(b) for this waltz.

Figure 9-8:
Chords for 'Waltz of the Little Girls'.

'White Hair and Wisdom' (see Figure 9-10 for the chords and Figure 9-11 and Track 46 for the full piece) uses a descending bass line that fits over the chord changes and acts as a counterpoint (harmony) to the melody.

As a mandolin player, usually you don't need to be too concerned with the bass part, because you leave that up to instruments that can play lower notes, but in this arrangement I suggest chords that include the descending bass line in order to add the extra colour of the *counterpoint* (an additional melody that fits with the original melody when the two are played together). This type of *voice leading* (moving from one chord to another) when played with the strumming pattern in Figure 9-7(a) creates a rhythm pattern that includes the counterpoint melody.

When the bass note or bass line is important, the chord symbol uses a slash chord. For example, a chord symbol written as G/B is telling you to play a G chord with a B note as the lowest note in the chord. If playing with a guitarist or bassist, you'd normally leave that low B note up to that person.

La Valse Pour Petites Jeunes Filles
The Waltz of the Little Girls

Figure 9-9: 'The Waltz of the Little Girls'.

I suggest playing this melody with all down-strokes.

Figure 9-10: Chords for 'White Hair and Wisdom'.

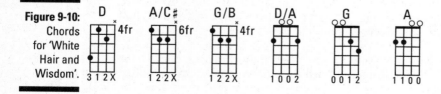

White Hair and Wisdom

Figure 9-11: 'White Hair and Wisdom'.

Playing all Raggedy on Purpose: Ragtime

Ragtime music or *rags* is usually associated with the piano music of Scott Joplin (famous from its use in the hugely popular 1970s film *The Sting*). But string bands often played ragtime in the early 1900s too, which means that mandolin players also get to play this joyful music (check out the nearby sidebar 'Getting hold of classic ragtime mandolin recordings'). With its blend of African rhythms and European melodic and harmonic structure, ragtime music was a uniquely North American new form of music, played by black and white musicians of the Deep South.

The term *ragtime* comes from the *syncopated* (uneven) melodies that were referred to as *ragged* time. Ragtime music consists of a rhythm pattern similar to a march (that is, 1, 2, 1, 2), with the bass note on beat 1 and the chord on beat 2.

The contrast between the syncopated melody and the strict marching rhythm is an important element in getting the ragtime sound, something this section can help you with.

Syncopating your mandolin melodies

Playing syncopated (uneven) melodies on the mandolin while using alternate picking creates some challenges, in that many of the accented notes are on the up-stroke (turn to Chapters 4 and 5 for more on finding the beat and learning pick direction, respectively). In addition, these tunes move along at a fair old lick, and so you need to have a well-organised, relaxed right hand to get these melodies sounding right.

Practise some of the exercises in Chapter 5 if you want to brush up in this area.

Practising ragtime chord progressions and patterns

Chord progressions (which I describe in Chapter 4) in rags can range from very simple to quite complex, and primarily use a variety of major, minor, seventh and the occasional diminished chord.

Getting hold of classic ragtime mandolin recordings

In order to fully appreciate rags played on the mandolin, listen to some of the original recordings of bands such as the Blue Boys, the Dallas String Band, the East Texas Serenaders, the Memphis Jug Band and the trio of Martin, Bogan and Armstrong.

Another classic recording is Dave Apollon's 'The Russian Rag'. Use the Internet to track down CDs or to download these tunes and many others at the touch of a button.

When playing rhythm mandolin in ragtime music, you can use either open (unfretted) or closed (fretted) chords, as long as you keep the rhythm steady. If you play open chords, try not to let all strings ring all the time. Instead, separate the bass note from the chord, as I show in the earlier Figure 9-1.

Here are the two most important things to bear in mind when playing rhythm on the mandolin:

✔ Keep good time; in other words, *don't slow down.*

✔ Play with confidence, but don't overpower the melody player or singer.

Although rags can have a complex form, in that they may have multiple sections, the two ragtime pieces that I present in this section have only one or two sections each.

'Stone's Rag' is a popular rag that many old-time fiddlers and mandolin players love to perform (a quick online search reveals downloadable versions by Eddie Pennington, Chubby Wise, Doc Watson, and the New Lost City Ramblers). As with all styles of music that are new to you, listen often and carefully to the masters. Figure 9-12 shows the chords that I use for 'Stone's Rag'.

Figure 9-12:
Chords for
'Stone's
Rag'.

The melody of 'Stone's Rag' uses a device called a *rhythmic motif* – a repeating rhythm pattern in which the melody notes keep changing while the rhythm pattern stays consistent. Rhythms are the responsibility of the right hand, and so in order to play a repeating rhythmic motif, you need to practise the physical motion required to play it. Figure 9-13 shows the rhythmic motif used in 'Stone's Rag' along with the proper pick-direction markings.

I demonstrate 'Stone's Rag' on Track 47 and show it in Figure 9-14.

Figure 9-13:
Right-hand
rhythm for
'Stone's
Rag'.

Figure 9-14: 'Stone's Rag'.

Using the circle of fifths

The ragtime type of chord progression is part of a musical concept called the circle of fifths. Although this sounds like a secret society with peculiar handshakes, the *circle of fifths* is a way of explaining the relationship of the 12 pitches in western music by using a graphic display that resembles a clock.

The numbers on the 'clock' represent each of the 12 musical notes. By following the circle around in a counter-clockwise motion, you can unlock the secret of many chord progressions. Notice in this figure that, when you start at B and go counter-clockwise, the chords match the progression (B, E, A, D) of the turnaround section of 'The Eight String Rag'.

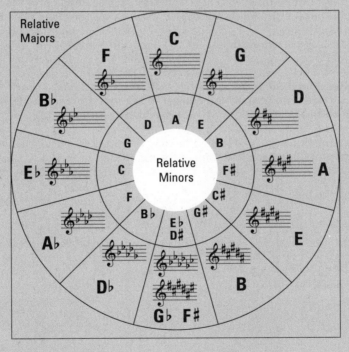

The next tune I look at is called 'The Eight String Rag', which uses a few techniques common in ragtime music. The opening melody is syncopated, starting on an off-beat, and you play it with an up-stroke. Follow the suggested pick direction in Figure 9-15 after you listen to Track 48.

Figure 9-15: 'The Eight String Rag' pick direction.

Another interesting element to this piece is the chord progression. The tune is in D but it starts on an A7 chord. (Seasoned musicians refer to this as starting on the 'V' (five).) I provide a secret insight into ragtime chord progressions in the nearby sidebar 'Using the circle of fifths'.

Also notice the way the chords change at the end of each part. This switch is called a *turnaround* and is part of the basic vocabulary of ragtime, blues and jazz styles. The turnaround consist of the series of chords: D, B7, E7, A7, D (which pros call a I/VI/II/V (one-six-two-five) turnaround).

Have fun playing 'The Eight String Rag'. Figure 9-16 shows the chords, and Figure 9-17 and Track 48 contain the full piece.

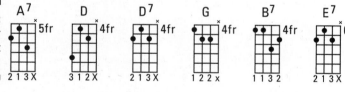

Figure 9-16: Chords for 'The Eight String Rag'.

The Eight String Rag

Figure 9-17:
'The Eight String Rag'.

Reproduced by permission of Don Julin

Playing away your Sorrows: The Blues

Blues came out of the Southern states of America in around 1900 and has been a major force in the development of music around the world ever since. Loads of regional dialects of the blues exist, including delta blues, Chicago blues, rock blues, jazz blues and many others. Rock and roll, country and jazz all grew out of the blues.

This music is particularly difficult to explain with the printed word, or even printed music for that matter. Blues is a feeling that you acquire by listening to the music. Fortunately, many recordings are available of the original blues masters along with a whole host of contemporary players.

My friend and blues scholar Rich DelGrosso (www.mandolinblues.com) supplied some guidance and a few anecdotes for this section. He's also written a great book on playing blues mandolin, called *Mandolin Blues: From Memphis to Maxwell Street* (published by the Hal Leonard Corporation), that includes songs for and historical facts about the blues mandolin.

Introducing the blues rhythm

Rhythm is one of the primary elements of the blues. Even if you play all the right *blue notes* (the style-defining notes usually considered to be the flatted third, fifth or seventh of a chord), without the right rhythm or an understanding of the blues feel the result isn't going to sound like blues. But don't worry, because this section is here to help you out with blues rhythms.

Good blues has a relaxed feel but never slows down. Musicians use phrases such as 'in the pocket' or 'in the groove' to describe when the beat is solid yet somehow laidback. Being able to relax when playing melody or playing a solo is the key to playing in the pocket. If you're the slightest bit nervous, you tend to play a bit ahead of the beat.

Listen carefully to the rhythms that I play in the audio recordings and immerse yourself in as many blues recordings as you can.

Swing/shuffle

Swing is a word that musicians use to describe a feel that affects the way that eighth notes (quavers) are played. The concept of dragging (or delaying) the up-beat a little so that that the down-beats are longer and therefore stronger is one of the defining elements of the blues and all forms of music that come from it.

Shuffle is a popular dance rhythm in the blues that is played with a heavy swing feel (see Figure 9-18) featuring an active bass line called a *boogie bass line* (see Figure 9-20). The dance creates the effect of shuffling the dancers' feet across the floor.

For the swing rhythm, think of the strong (numbered) beats as being a bit longer than the weak beats (the 'ands'). You can adjust the amount of swing by making the down-beats longer, resulting in shorter up-beats. This feel can be played with all down-strokes and with alternate picking, depending on the speed of the song. In fact, the blues mandolin master Yank Rachell played this feel with all up-strokes.

Figure 9-18 shows a visual demonstration of swing. In example (a), the numbers and 'ands' are all evenly spaced, but in example (b) the 'ands' have 'moved' to the right and therefore are slightly delayed, while the numbers haven't moved (thus creating what's called *medium swing*). The numbered beats are, in essence, longer than the 'ands'. In example (c), the 'ands' are delayed even more, creating a *heavy swing*.

The swing feel can't be written into the music, because swing eighth notes (quavers) look exactly like even eighth notes, which is why I say that the blues sound is very difficult to write about (but very easy to hear).

Figure 9-18:
Three examples to show swing rhythm: (a) straight time; (b) medium swing; (c) heavy swing.

(a) 1   +   2   +   3   +   4   +

(b) 1   +   2   +   3   +   4   +

(c) 1   +   2   +   3   +   4   +

Boogie

The term *boogie* implies a rhythm style where the bass part (originally the left hand of the piano player) is played using a pattern made of mostly *chord tones* (the notes in a chord) using a heavy swing feel. This boogie piano style has been adapted to many instruments, including upright bass and guitar, and works well on the mandolin.

The arrangement in Figure 9-19 and on Track 49 uses slides, a big part of the blues sound. You can read all about how to play slides in Chapter 6.

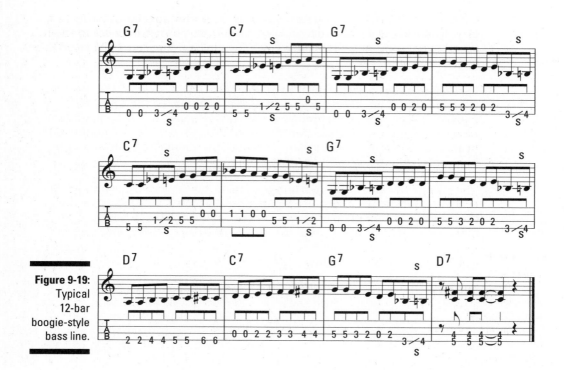

Figure 9-19: Typical 12-bar boogie-style bass line.

Backbeat

Backbeat indicates that the accent (or driving part) of the rhythm is on the 'back' side of the beat (on beats two and four). Many blues-based rhythms accent these two beats by choking or muting the notes on the backbeat. (I discuss muting in Chapter 6.) Feeling this backbeat is essential to getting a good blues feel.

Backbeat is illustrated in Figures 9-21 and 9-33 by the short (eighth) notes being played on beats two and four, creating an accent on the backbeat.

Chording up for the blues

Usually blues songs don't use many chords; in fact, some blues songs can be played by staying on one chord for the entire song. In addition, seventh chords (which I cover in Chapter 6) are a big part of the blues sound; in many cases all the chords in a blues song are seventh chords.

Chord progressions in blues vary, but the most common chords are built on the first, fourth and fifth notes of the scale. So in the key of G, the chords are G (G7),

C (C7) and D (D7). Figure 9-20 shows two common seventh chord shapes for playing blues rhythm. Notice that these three-string chords don't use the high (E) string at all. (Check out Chapter 7 for more info on three-string chords.)

Figure 9-20:
Two sev-
enth chord
shapes.

Twelve-bar blues

One of the most common chord progressions in the blues is called the 12-bar blues. I like to think of this form as three four-bar phrases, in which each four-bar phrase is like a sentence or statement. (Listening to blues singers is a great way to hear the sentence structure clearly.)

The basic 12-bar rhythm feel for blues mandolin is a pattern of four down-strokes (one per beat), letting beats one and three ring longer, while cutting beats two and four shorter by muting with the left hand. This approach puts a small silence after beats two and four, re-enforcing the backbeat (see the earlier section 'Backbeat' for more). When played correctly, the result is a long-short-long-short feel to the rhythm.

Figure 9-21 shows the basic 12-bar blues, and Track 50 Part 1 has a demonstration. Listen for the backbeat. Play the example rhythm using the three-note chords shown in the earlier Figure 9-20.

Figure 9-21:
Basic 12-bar
blues chord
progression.

When listening to vintage blues recordings, you may well notice that the 12-bar pattern can become quite distorted. It may be 13 bars or 11 bars, and one blues musician may hold one chord a little longer, and another make that chord a little shorter. Although the blues is loosely based around the 12-bar chord pattern, be prepared for some variations.

Plenty of variations exist on the 12-bar blues format, and the following list describes three of the most common (see also Figure 9-22 and Track 50 Part 2):

✔ **Quick to the four:** Bar 2 of the progression is a quick chord change to the IV (four) chord, which is the chord built on the fourth note of the scale. In G, this chord is C. This chord lasts only for one measure, returning back to the root chord for the duration of the first four-bar phrase.

✔ **The walkdown:** The V (five) chord in bar 9 moves down to the IV (four) chord for bar 10, instead of holding the V chord for two measures.

✔ **The turnaround:** In its simplest form, the last bar in the 12-bar form becomes a V (five) chord to indicate that you're going to go back to the beginning of the form (bar 1) and keep playing. One function of the turn- around is to do as the name implies and turn the song around from the end of the form back to the beginning and continue playing.

Turnarounds can be quite complex but are one of the more dramatic or colourful parts of a chord progression. They can help create the feeling of movement in a song. Another chord change that can create move- ment or anticipation is going from the standard major chord (G in bar 1) to the seventh chord of the same name (G7 in bar 2). Figure 9-23(c), in the next section, shows an eight-bar blues with a I/VI/II/V turnaround.

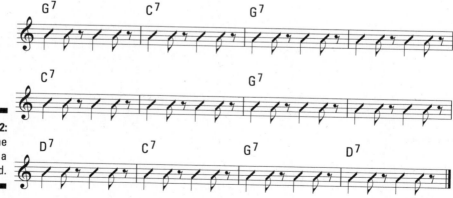

Figure 9-22:
Quick to the
four with a
turnaround.

Eight-bar blues

The second most common blues form is an eight-bar chord progression. 'Sittin' on Top of the World', 'How Long Blues' and 'Trouble in Mind' are just three well-known eight-bar blues forms.

Track 51 Parts 1, 2 and 3, and the three parts of Figure 9-23 demonstrate some basic eight-bar blues patterns in the key of G.

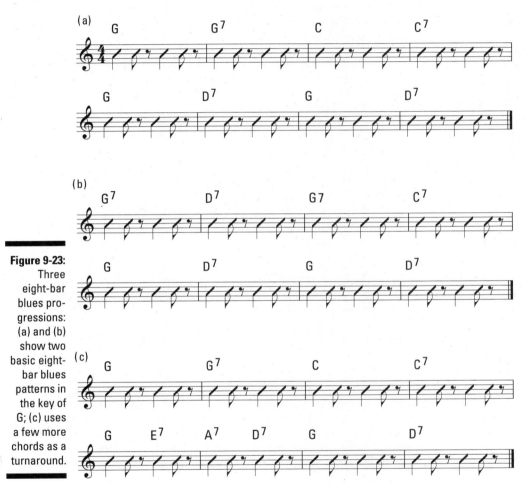

Figure 9-23: Three eight-bar blues progressions: (a) and (b) show two basic eight-bar blues patterns in the key of G; (c) uses a few more chords as a turnaround.

Playin' the blues: Some tips and techniques

Melodies used in blues music are a mystery to many highly educated music scholars, because most blues melodies aren't based on scales, at least not the major and minor scales they teach people in music school.

Blues melodies (the notes and riffs that I describe in this section) primarily come from *chord tones* (the notes in a chord) and what are called *blue notes*: chord tones or scale tones that have been lowered or flatted by one fret (one half step). Flatted thirds and sevenths are the most common blue notes, followed by the flatted fifth. When combined with the standard notes in a chord or scale, these blue notes give a group of notes from which many blues melodies are constructed.

To illustrate, Figure 9-24 shows the traditional (legitimate) notes for the key of G major, along with the chord tones for the chords G, C and D in open position. The G major scale is also shown as a way to demonstrate that the notes of these chords are included.

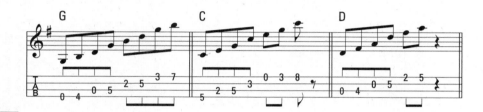

Figure 9-24:
G, C and
D chord
tones —
open and
scale.

Slurred third

The third of a chord is where you determine whether the chord is major or minor. In general, major things sound happy, and minor things sound sad. For instance, a chord containing the notes G, B and D would be a G major chord, while a chord containing G, B♭ and D would be G minor. (See Figure 6-27 in Chapter 6 for a table of chord tones for all major and minor chords.)

One of the main elements of the blues sound is a *slurred* (ambiguous) third. Blues melodies often include the flatted third over a major chord. For example, a blues band's rhythm guitar or rhythm section plays a G major chord, but the melody includes B♭. This can be very confusing, because the B♭ would indicate that the G chord should be G minor, but it isn't. This technique suggests the blend of sadness and optimism that makes the blues appeal to people around the world.

Flatted seventh and fifth

Another element of the blues sound is the flatted seventh note. Remember that in a G major scale, the seventh note is F♯. Flatting this note to F♮ gives a darker, less resolved type of sound. When you add F♮ to a G chord, it becomes G7.

The flatted fifth is less common in blues than the other blue notes, but it is used. Figure 9-25 demonstrates chord tones and blue notes for the chords G, C and D.

Figure 9-25:
Blue notes and chord tones.

Riffs

A *riff* or lick is a short melody that fits a specific musical style or genre. 'Workin' That Riff' uses one riff and transposes (moves) it to fit the chord progression. Notice how the opening G riff is played mostly on the A and D strings. By moving this riff to the G and D strings in measures 3 and 4, you're transposing it to C to match the chord progression. Also notice that in measure 6 the riff is moved to the A and E strings to match the D chord, but the riff is cut short because the D chord lasts only one measure. This symmetry is one of the wonders of the mandolin. You can also move riffs up the neck to transpose them into whatever key you need.

For tracks 52, 53 and 55, I play a 1970s vintage Harmony Batwing electric mandolin with a Steve Ryder pickup.

'Workin' That Riff' in Figure 9-26 is an eight-bar blues with a first and second ending. This tune uses two types of slide and tremolo from Chapter 6. Listen to Track 52 and try to play 'Workin' That Riff'.

Workin' That Riff

Figure 9-26:
'Workin'
That Riff'.

Reproduced by permission of Don Julin

Heavy triplet feel

The heavy triplet feel is a fundamental element to the blues. A *triplet* is simply three notes played in the space in which you'd normally play two. For this heavy triplet feel you want to play a triplet for each strong beat. I use the word 'triplet' broken into three syllables to get the right feel (tri-pl-et, tri-pl-et). Look at Figure 9-27 and listen to 'Three Shots of Rye Whiskey' on Track 53 for a better understanding of the triplet.

Depending on the musical style being played, triplets are performed differently. In this heavy triplet blues feel, I suggest using all down-strokes.

The 'Three Shots of Rye Whiskey' riff (see Figure 9-28) uses all the elements I present in this section, including chord tones, a slurred third and flatted seventh, along with triplets, double stops and slides (phew!). Also notice that in this tune, the melodies or riffs follow the chord changes, so that when the rhythm section changes to the C chord, the melodies also switch to C.

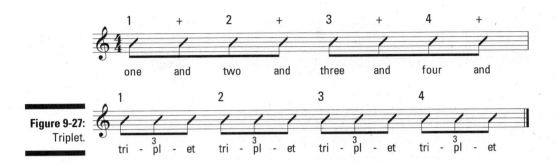

Figure 9-27:
Triplet.

Three Shots of Rye Whiskey

Figure 9-28:
'Three
Shots of Rye
Whiskey'.

Don't worry if you have trouble figuring out this music from the sheet music and tab. In general, blues musicians don't read music, and the blues feel doesn't transfer to the printed page very well, which is another reason to listen to all those classic blues records (hardly a chore!).

Influencing other genres

You can detect blues influences in all sorts of musical styles including, as I demonstrate in this section, country and rock.

Country blues

Figures 9-29 and 9-30 and Track 54 demonstrate how to play 'Country Boy Blues', a country-style blues with a peppy two-beat rhythm (um-pa, um-pa) similar to fiddle tunes or rags (check out the earlier sections 'Searching out the Past: Old-Time Music' and 'Playing all Raggedy on Purpose: Ragtime', respectively).

This tune uses the alternate-picking technique (flip to Chapter 5 for a description). The melody is constructed using the major pentatonic scale (see Figure 9-31) with a slurred third for each chord (see the earlier 'Slurred third' section), while following the chord progression.

For Track 54 – 'Country Boy Blues' – I play an Eastwood Mandocaster electric solid-body mandolin, which you can see in Figure 15-5(b) (in Chapter 15).

Figure 9-29:
Chords for
'Country
Boy Blues'.

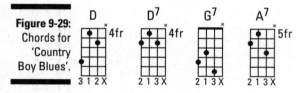

A note that country musicians like to use, along with all the other blue notes that I mention, is the sixth note of the scale, applied to each chord. You can think of this as a major pentatonic scale (see Figure 9-31) with a flatted third in addition to the regular third used for each chord.

This type of thing is easier to play than talk about, and so take a look at Figure 9-31 and try to play the fingerings and hear the major pentatonic sound. By using notes in the D pentatonic over the D chord, the G pentatonic over the G chord, and the A pentatonic over the A chord, you're *playing the changes*, which means playing a new set of notes for each chord in the song.

Country Boy Blues

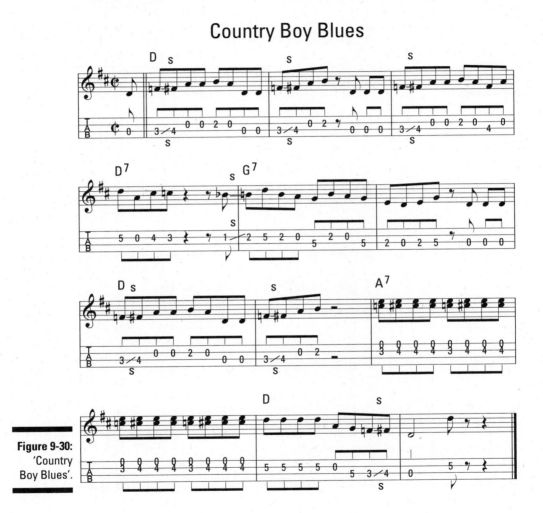

Figure 9-30: 'Country Boy Blues'.

Figure 9-31:
Three major
pentatonic
scales – (a)
D major; (b)
G major;
(c) A major
– with an
added blue
note in each.

Slow blues

Slow blues is an important style of blues. The slower tempo allows for a different style of expression and gives mandolin players an excuse to play more tremolo. The rhythm part of a slow blues blends elements of the boogie-woogie pattern with the heavy triplet feel (which I discuss in the earlier 'Boogie' and 'Heavy triplet feel' sections, respectively), while maintaining a slow grinding beat.

Yank Rachell and tuning

Rich DelGrosso tells the following story about the great Yank Rachell.

'When I lived in Detroit, I had the opportunity to bring Yank up from Indianapolis for a gig. I pulled together a band, but we didn't have time to rehearse. I was aware that Yank tended to tune the mandolin strings by ear. His strings were tuned to fifths in the traditional manner, but his bass strings weren't always tuned to G. He'd tune them to where his voice was that day: maybe G, maybe F, maybe E.

'That night, he tuned them to E, one and a half steps down. We took the bandstand and started the show. I leaned over to Yank and asked him "What key is the song?" He responded "G". I turned to the band and said "It's in E", and they looked at me like I was crazy. They learned quickly to wait for my translation, before grabbing capos or harmonicas to retune. It turned into a great night!'

Rock and roll: Blues pentatonic scale

The blues (or minor) pentatonic scale is the quintessential rock-and-roll lead-guitar sound that comes directly from the blues. The blues pentatonic scale is a five-note scale that includes many of the blue notes that I describe earlier in this section, but in a slightly different format in that it's used as a scale. This method allows you to play an entire song or solo using only the notes in the pentatonic scale, without worrying about flatting thirds or sevenths or even knowing the chord tones in each chord.

With the blues pentatonic scale, you're actually playing a minor (dark) sound over major (happy) or seventh chords. Figure 9-32(a) shows a G minor pentatonic scale. By adding one more blue note to this pentatonic scale, you get what jazz players call a blues scale (see Figure 9-32(b)).

Figure 9-32:
Blues
(minor)
pentatonic:
(a) G minor
pentatonic
scale; (b) G
blues scale.

Using *guide tones* is a way of playing the blues using only the blues pentatonic scale but still paying attention to the chord changes. It's essentially quite simple: when the chord switches to C, you use the C note a bit more; when it changes to D, you use the D note a bit more.

For this slow blues, I play a slow rhythm part that includes two-note chords that include one moving or rockin' note. This sound is used in rock and roll and provides a bit more motion to the sound than just strumming the chord. Check out Figure 9-33 and Track 55 to hear how this type of rhythm part works.

Figure 9-33:
Slow blues
rhythm.

'Slow Cookin' (see Figure 9-34) is a slow blues in the key of G. Listen to Track 55 to hear how the slow rhythm part works with the melody. Other techniques used in this tune are down-strokes, tremolo and slides (which I describe in Chapters 5 and 6).

Slow Cookin'

Figure 9-34: 'Slow Cookin' blues.

Rock and pop mandolin

Just as rock and roll came after the blues went electric, so the mandolin followed. In general, rock mandolin is played by guitarists who double on a mandolin for a song or two. It provides colour, although the 'heavy lifting' is still up to the electric guitars. The following are some examples of mandolin used in rock music:

✔ Led Zeppelin uses mandolin on tunes such as 'Going to California', 'The Battle of Evermore', and 'Boogie With Stu'.

✔ Probably the best-known mandolin riff in pop music is the one from Rod Stewart's 'Maggie May'. The part was played by Ray Jackson.

✔ The R.E.M. hit 'Losing My Religion' features a very simple strummed mandolin part played by guitarist Peter Buck.

✔ Levon Helm, best known as the drummer/ singer for The Band, can also play the heck out of the mandolin. Listen to 'Rag Mama Rag' on his recent solo CD *Dirt Farmer*.

Other pop/rockers to use mandolin include: Seals and Crofts, Eddie Vedder, The Grateful Dead, The Rolling Stones, Ry Cooder, Fairport Convention, Rory Gallagher, Jethro Tull, Cowboy Junkies and Paul McCartney. Also, Punch Brothers, featuring the phenomenal Chris Thile on mandolin, are producing great pop songs using mandolin and other traditional bluegrass instrumentation.

You can find some of today's best rockin' mandolin music. Jim Richter has many videos of blues and rock mandolin, including tunes by Jimi Hendrix, and Eva Holbrook shreds on her solid-body electric mandolin – check out her video titled 'Slash's Little Sister'.

Chapter 10

Giving your Mandolin a Speedy Workout: Bluegrass

From the traditional Del McCoury Band (with Ronnie McCoury on mandolin) to the progressive sound of the Boxcars (featuring Adam Steffey on mandolin), bluegrass is a constantly evolving musical genre that holds something for every generation and all musical tastes. Today, people such as Hollywood star Steve Martin (who also happens to be a very fine banjo player!), the Steep Canyon Rangers (with Mike Guggino on mandolin), and the Punch Brothers (featuring Chis Thile on mandolin), are breaking all the rules, reaching new and exciting levels in pop music using standard bluegrass instrumentation.

Bluegrass music first appeared in North America in and around the state of Kentucky in the 1940s. The classic bluegrass band includes mandolin, guitar, bass, banjo and fiddle. The music features a distinctive high lonesome vocal sound with fiery instrumental breaks.

Mandolin player Bill Monroe is considered the creator of bluegrass, and in this chapter I cover some of his signature mandolin-playing techniques that bluegrass mandolin players commonly use.

The audio tracks from this chapter are played on a 2010 Northfield Workshop F-5 standard #79 mandolin.

Getting a Grip on that Bluegrass Rhythm

The mandolin has a very specific function in a bluegrass band as regards playing rhythm (for an introduction to mandolin rhythm, check out Chapter 4). Many people refer to this bluegrass rhythm sound or technique as *chopping*. Here's a step-by-step guide to playing the classic bluegrass chop-style rhythm:

1. **Make a four-finger G chord with your left hand, as I show in Figure 10-1(a) and (b).**

2. **Play the fourth string with a single down-stroke of the pick.**

3. **Strum or brush quickly across all four strings with another down-stroke fast enough so that all four strings make one sound (or chop), as if they're all being struck simultaneously.**

4. **Mute with your left hand by releasing pressure on the strings immediately after brushing all four strings, creating a very short staccato sound.**

5. **Repeat the pattern of picking the fourth string on beats 1 and 3 and the complete chord (muted) on beats 2 and 4.**

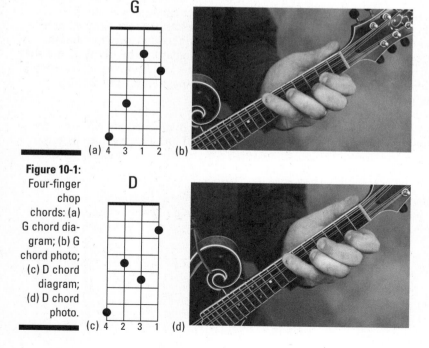

Figure 10-1: Four-finger chop chords: (a) G chord diagram; (b) G chord photo; (c) D chord diagram; (d) D chord photo.

I demonstrate a bluegrass chop in Figure 10-2 and on Track 56.

Figure 10-2:
Playing
the chop
rhythm.

One of the keys to a good chop sound is the ability to brush the strings very quickly on beats 2 and 4. Imagine having a burning match between the index finger and thumb of your right hand. As the match burns down, you feel the heat on your fingertips. To avoid burning your skin, you naturally do a fast flick with your wrist to extinguish the match. This flicking motion, followed by the left-hand mute, is how you get a good bluegrass mandolin chop sound.

As well as the difficult four-finger G chop chord, Figure 10-1 also shows the equally dreaded four-finger D chop chord – see Figure 10-1(c) and (d). Although quite a stretch at first, with a bit of practice most people can make these chords.

If you prefer, like many players you can choose the more economical three-finger chop chords (shown in Figure 10-3), which are played with the same technique. One difference is that with the three-string chords, you need to make sure you don't hear the e-string when you brush all the strings. Options are to strum in such a way that your pick doesn't hit the e-string, or mute that string with the edge of the finger that's fretting the a-string.

These chords are moveable (something I cover in Chapter 7). So the C chord moved two frets higher is a D chord, the G chord two frets higher is A, and so on. Use these chop chords for all songs in this chapter or whenever you're playing bluegrass rhythm.

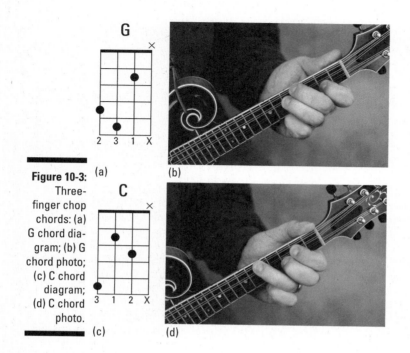

Figure 10-3: Three-finger chop chords: (a) G chord diagram; (b) G chord photo; (c) C chord diagram; (d) C chord photo.

Gathering Together the Bluegrass Elements: An Original Mandolin Style

If you compare bluegrass mandolin with rock-and-roll guitar, you may be surprised by the similarities, but you needn't be. Both styles are fairly recent, with bluegrass being formed in the 1940s and rock-and-roll in the 1950s, and both are the result of incorporating African-American rhythms into a new musical form. Elvis Presley recorded (and had a hit with) a version of Bill Monroe's 'Blue Moon of Kentucky' very early in his career, and when you listen to some of the early Bill Monroe recordings, you can hear what sound like Chuck-Berry-style riffs being played on the mandolin. Bill, though, was playing these licks about ten years before anyone ever heard of rock 'n' roll.

Here's the classic bluegrass mandolin recipe (serve with cornbread!) that I describe in this section: a blend of Scottish and Irish fiddle tunes, blues from the Deep South of North America, and a new interpretation of the Italian tremolo technique. Add in some individual solos as you'd hear in a jazz group, and play at blurring speeds. No wonder that most people playing mandolin today were drawn to it by listening to bluegrass!

Fiddling about with fiddle tunes

One of the main elements of bluegrass is fiddle tunes, which I discuss in Chapter 9. But playing fiddle tunes alone doesn't make you a bluegrass picker. The following is a checklist of techniques for transforming a traditional fiddle tune into a bluegrass-style fiddle tune. As you become increasingly comfortable with these techniques, your playing will begin to sound more and more like bluegrass:

✔ Remove notes that aren't needed to identify the melody, thus reducing the melody to a skeleton of its former self.

✔ Play the new, reduced melody using a steady stream of down-up picking strokes, adding in rhythmic patterns such as the ones shown in Figure 10-6.

✔ Add slides and double stops (from Chapter 6), blue notes (see Chapter 9) and drone strings (I drone in Chapter 8!) while playing in the positions I cover in this chapter, all the while keeping the original song in mind.

✔ Pass the reduced melody around from one player to the next, allowing each musician to present the tune in a unique, arranged version.

Here's an example of a common fiddle tune. I present the 'A' part of 'Whiskey Before Breakfast' in Figure 10-4 in a traditional Irish or old-time manner, and then a bluegrass-style version of the same tune in Figure 10-5 (also listen to Track 57).

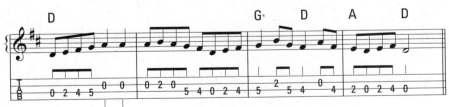

Figure 10-4: Old-time fiddle version of 'Whiskey Before Breakfast'.

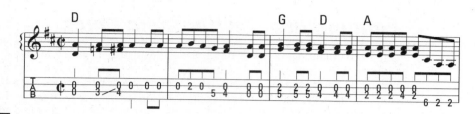

Figure 10-5: Bluegrass-style 'Whiskey Before Breakfast'.

Don't play these free-spirited interpretations of fiddle tunes when you're at an Irish or old-time session. Those folks may not find your interpretations and blues-based licks very enjoyable.

Meeting the father of bluegrass

Bill Monroe and the Bluegrass Boys created the sound that paved the way for all other bluegrass bands. On first listen, you may find the early Bluegrass Boys' recordings harsh, raw and even difficult to listen to. But to get a grip on the band's importance, think of Bill Monroe as the Robert Johnson (blues guitar great) of mandolin, because he influenced the course of mandolin history just as Johnson did for guitar. Monroe has influenced nearly every person who decided to play mandolin in the last 70 years. Following are a few facts about one of the most important figures in American music:

- William Smith Monroe was a cross-eyed kid who was picked on by his siblings and classmates. His poor eyesight caused him to be seen as slow, and he was made to sit at the back of the class. He carried his childhood experiences throughout his life, at times feeling the need to prove himself.

- He started playing professionally with his brothers in the early 1930s.

- He worked as a professional dancer early in his career, and many of his right-hand rhythms come directly from dance steps.

- He invented a musical genre in bluegrass that includes a distinct vocal style and an instrumental style featuring the mandolin; he even wrote much of the standard repertoire.

- He's currently the only person to be inducted into the Bluegrass Hall of Fame, the Country Music Hall of Fame *and* the Rock and Roll Hall of Fame.

Adding the blues style

The blues is a major component of bluegrass. If you aren't familiar with blues from the early 1900s, you may want to listen to and study that music a bit before trying to understand bluegrass. Chapter 9 demonstrates some of the early American string-band styles from which bluegrass evolves. Here are a few basic elements of the blues techniques used in bluegrass mandolin playing:

- ✔ Playing melodies, licks, fills and rhythms using primarily down-strokes.

- ✔ Using blue notes and chord tones instead of standard notes of the major scale (as the later sections 'Exploring other left-hand ornamentations' and 'Playing out-of-chord positions: The left hand' show).

- ✔ Ornamenting with left-hand articulations such as slides, hammer-ons and pull-offs (check out Chapter 6 for details).

- ✔ Creating the sound of steel strings smashing against the steel frets.

In many styles, you'd want to avoid the sound of strings hitting the frets because it can be considered as having a poor tone, but it has the same exciting effect as overdriving an electric guitar. It's a form of distortion that many people (including me!) think sounds just great.

Using tremolo

Bluegrass mandolin tremolo refers to the act of keeping the pick moving in a down-up fashion while playing. In general, the use of tremolo is timed to fit the beat of the music; it may turn out to be eighth, sixteenth or thirty-second notes (quavers, semiquavers or demisemiquavers, respectively) or a triplet figure, but it's steady and in time with the music. A good tremolo is one of the toughest skills mandolin players need to develop.

Chapter 5 demonstrates many types of tremolo and exercises including this bluegrass-type timed tremolo.

Adding extra bars: Irregular time

When listening to bluegrass music, you may notice that some tunes seem to have an extra measure or even an extra half of one measure (or sometimes a missing measure). These kinds of tunes are called *crooked tunes*. Many of the authors of these melodies weren't technically trained musicians, and just played by ear. As a result, some tunes have a little hiccup, or a place for a short guitar run between verses. This doesn't happen in all bluegrass songs, but knowing that it can is important; keep your ears open and be ready for some surprises.

Picking up Bluegrass Melodic Techniques

Melodies come in many forms in the bluegrass world: they can be in the form of an instrumental break, an intro or ending lick, fills behind a vocalist or long soaring tremolo lines. In this section, I present some concepts to get your melodies sounding all bluegrassy using your left and right hands.

Using the right hand

The right hand is where bluegrass mandolin players get the speed, tone, volume and rhythm that are so identifiably bluegrass. I cover many of these basic skills in Chapter 5 but, in addition, bluegrass requires that your right hand performs like an Olympic athlete. Whether you're playing a breakdown at warp speed using alternate picking, using tremolo in an old gospel tune, or playing a bluesy piece using all down-strokes, the right hand plays a major role. Underestimate it at your peril!

Constant motion

The object here is to be able to keep a steady pattern of down-up strokes with your right hand while playing. Even when you *ghost* a note (meaning that your pick doesn't play a string), keeping your hand moving while following the melody of the tune is important.

When you can keep a steady flow of notes while playing a melody, you're ready to make your playing more interesting by adding some rhythmic patterns. Bill Monroe disciple Mike Compton (check out his website, www.mike-compton.net) transcribed hours and hours of Bill's playing and noticed some rhythmic patterns that Bill used in his unique mandolin playing. Figure 10-6 and Track 58 demonstrate a few of these patterns.

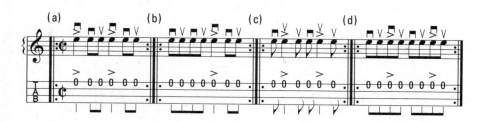

Figure 10-6: Some Bill Monroe rhythmic patterns.

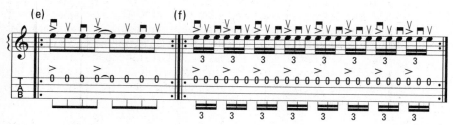

Practise these patterns with alternate picking and with all down-strokes.

Now try applying this concept to the traditional song 'Bury Me Beneath the Willow'. Figure 10-7 shows the chorus of the song as you'd sing it. Listen to Track 59 for a demonstration of this basic technique. I play the song the first time as it would be sung, followed by a simple mandolin version using alternate picking, incorporating some of the accents and patterns from Figure 10-6.

Bury Me Beneath The Willow

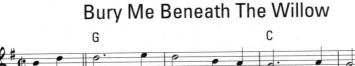

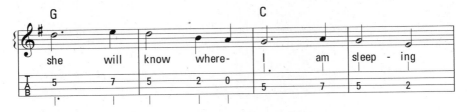

Figure 10-7: 'Bury Me Beneath the Willow'.

Down-strokes

Hard driving down-strokes are a key element of the Monroe style of mandolin playing. He often used this picking style to play blues-influenced licks both in instrumentals and when accompanying a vocalist.

Figure 10-8 and Track 60 demonstrate a Bill-Monroe-style mandolin blues tune. Notice how the melody incorporates a few of the rhythmic patterns from Figure 10-6. Remember to play this tune with all down-strokes, except where noted.

Uncle Bill

Figure 10-8: 'Uncle Bill' using down-strokes.

Reproduced by permission of Don Julin

Playing out-of-chord positions: The left hand

The basic left-hand techniques needed to play bluegrass mandolin include playing out-of-chord shapes, playing up the neck, and using slides, hammer-ons and double stops containing chord tones. I describe all these techniques in Chapter 6, except for playing out-of-chord shapes. In this section, I explain what I mean by this term.

Many bluegrass mandolin players use the out-of-chord-shapes technique, and it's a major part of the bluegrass sound. This method of playing focuses much more on the chord–melody relationship than the scale–melody relationship.

Finding the chord positions on the fingerboard requires knowing the location of the root notes of chords used in the song, along with an understanding of the two shapes shown in Figure 10-9. Flip to Chapter 6 if you need help remembering the note names.

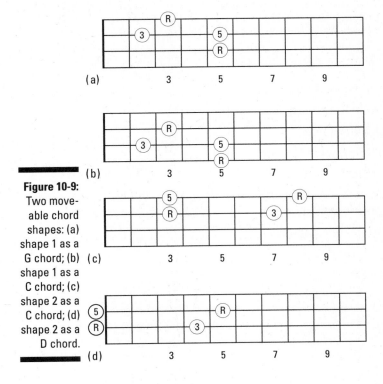

Figure 10-9: Two moveable chord shapes: (a) shape 1 as a G chord; (b) shape 1 as a C chord; (c) shape 2 as a C chord; (d) shape 2 as a D chord.

'Speaking' bluegrass mandolin!

To discover the language of bluegrass mandolin, ideally you need the musical vocabulary, which is made up of tunes, licks and breaks that you pick up by listening to the pros. All your mandolin heroes, including Sam Bush, David Grisman, Ronnie McCoury, Mike Compton, Adam Steffey, Chris Thile and John Reischman, learned by imitating their heroes.

When learning songs or licks from recordings or in workshops, analyse the lick or melody in reference to the chord changes and chord positions. This way, if you know that this one lick works over a G chord, you can try placing it in a break over a G chord.

Playing two primary chord shapes

In essence, you can play two primary arpeggio (chord tone) shapes for major chords on the mandolin. By combining and overlapping chord shapes, and shifting from one shape to another, or by moving a shape over one string, you're able to follow the chord progression of a song in a melodic way. Figure 10-9 shows the two primary shapes. The notes are labelled root third or fifth. (For a table of chord tones for all major and minor chords, check out Chapter 6.)

For shape 1 in Figure 10-9(a) and (b), practise your fingering in two ways:

- **Fingers one, two and three:**
  - Low root: Ring finger
  - Third: Index finger
  - Fifth: Ring finger
  - High root: Second finger

- **Fingers two, three and four (this fingering applies more when playing in higher positions):**
  - Low root: Fourth finger
  - Third: Second finger
  - Fifth: Fourth finger
  - High root: Ring finger

Also practise your fingering for shape 2 in Figure 10-9(c) and (d) in two ways, as follows:

✔ **Closed position:**

- Low root: Index finger
- Third: Ring finger
- Fifth: Index finger
- High root: Fourth finger

✔ **Open position:**

- Low root: Open string
- Third: Second finger
- Fifth: Open string
- High root: Ring finger

Notice how both of these shapes can move across the string or up the neck. The trick is to remember where the root notes are and what finger should be playing them.

Staying in position

Playing *in position* refers to keeping your left hand in one place while playing, as opposed to flying up and down the fingerboard. Figure 10-10 shows all the available chord tones in first position (up to the seventh fret) for G, C and D chords.

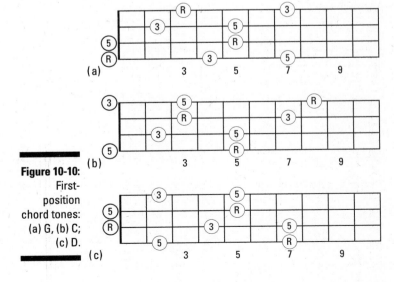

Figure 10-10: First-position chord tones: (a) G, (b) C; (c) D.

Moving up the neck

As you move up the mandolin's neck, you start to see the same patterns or shapes appearing over and over. Each range or arpeggio shape has its own unique sound quality, and by learning to transition (shift) from one position or shape to another, you broaden your palette of sounds and the keys in which you can play.

Shifting smoothly requires knowing which left-hand finger to land on when you arrive at the new position, and where the root notes of each chord are.

Figure 10-11 is a diagram of the mandolin neck, showing all the chord tones for G, C and D chords up to the 12th fret. Seeing these primary shapes when looking at the entire neck can seem a bit like playing the word-search game, but be patient because they reveal themselves one at a time.

Another way to learn where these shapes are located is to learn the arpeggios for each chord in four different positions (see Chapter 6 for positions). Using this method enables you to see the two arpeggio shapes used by many bluegrass mandolin players, in different locations on the fretboard. For example, Figure 10-12 demonstrates four positions for the C major chord tones. I include finger numbers above the standard notation:

✔ Measure 1 shows the C chord tones using shape 1 in first position.

✔ Measure 2 shows the C chord tones using shape 2 in second position.

✔ Measure 3 shows the C chord tones using shape 1 in fourth position.

✔ Measure 4 shows the C chord tones using shape 2 in third position.

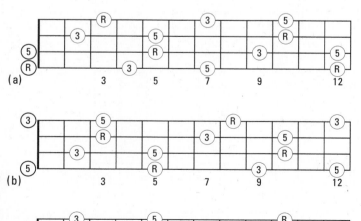

Figure 10-11:
Open to
12th-fret
chord tones:
(a) G, (b) C;
(c) D.

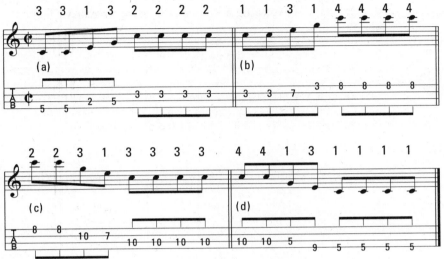

Figure 10-12: C major chord tones in four positions: (a) shape 1 in first position; (b) shape 2 in second position; (c) shape 1 in fourth position; (d) shape 2 in third position.

Don't forget about open strings. Open or first position is a little different because some of the chord tones are the open strings requiring no left-hand fingers, and so making these shapes feels a bit different. Open strings on the mandolin have a great sound, and so feel free to use them without shame.

Exploring other left-hand ornamentations

In addition to understanding and memorising chord shapes for both rhythm playing and melody or instrumental breaks (as I describe in the preceding section), you also need a strong left hand to accomplish a few other important elements of bluegrass mandolin.

Slides

Slides, which I cover in Chapter 6, can be an effective way of moving from one position to another. You can also use them while staying in one position to connect or slur two notes together or to slide into or away from a chord tone. Normally the slide is focused on the chord tone and a fret or two below that chord tone.

Double stops

I describe the basic concept of double stops in Chapter 6. For the bluegrass mandolin player, double stops played with tremolo are pretty much a mandatory skill for melody or an instrumental break; they make one of the defining sounds in classic bluegrass mandolin.

Mike Compton has generously offered the following exercise in double stops, which gets you exploring new areas of the fingerboard. The concept is fairly simple.

In this exercise you use the notes of the G chord, but do so over the full length of the fretboard. Start with lowest possible double stop (two notes of a chord) and work your way up the fingerboard by replacing one note at a time. For extra credit, try playing this exercise with an even tremolo (see Figure 10-13 and listen to Track 61). When you can do this for the G chord, expand your vocabulary by adding this technique to more chords.

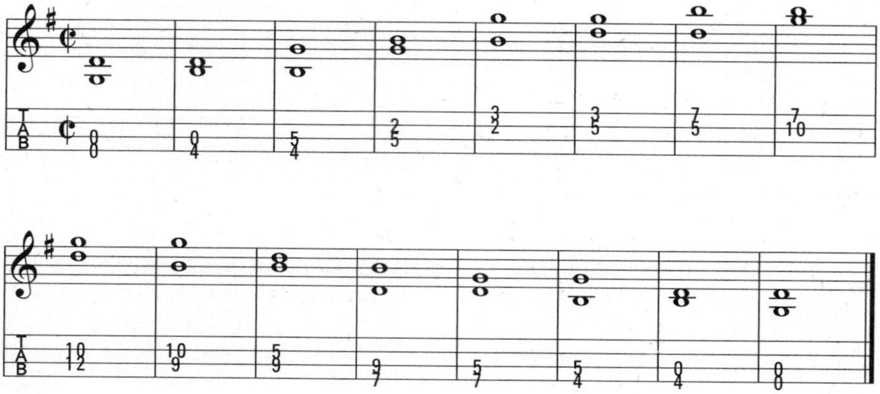

Figure 10-13:
Double-stop
crawl.

Blue notes

Blue notes are simply the notes that are outside the chord or the scale. They can create colour, tension and sadness. Check out Chapter 9 for much more on blue notes.

People like to say that the *flatted* third, fifth and seventh notes of a chord are the blue notes. The translation is one fret below the third or fifth of a chord and two frets below the root of the chord.

Figure 10-14 and Track 62 feature a Monroe-style mandolin instrumental I call 'Kickin' Mule'. Notice how each lick or phrase of the tune is built for one of the arpeggio shapes I present in this chapter.

Pay close attention to pick direction in the B section, as changing from one string to another on the up-stroke can be challenging (see Chapter 5).

Kickin' Mule

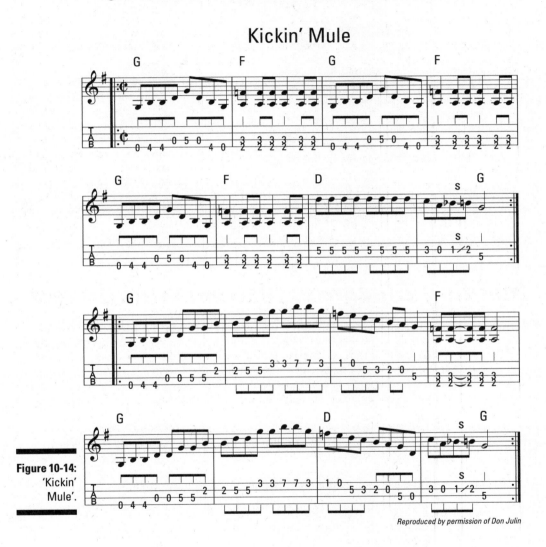

Figure 10-14: 'Kickin' Mule'.

Reproduced by permission of Don Julin

Newgrass

In the late 1960s and early 1970s, progressive bluegrass or *newgrass* music was introduced to a new generation by artists such as John Hartford, Newgrass Revival (featuring Sam Bush), Old and in the Way (featuring David Grisman, Jerry Garcia and Peter Rowan), and the Nitty Gritty Dirt Band. These long-haired hippies had authentic bluegrass chops and took the music to the rock-and-roll audience on the coat tails of Jerry Garcia's popularity from the Grateful Dead.

The seeds of this movement actually lay in the early 1960s, when Bill Monroe and the Bluegrass Boys started to play college campuses.

Folk music was experiencing a revival, and it seemed like a good way to expand the awareness of bluegrass.

By the early 1970s, this new generation of progressive bluegrass bands was fusing bluegrass with pop, rock and jazz styles, straying away from traditional fiddle-based rhythms. Some elements of this new music included the use of non-traditional bluegrass instruments, chord changes that sounded more like pop music, and extended improvisational solo sections. Even though these modern musicians broke away from the tradition, many are great musicians and studied the masters.

Building Bluegrass Instrumental Breaks

Constructing an instrumental bluegrass-style break in a vocal song can be a bit of a mystery — which this section can help you with. The first thing you need to know is that the instrumental sections of bluegrass songs are really just the vocal sections of the songs without the vocals. Some simple songs have only one part or section (a verse), whereas others may have a second section (a chorus). You can play an instrumental break over either part.

The instrumental break can be the most exciting bit of a bluegrass song and can even receive applause from the audience, like a jazz solo. Bluegrass breaks vary greatly:

- Some are simply the melody played on an instrument.
- Some are the melody played with ornaments or embellishments.
- Some are the melody changed around so much that it's only vaguely recognisable.
- Some don't even hint at the original melody.

These breaks can be improvised or planned out. In either case, they're creative, in that musicians have their own individual ways to play a break in any given song. In this section, I help you to understand the concept and the process of creating a bluegrass-style break.

Learning the song

The first step in building a break in a bluegrass song is to know the song well, including playing, singing or even humming the melody, and committing the chord changes to memory. Here's a three-step programme designed to get you started:

1. **Memorise the melody by humming or singing along with a recording of the song.**

2. **Practise playing the chords (in time) while you're humming or singing the melody.**

3. **Learn to play the melody fairly close to the way you'd want to sing it.**

Although this advice sounds obvious, I've seen many students try to play very complex breaks from printed sources for songs that they can't sing or play the chords to. I've never seen that approach work!

When you know the song, I encourage you to learn as many of your favourite mandolin players' breaks as you can. By learning and comparing how some of your heroes played a song, you start to see how the top players use some of the left- and right-hand techniques I cover in this chapter. When you're able to imitate some of these *licks* (short musical phrases), you can then incorporate them into your own instrumental breaks. As you discover breaks from recordings or sheet music, it's very important to see how these licks relate to the original melody or chords of the song.

Making your break sound like bluegrass

The following tips help you to produce a break that sounds authentically bluegrass:

- **Get your right hand moving:** Bluegrass mandolin players use their right hands to shape the rhythm of a song. The first choice is to determine whether this song is best served by down-strokes or alternate picking. This decision has a lot to do with the speed of the song, with slower to mid-tempo tunes using more down-strokes and faster hoedown tempos using alternate picking. After you determine the basic picking style and can play the melody using it, try to add some life by incorporating one or more of the rhythm patterns shown in the earlier Figure 10-6.

- **Play out of position:** By playing out of the suggested chord positions, you have a shape under your fingers that contains the all-important chord tones. Flip to the earlier 'Playing out-of-chord positions: The left hand' section for more.

✔ **Use blue notes:** These notes put the blue in bluegrass. Instead of using scales to fill out the spaces or connect melody notes, using chord tones and blue notes gets you closer to a bluegrass-sounding harmony. Chapter 9 contains much more information on blue notes.

✔ **Add some tremolo:** Although tremolo can mean a lot of different things to different people, I mean a rapid alternate stroke (still in time with the music) with a longer soaring type of melody, often made up of double stops that follow the chord progression. You need to decide where or whether you want to use this colour in your own bluegrass break. Check out Chapter 5 for everything about tremolo.

✔ **Remember the melody:** You can build up a collection of licks, chord positions, blue notes and tremolo and develop the courage to stray from the melody, and yet find that you're not really representing the song. To work the song back into your break, let the melody influence your right-hand patterns while your left hand chooses notes from chord positions and double stops. By using the rhythmic contour of the melody, the harmony notes make more sense and listeners still hear the melody even though you aren't completely playing it.

Bluegrass mandolin players often tremolo two or even three pairs of strings at a time. I suggest you review Chapter 5 and practise picking each pair of strings. For example, run through the tremolo exercises picking the e- and a-strings, followed by the a- and d-strings and then the g- and d-strings.

Figure 10-15 and Track 63 demonstrate a fairly simple finished bluegrass-style instrumental break for 'Bury Me Beneath the Willow' (which I describe in the earlier section 'Using the right hand'). This break consists almost entirely of eighth notes (quavers). I suggest using the accents shown in the earlier Figure 10-6(d) to give this break more life.

Notice that the first half of this break is in first position and uses shape 1, but also uses the fourth finger to complete the melody during both G and C chords. The second half moves to third position and uses shape 2 for both chords. (I describe shapes 1 and 2 in the earlier section 'Playing two primary chord shapes'.)

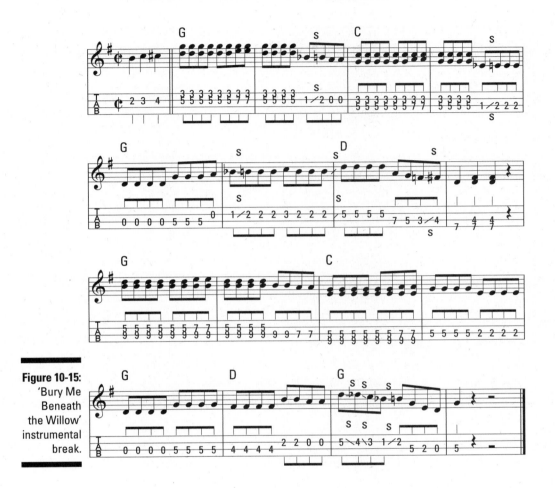

Figure 10-15:
'Bury Me
Beneath
the Willow'
instrumental
break.

Meeting a mandolin *wunderkind*

Faster than a speeding breakdown! More powerful than a four-finger chop chord! Able to leap from bluegrass to Bach to Radiohead in a single bound! Look in the sky: it's a bird! it's a plane! It's Chris Thile!

Chris Thile is clearly the superhero of the modern mandolin world, a child prodigy who had his first recording contract at 10 years of age. Now, in his early 30s, he's changing the path of the mandolin for future generations. Even though his music far exceeds the boundaries of bluegrass, he comes from a bluegrass and traditional country-music background.

Prolific doesn't do justice to describing him. Recently, in one year, he released three albums as diverse as one blending the blood-curdling ancient tones of the Monroe Brothers with the reckless energy of a punk band (*Sleep With One Eye Open*, with Michael Daves — www. thiledaves.com); a mix of classical, Americana and incredibly clean playing (*The Goat Rodeo Sessions*, with Yo-Yo Ma, Stuart Duncan and Edgar Meyer — www.yo-yoma. com/news/goat-rodeo-sessions); and contemporary pop music played on bluegrass ensemble instruments (Punch Brothers' *Who's Feeling Young Now?* — www.punch brothers.com).

When not on tour with one of the supergroups, he's playing solo gigs and his mandolin concerto 'Ad astra per alas porci' ('to the stars on the wings of a pig') with many of the world's top orchestras. Whatever he does is likely to include some of the best mandolin playing of the last hundred years or so.

Chris is inspiring the new generation of mandolin players and, like Bill Monroe did, is changing the course of mandolin history. The new breed of post-Thile mandolin stars include Sierra Hull, Scott Gates, Sarah Jarosz, Dominick Leslie and soon many others who've not even picked up the mandolin yet.

Chapter 11

Travelling to the Emerald Isle: Irish Mandolin

The mandolin has an interesting relationship with Irish music. Even though fiddle tunes are a big part of their standard repertoire, mandolins aren't considered to be core instruments in an Irish traditional music *session* (a gathering of musicians playing Irish tunes, drinking a few pints, and in general enjoying life). In recent years, though, mandolins have been welcomed into sessions for melody purposes.

In this chapter, I introduce you to a few beautiful Irish melodies and modes (or scales), some toe-tapping rhythms, and the mandolin techniques needed to play Irish music. I also let you in on the required etiquette of joining in with an Irish session – a rewarding opportunity to take, if you get the chance.

A world unto itself: Irish music

Irish music is a style with its own specific rules. You need to prepare in order to play it properly, more so than some other styles. Being an American-music-style mandolin player, I did just that and consulted my colleague and Irish mandolin musician Marla Fibish on this chapter, so you can be sure that what you read comes from a real expert in the world of Irish mandolin. Marla suggested the four tunes that I demonstrate. If you get a chance to take a workshop or attend a concert of Marla's, make a point of going (check out www.marlafibish.com).

Following the Melody One Note at a Time

On the whole, traditional Irish music is *monophonic*, which means that only one note is played at a time. As a mandolin player, you can forget all about harmony parts, counterpoint, fancy chord changes or improvisation in Irish music – it's all about the melody and knowing a lot of tunes. In this section, I share with you the best way to learn Irish tunes, demonstrate a few common rhythms – jigs, reels, slip jigs and hornpipes – and offer a quick look into the *triplet*, the most common ornament used in Irish music.

Listening to learn Irish tunes

The goal when playing Irish music is to learn tunes and commit them to memory, and the best musicians are clear that learning by ear is the best way to master Irish music.

If at all possible, you want to learn these tunes from musicians during a live Irish music session. Take along a pocket-sized digital recorder to the session (as I describe in Chapter 16) and record some tunes (after asking for permission) so you can learn them when you get back home.

Unfortunately, most people don't have access to regular Irish sessions in their neighbourhood and need to resort to other tactics. Listening to commercially available recordings is a great way to pick up tunes. If you prefer to learn from a book, *O'Neill's Music Of Ireland* by Francis O'Neill is seen by many people as the bible of Irish tunes, although it's available in standard music notation only. Mandolintab.net at http://www.mandolintab.net has over 10,000 tunes available in PDF form in standard notation and tablature.

All good things come in threes

Irish tunes are normally played in groups called *sets*. A set of tunes can be any group of tunes, but the most common sets contain three tunes of the same type strung together without a pause. So a set may be three jigs or three reels and so on. Each tune can be played any number of times before switching to the next tune, but three times for each tune is the most common approach.

If you do choose to learn a tune from a printed page, be sure to commit it to memory. You get some funny looks if you show up at an Irish music session with a music stand and sheet music!

Swinging with triplets and the lilt

Triplets are simply three notes played in the space that would normally be occupied by two notes.

In Irish music, *eighth note triplets* (where three notes are played in the space of two eighth notes) are performed with either a quick down-up-down or, in some cases, an up-down-up pattern, depending on where in the beat the triplet is placed (see the 'Reel triplets' and 'Jig triplets' sections later in this chapter). Jigs and slip jigs use the same down-up-down picking pattern for eighth notes (see Chapter 5) and aren't considered triplets, technically speaking, because they aren't three notes played in the space of two. Instead, they are dividing one beat by three (see Chapter 4) with a specific picking pattern of down-up-down. In either case, learning to play notes in groups of three (whether triplets or not) by getting comfortable with down-up-down or up-down-up picking makes Irish playing much more fun. (In other styles of music such as bluegrass or swing, players usually perform triplets by using left-hand effects such as hammer-ons and pull-offs instead of down-up-down picking; see Chapter 6.)

Another important rhythmic element to Irish music is the *lilt*, or what some people would call a *dotted feel*. (Remember that a dot after a note makes it longer; see Appendix B.) In the hornpipe, the melody is comprised of eighth notes, but the flow of notes has an underlying triplet or dotted feel. This all boils down to the fact that the strong beats (or down-strokes) or numbered beats are actually a bit longer than the weak beats (or up-strokes) or 'ands'. This is very similar to what blues and jazz players call *swinging eighth notes* (see Chapter 13).

Listen to Track 64 and check out Figure 11-1 for an example of straight or evenly played eighth notes (quavers) with alternate picking (which I describe in Chapter 5) as you'd use in a reel, down-up-down picking as used in jigs or slip jigs, and a visual representation of lilt or hornpipe rhythm.

This last example is a visual aid (music wouldn't be printed this way) to help you understand the lilt, which is essentially the hornpipe rhythm. Even though hornpipes are written as eighth notes (quavers) when printed in tab or sheet music form and look very similar to reels, hornpipes are played with a different feel.

Using triplets as ornamentation

The judicious use of triplets is a common way to *ornament* (spice up) a tune. You can play the triplet by repeating the same note for all three strokes or with a combination of notes. You can get your pick tangled up in the strings playing triplets if you aren't careful, so go slow, adding these ornaments gradually into your playing.

Triplets are placed differently in the measure depending on the rhythm of the tune. I give some basic guidelines for using triplets in the four basic rhythms that I describe in the later section 'Playing Irish Rhythms and Tunes'.

I talk more about reels, jigs, hornpipes and other rhythms in the later section 'Playing Irish Rhythms and Tunes'.

Don't worry if this description sounds a little complicated; rhythms are much easier to hear than to read about, and make more sense when you listen to Track 64.

Figure 11-1:
(a) Straight eighth notes (quavers), as used in reels; (b) eighth notes, as used in jigs; (c) lilt or hornpipe.

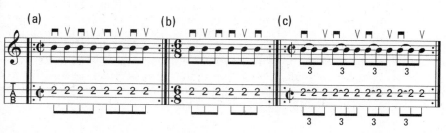

Discovering the Irish Music Modes

A mode is a fairly simple concept that can seem a bit confusing at first. Simply put, a *mode* is a type of scale starting on a note other than the *tonic* (root note) of the scale. Chapters 7 and 8 have all about scales and root notes, which may help you when approaching modes.

As an example, take the key of D, which is the most popular key for Irish music. A scale that goes from D to D using the notes of a D major scale is simply a D major scale. If you use the notes of a D major scale but play them from E to E (E, F♯, G, A, B, C♯, D) you're playing a type of E minor scale (or Dorian mode).

In this section, I describe the four most popular modes in Irish music.

Using a standard major scale (Ionian mode)

This scale isn't really a mode at all, just a regular everyday D major scale (with a Greek name) containing the notes D, E, F#, G, A, B, C# and D. Musicians usually just call this *major* (see Figure 11-2). The most common major keys (scales) for Irish tunes are D, G, and A with fewer in C and F.

Figure 11-2: The major scale (Ionian).

Tackling a standard minor scale (Dorian mode)

Often just called *minor*, the E Dorian mode starts on the second step of the D major scale. Some people choose to remember these modes by altering a major scale – for example, by starting with an E major scale and lowering or flatting the third and seventh notes in the scale. (I prefer to think of this as a D major scale starting at E or the second degree of the scale.) Use whatever method makes the most sense to you.

The notes of this type of E minor scale are E, F#, G, A, B, C#, D and E. The most common minor keys for Irish tunes are Am, Em, and Bm, with fewer in Dm and Gm.

TECHNICAL STUFF

Meeting some big fat Greek words

Each mode has a Greek name just to make it seem more complicated than it really is. The four modes that I cover in this section are also called Ionian, Dorian, Mixolydian and Aeolian.

Don't worry about memorising these names. And you don't need to know that most of them relate to places in Ancient Greece, unless you intend to use this area as your specialist subject on a TV quiz show!

This type of minor scale has been used in a variety of well-known melodies such as 'Drunken Sailor', 'Scarborough Fair' and 'Eleanor Rigby', and is quite popular in Irish music (see Figure 11-3).

Figure 11-3:
The minor scale (Dorian).

Meeting the other major scale (Mixolydian mode)

Even though the term *Mixolydian* is rarely used by traditional Irish musicians, many Irish tunes use this scale, and Irish musicians refer to this sound simply as *modal*. This scale (which has a major third and flatted seventh) has an old-world, enchanted, unresolved and almost bluesy quality. Irish music tunes in this scale are usually called *modal tunes* (see Figure 11-4), and the most common modal keys for Irish tunes are D, G and A.

You can arrive at the Mixolydian mode by using a major scale but starting on the fifth step of that scale – so, A to A using the D major scale. The other method is to start with an A scale and flat the seventh step or note in the scale. The notes of this type of major scale (as shown in Figure 11-4) are A, B, C♯, D, E, F♯, G and A.

'Old Joe Clark', 'Norwegian Wood' and the traditional folk song 'She Walks Through The Fair' are good examples of modal melodies.

Figure 11-4:
The other major scale (Mixolydian).

Encountering the relative minor scale (Aeolian mode)

This scale (see Figure 11-5) isn't as common as the other three examples in this chapter, but it does exist in Irish music. The Aeolian mode starts on the sixth step of the major scale and can be referred to as the *relative minor*. As with the other modes, you can arrive at this mode by starting with the B major scale and flatting the third, sixth and seventh notes. I find it much easier to think of this as a D major scale starting on the sixth note (B).

The notes for this relative minor scale (as shown in Figure 11-5) are B, C♯, D, E, F♯, G, A and B. The most common relative minor keys for Irish tunes are Em, Bm, and Am, with fewer in Dm and Gm. Don't worry too much about this mode, though, as it is used less frequently and none of the tunes in this chapter feature it.

You can hear this relative minor scale in Bob Dylan's 'All Along The Watchtower' and R.E.M.'s 'Losing My Religion' (which, by the way, features a nice mandolin part!).

Figure 11-5:
The relative minor scale (Aeolian).

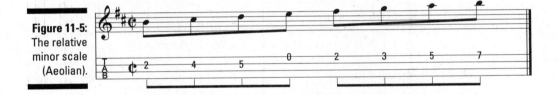

Playing Irish Rhythms and Tunes

No doubt you're itching to start playing a few Irish tunes, and this section shows you how. Each of the four tunes features a traditional Irish rhythm – reel, jig, slip jig and hornpipe.

'Reeling in the Years'

Yes, I know 'Reeling in the Years' isn't an Irish tune, but I couldn't resist the pun.

Mandolin types and models

The favoured mandolins of Irish players tend to be the carved-top Gibson A models with round soundholes. Octave mandolins, mandolas and even Irish bouzoukis are also fairly common in Irish music. These overgrown mandolins are used primarily as accompaniment instruments, but some daring souls with large fingers can manage to play melodies with them as well.

I play the tracks in this chapter on a 1923 Gibson A snakehead mandolin. On these audio tracks, I play the tunes straight (as written) first time,

and follow them with versions featuring triplets as ornaments. I include a section of the tune with examples of triplets in the figure that follows each tune. Feel free to experiment with placing your own triplets in these tunes, once you get the melodies down. I play these tracks at a moderate tempo, but you still may need to slow them down a bit at first (see Chapter 16). I've also recorded basic accompaniment tracks for these tunes using an octave mandolin.

The reel is the most common type of Irish dance tune. Reels are in *cut time*, which is written like 4/4 time (see Chapter 4 for all about time signatures) but counted with two strong beats per measure (and so is technically 2/2). The notes of a reel are in general even eighth notes with little or no lilt, and can be played at fairly brisk tempos, ranging from 90 to 120 beats per minute (bpm) on your metronome (check out Chapter 16 for more on metronomes).

Reel picking and accents

Picking in reels is straight ahead alternate picking (for more information and exercises in alternate picking, see Chapter 5). Accenting certain beats, called *stressed* beats, adds life and a rhythmic drive to these melodies. The primary beat in reels lands on beat one of a measure, and a secondary or lighter-stressed beat appears halfway through the measure on beat two (remember we are in cut time here).

'The Drunken Landlady' is a reel in E minor (flip to the earlier section 'Tackling a standard minor scale (Dorian mode)'. Just as a reminder, I include pick direction marks for the first two measures. Check out Figure 11-6 and Track 65 Part 1 for 'The Drunken Landlady'.

The Drunken Landlady

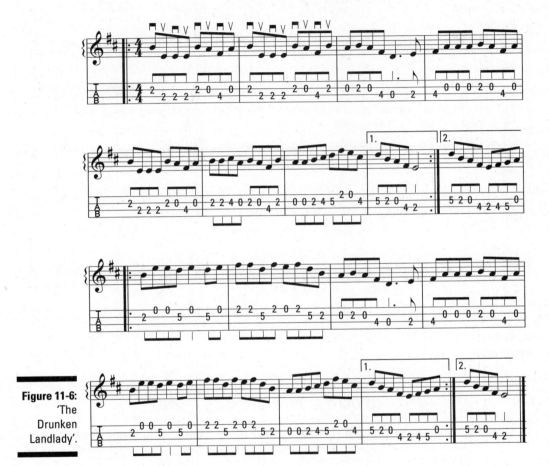

Figure 11-6: 'The Drunken Landlady'.

Reel triplets

Triplets are used in reels as ornaments and are placed on the down-beat. When playing triplets in reels, you replace the standard down-up stroke with a quick down-up-down. You may need to slow the tempos down in order to fit many triplets in. Figure 11-7 shows a section of 'The Drunken Landlady' with a few triplets, as played on Track 65 Part 2.

Varying the melodies

As you listen to different versions of the same Irish tunes, you find that not everyone plays the tune the same way. Some of the differences are due to one player's melodic embellishments of the melody, and yet other versions vary from region to region. So a tune can sound quite different when played a few miles away.

These regional differences may be because these tunes are learned by ear and played from memory. Multiply this by thousands of miles and hundreds of years, and how anyone knows the same melodies is a wonder. This is just one of the fascinating mysteries of Irish music.

The trickiest part of playing triplets is recovering from the quick down-up-down when returning to the standard down-up stroke, due to the fact that you have two very quick down-strokes in a row.

Figure 11-7: 'The Drunken Landlady' with triplets.

Jigging around the dance floor

Jigs are written in 6/8 time, but you really feel two strong beats per measure. Each strong beat is divided into three smaller beats. Jigs are normally played between 90 and 120 bpm with two clicks per measure on your metronome.

Jig picking

Picking when playing a jig is similar to triplet picking in that the pattern is a series of down-up-down strokes, even though this pattern is not considered a triplet. Each measure contains two sets of this down-up-down picking pattern, which is counted as '**1**, 2, 3, **2**, 2, 3'. The large stressed (or accented) beats are on beats one and four, and the secondary stress or lighter accent is on beats three and six.

'Hag at the Churn' (see Figure 11-8) is a jig in D modal (see the earlier section 'Meeting the other major scale (Mixolydian mode)'), and I demonstrate it in Track 66 Part 1 (remember to use the down-up-down picking pattern shown in Figure 11-1(a)). I include the pick direction for the first two measures.

Hag At the Churn

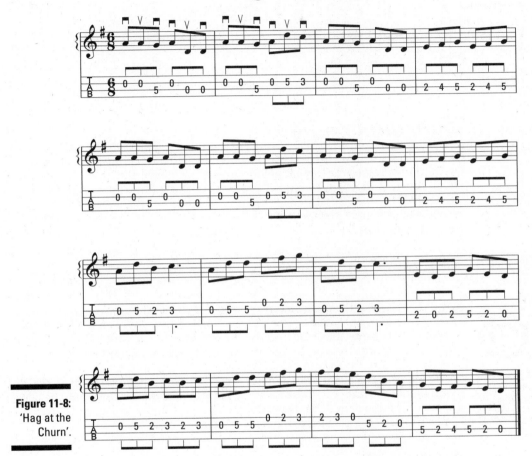

Figure 11-8: 'Hag at the Churn'.

Jig triplets

You can use triplets in jigs as rhythmic accents, but unlike reel-style triplets from the earlier section 'Reel triplets', they can be placed on the down-beat or the up-beat part of the picking pattern. As shown in Figure 11-9, the up-beat triplets are played with a quick up-down-up pattern placed between the stressed beats. Listen to 'Hag at the Churn' in Track 66 Part 2 to see whether you can hear the triplets in the second run through the tune.

Figure 11-9:
'Hag at the Churn' with triplets.

Slipping in a jig

A *slip jig* isn't where you're trying to play a jig and make a mistake, but a tune written in 9/8 time; for the unfamiliar listener or player, this time can be a difficult one to find a beat in. Similar to the jig (see the preceding section), and counted '**1**, 2, 3, **2**, 2, 3, **3**, 2, 3', the slip jig divides the strong beats into three equal smaller beats, the difference being that the slip jig has three strong beats per measure.

Slip jig picking

Picking for slip jigs amounts to three down-up-down patterns per measure.

I find that keeping this beat straight is easier if you count only the three strong beats; in other words, don't try to count to nine for each measure. The stressed or accented beats are on the three strong beats, with beats one and three being more stressed, and beat two being a bit more subtle.

'A Fig for a Kiss' is a slip jig in E minor (read 'Tackling a standard minor scale (Dorian mode)' earlier in this chapter for more). Remember that a slip jig uses three sets of down-up-down picking per measure. Check out Figure 11-10 and Track 67 Part 1 for a demonstration of the tune.

Slip jig triplets

Slip jig triplets are very much like jig triplets in that they can be played on the down beat or stressed part of the beat or on the up-stroke part of the picking pattern. Figure 11-11 contains a section of 'A Fig for a Kiss' that includes a few triplets as ornaments. You can hear this on the second version of 'A Fig for a Kiss' on Track 67 Part 2.

A Fig For A Kiss

Figure 11-10:
'A Fig for a Kiss'.

Figure 11-11:
Slip jig triplets in 'A Fig for a Kiss'.

Deciding on the tempo

Many a pint has been consumed discussing the topic of the correct tempos for Irish tunes. It seems to boil down to this: dancers like jigs, reels and slip jigs to be a crisp 115 bpm, give or take a few (in other words, fast). At that speed only the finest musicians can even think about embellishments or anything else for that matter. Many pro players who can play very fast choose to play slower and add more ornaments and detail when playing concerts or in sessions.

So if you aren't playing for dancers, feel free to slow these tunes down a bit.

Being all at sea in a good way: The hornpipe

The hornpipe is similar to the reel but in general played a bit slower (flip to 'Reeling in the Years' earlier in this section for more on reels). The eighth notes (quavers) in a hornpipe aren't as even as the eighth notes in a reel. They're played with what's called a lilt or a dotted feel (check out the 'Swinging with triplets and the lilt' section for a description of lilts), meaning that the down-strokes tend to be a bit longer than the up-strokes.

Hornpipes are written with standard eighth notes (quavers), and when printed in sheet music form they look very similar to reels, even though the notes are played with a lilt or dotted feel. See Figure 11-1(c) for a visual representation of the hornpipe rhythm.

Hornpipe picking

Picking for a hornpipe follows the down-up pattern, similar to reels, but the eighth notes (quavers) have an underlying triplet feel and aren't even. I think of a hornpipe as somewhere between a reel and a jig, played at a slightly slower tempo.

'Little Stack of Wheat', which I demonstrate in Figure 11-12 and Track 68, is a hornpipe in G major. Notice that this arrangement or *setting* includes a few triplets in the melody already.

Hornpipe triplets

Hornpipe triplets are very much like reel triplets in that they're played on the down-stroke beats and with a quick down-up-down picking pattern. Measures 2 and 6 of 'Little Stack of Wheat' have triplets incorporated into the melody.

The Little Stack of Wheat

Figure 11-12: 'Little Stack of Wheat'.

Current players to check out

If you think that Irish mandolin may be your cup of tea – or glass of stout – I suggest you listen to recordings by Marla Fibish, Luke Plumb, Andy Irvine, Mick Moloney, Dan Beimborn, Simon Mayor, Kevin Macleod, Kevin McElroy and Dagger Gordon. Thanks to the digital age, `www. amazon.com`, iTunes (`www.apple.com/ itunes`), CD Baby (`www.cdbaby.com`) and many other online music sellers make finding obscure independent artists easier than ever.

Playing Irish Tunes with Other Musicians

Playing music with other people is really what learning to play an instrument is all about. Along with knowing the tunes and being able to listen and follow others while playing, Irish music has its own set of arcane rules with regards to playing this music with others.

The session is the most common place to play with others, but some of the guidelines that I provide in this section work just as well if you're playing with one other musician in your living room. The following is a list of common questions about playing in an Irish music session:

- ✔ **Do I need an invitation?** You may. Some sessions are open and new-comers (who know the tunes) are welcome to join in, but others are more structured and the players are set.

- ✔ **I pick stuff up pretty fast; can I just strum along?** In a traditional Irish session, the answer is a resounding *no*! Only one chord-playing instrument is allowed in a traditional session. This instrument can be a guitar, octave mandolin or even a piano, but only one is permitted. The chords or accompaniment to Irish music is a much-discussed subject that arouses strong opinions, and as a mandolin player my best advice is to leave it alone. Just learn the melodies.

- ✔ **I love to jam; will I get to take any solos?** No. If you do, you'll be asked to stop.

- ✔ **Can I sit in the background and 'noodle' while trying to learn a tune?** No, this is viewed as a distraction. Learn the tunes at home.

- ✔ **How long is a session?** At least a few pints.

- ✔ **I'm a good sight-reader; can I bring my book of tunes and read them at a session?** You'll raise a few eyebrows if you do. Memorise what you can and leave the book at home.

Chapter 12

Taking a Quick World Tour

People across the globe – from Auckland, New Zealand, to Accrington, UK, and from Tokyo, Japan, to Tacoma, Washington, USA – enjoy playing and listening to the mandolin. In fact, you may be surprised just how much of the world and how many different cultures have fallen under the seductive charms of the mandolin over the centuries.

In this chapter, I focus on just three of the many mandolin styles from around the world: Italian folk music, European classical and Brazilian choro. So get your hiking boots (and, in fact, your time machine) ready!

For those of you who like the details, I play the Italian and classical audio tracks for this chapter on a 1916 Vega bowlback mandolin (you can see it in Figure 15-7, in Chapter 15).

Returning to the Mandolin's Birthplace: Italy

The mandolin evolved from the lute family of instruments in Italy during the seventeenth and eighteenth centuries. By 1780 in Naples, the instrument had arrived at what's called the *Neapolitan mandolin*, having four pairs of strings tuned G, D, A and E. This tuning (the same as a violin) opened the door for violinists to cross over to the mandolin, and also made a large amount of violin music available to mandolin players.

As well as becoming a popular instrument among the European aristocracy, the mandolin also gained popularity with the citizens of Italy for playing folk music, the subject of this section. It's suitable for use in tarantellas, lullabies, polkas, serenades, waltzes, mazurkas and love songs.

Strolling to play

For many people, the sound of Italian mandolin music invokes the smell of garlic and tomato sauce and the taste of red wine; Italian restaurants keep such associations alive by hiring mandolin players. The strolling (or sitting) mandolin player usually performs a combination of folk tunes, themes from operas and popular melodies.

If you fancy the life of a strolling café mandolin player, one technique that you need to perfect is tremolo . . . in which case, check out the following section.

Making great use of tremolo

The best-known sound of the mandolin is tremolo, which I discuss in Chapter 5. This rapid back-and-forth motion of the pick while the musician is playing singing-style melodies can be credited to the Italian folk mandolin players. The tremolo that I demonstrate in this section is a style that changes speed based on dynamics or intensity.

Tremolo to your heart's content on 'O Sole Mio', written by Eduardo di Capua in 1898 (see Figure 12-1 and Track 69). This classic (see Figure 12-1) has two distinctive parts, with the first part being quieter (with slower tremolo), and the second part being louder (with faster tremolo), before quietening down (so, slower tremolo again) at the end of the song. The chords for 'O Sole Mio' are played using the arpeggio-type accompaniment shown in Figure 8-6(a) (in Chapter 8).

Tremolo for too long can get monotonous, so experiment with breaking up the tremolo by playing some of the melody notes with a single pick stroke.

Despite my best efforts, whenever I hear this song I can't help but think of the Elvis song 'It's Now or Never', which has the same melody but with new lyrics added by Wally Gold and Aaron Schroeder. As much as I love the sound of Italian mandolin, I can't shake my American roots, and I fear I may have invented a new genre of mandolin playing on Track 69 called 'Spaghetti Mid-Western'!

No mandolin player can get a gig in an Italian bistro without knowing how to play 'Torna a Surriento' ('Come Back to Sorrento'). Written in 1902 by Ernesto De Curtis, this song is enough to get you salivating in anticipation of a great Italian meal! Check out Figure 12-2 and listen to Track 70.

Figure 12-1:
'O Sole Mio':
(a) chords;
(b) melody.

Figure 12-2:
'Torna a
Surriento':
(a) chords
and (b)
melody.

This arrangement calls on you to use your fourth finger a fair amount. You also need to shift to third position in three places, playing the fifth fret with your first finger. Play measures 3, 5 and 21 in this third position.

You can play the chords for 'Torna a Surriento' with the waltz strumming pattern I show in Figure 9-7 (in Chapter 9).

Varying the tremolo speed

Tremolo, as I use it in this chapter, is a type of free tremolo (see Chapter 5) that is based not on tempos or beats but on dynamics or the intensity of the melody. So when you come to a louder part, you increase the tremolo speed to create excitement. The speed of the tremolo, however, is less important than playing each new melody note with a down-stroke. This is called an *expressive tremolo*, because you use it to add expression to the melody.

Visiting the Concert Hall: Classical Mandolin

Just as not all mandolin players play bluegrass, so they don't all wear denim dungarees; in fact, some dress up in dinner jackets and posh frocks. The classical *mandolinist* is a conservatory-trained mandolin player who specialises in the techniques needed to perform a specific repertoire composed for mandolin.

Mandolin For Dummies isn't intended to replace many years of study at a conservatory (that would be one very big book!), but I do hope to introduce you to some mandolin music that perhaps you didn't know about when you picked up this book. For example, I describe a classical mandolin technique called the glide stroke. I also look at a section of Beethoven's 'Sonatina in C Major' for mandolin and piano, which uses primarily a series of arpeggios for the mandolin part. Lastly, I introduce you to the very accessible mandolin orchestras.

Gliding towards acquiring a classical mandolin technique

Far too many classical mandolin techniques exist to cover in this book, let alone in a short chapter. Here I include two variations on one technique called the *glide stroke,* which is one of the techniques used in duo-style and played by such classical mandolin luminaries as Chris Acquavella (www.chrisacquavella.com). This is usually the first classical mandolin technique that young children are taught.

Duo-style is a classical mandolin technique where you play two independent melodies at the same time, giving the impression of a duet or of two melodic parts being played simultaneously. Many specific techniques are involved in duo-style, but the glide stroke is a great place to start.

The glide stroke is simple in concept but quite difficult to master. The type of glide stroke I cover is the triple stroke, meaning that the picking pattern involves plucking three notes per beat. This pattern consists of a down-stroke that plucks two notes (on two separate strings) and an up-stroke to play the third note of the triplet (in fact the second note played again):

1. **Start by tilting the pick to about a 45-degree angle so that it easily glides over the strings.**

2. **Rest the pick against the d-string and support the pick with thumb pressure only – try not to squeeze the pick with your finger and thumb.**

3. **Let gravity pull the pick down over the d- and a-strings, followed by an up-stroke on the a-string (because of the angle of the pick, the up-stroke should only hit one of the a-strings, giving the up-stroke a lighter sound).**

Practise the glide stroke using your metronome. Set it to click for each note of the triple glide stroke, going very slowly, because getting the notes perfectly even is very important. When you can do this, change the metronome speed so that it's only clicking once per beat; that is, on each quarter note (crotchet).

Figure 12-3 and Track 71 Part 1 include two glide-stroke exercises. I'm afraid my Midwestern roots show up again on this recording. When I played this exercise for Chris, his comment was 'you're swinging everything', which I usually think of as a compliment, but I'm not sure he meant it as one!

Figure 12-3: (a) Triple glide stroke with d-string as bass; (b) triple glide stroke with g-string as bass.

Reproduced by permission of Chris Acquavella.

Meeting the great composers and the mandolin

Even though the classical period is considered to be a fairly dead time for the mandolin, many celebrated composers wrote original works for the mandolin in a variety of settings. Check out recordings of them.

Beethoven is believed to have composed six pieces for mandolin and harpsichord/piano, of which four remain, and Vivaldi's 'Mandolin Concerto in C Major' is the world's most popular classical work featuring mandolin. Mozart used the mandolin primarily to accompany singing (such as briefly in the opera *Don Giovanni*), and Hummel's 'Concerto for Mandolin in G Major' is one of the most colourful mandolin concertos.

Figure 12-4, which you can hear on Track 71 Part 2, is an excerpt from 'La Fustemberg Variations' by Antonio Riggieri (an eighteenth-century composer). It uses the triple glide stroke with the g-string as bass note.

Figure 12-4: An excerpt from 'La Fustemberg Variations'.

Exploring arpeggio uses in classical music

Arpeggios are simply chords played one note at a time. In folk music, you strum chords as accompaniment, but in classical music, chords are usually incorporated in the melodies or parts in the way of arpeggios. (Flip back to Chapter 10, where I look at arpeggios under the name *chord tones*, for more info, and take a look at Figure 6-27 in Chapter 6 to determine which notes belong in each major and minor arpeggio, or chord. You may also want to visit Figure 10-9 in Chapter 10 for two common major chord shapes or hand positions for playing these arpeggios on the mandolin.)

The melody of Beethoven's 'Sonatina in C Major' in Figure 12-5 and on Track 72 uses a series of arpeggios combined with a few scale passages (or runs). Some of these arpeggios require you to shift to second position (which you can read about in Chapter 6). Each position shift happens quickly while the open e-string is ringing, giving you one sixteenth note to move your hand to the next position. If you do it correctly, each new note will be played by a different left-hand finger, meaning that you don't use the same finger for any two consecutive notes. To help you get it right, here are the individual steps you need to take:

1. **Start measure 1 with a two-octave C arpeggio using shape 1 (see Chapter 10) for the first octave, shifting at the open e-string to shape 2 in second position (with your first finger on third fret of the e-string) for the higher octave.**

2. **Stay in second position 2 (index finger on the third fret) for measure 2, starting on an F arpeggio using shape 1 (see Chapter 10) and fingers 2, 3 and 4. Follow this with a C arpeggio played using shape 2 and fingers 1, 3 and 4.**

3. **Still remaining in second position, start measure 3 with a G7 arpeggio using fingers 1, 2 and 4, followed by a C major arpeggio using fingers 1 and 3.**

4. **When you play the last note in measure 3 (the open e-string), quickly move your left hand back to first (open) position, landing on your third finger (fifth fret), and play the descending (downward) C major scale from D to D.**

5. **Repeat measures 1 and 2 for measures 5 and 6.**

6. **For measure 7, use the C major scale that begins in second position and shifts to first position halfway through the measure on the open e-string. Land on you third finger on the fifth fret (a-string) and continue in first position.**

7. **For measure 8, use another C major arpeggio in first position using shape 1.**

8. **For measures 9–14, stay in first position using the G7 arpeggio and C major scale with an occasional use of the F♯ note, returning to the main theme for measures 15–18.**

Sonatina in C major

for mandolin and piano

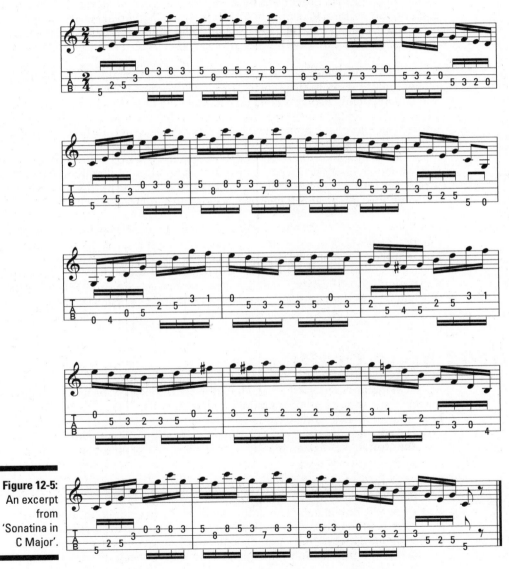

Figure 12-5:
An excerpt
from
'Sonatina in
C Major'.

Introducing mandolin orchestras

Mandolin orchestras are the link between trained classical players and amateur players who perform in community groups for fun. Mandolin orchestral music is arranged for mandolin, mandola, mando-cello, guitar and bass, or sometimes even mando-bass. Some orchestras also use percussion and even woodwind.

Mandolin orchestras range in size from 10 or 12 players up to the 100-plus player En Masse orchestra. They also range in performance level, with some being highly professional and others being more of a community get-together. The community style ensembles enable members of most ability levels to get involved. Some even have reduced or easier parts for beginners.

Music for mandolin orchestras, which ranges from serious classical to rags or famous movie themes, is written in standard notation but, depending on the group, the music may be available in tablature also. You may want to brush up on your reading skills if you plan on joining a mandolin orchestra.

Mandolin orchestras are alive and well in many parts of the world. Michael Reichenbach's blog www.mandoisland.com contains a wealth of information. The site lists mandolin orchestras around the world, including over 200 in Germany alone. Today, mandolin orchestras are actively performing in the USA, Switzerland, France, Japan, Great Britain, Australia, New Zealand, Spain, Poland, Belgium, The Netherlands and Austria. Why not find one near to you and join in.

Heading to Brazil

Brazilian mandolin music has a rich history and is one of the hottest happening genres in today's global mandolin community. Here are a few terms to help you get a basic understanding of the music:

✔ **Bandolim:** A Brazilian mandolin that's strung like a regular mandolin (G, D, A, E) but has a bigger body than the European bowlback or American-style mandolins. Some bandolims also add a fifth course with a pair of C strings in the bass, making them ten-string bandolims.

✔ **Choro:** A Brazilian instrumental music style, developed in the late nineteenth century, which features syncopated rhythms (Chapter 13 explains syncopation), complex melodies, frequent key changes, and a style of improvisation that involves altering the melody without completely replacing it with a new one. Just to confuse you, the word 'choro' also indicates a tune in the choro music style.

Choro music is a passionate blend of European classical-style melodies and Afro-Brazilian syncopated rhythms. The most popular choro in the world is 'Tico-Tico no Fubá', due to the fact that Carmen Miranda performed it on screen in the 1947 film *Copacabana*.

In one way, choro is like classical music in that the tunes are all composed and written out, as opposed to blues or Irish styles that you learn by ear. In another way, a choro ensemble is a bit like a jazz combo in that the melody is played by one person at a time, allowing for a great amount of personal expression and even improvisation.

Getting hold of some basic choro rhythms

Even though purists often think of the bandolim as a melody instrument, most choro players are equally comfortable playing chords. The rhythm patterns played on the bandolim were traditionally played by the cavaquinho, however, which is basically a steel-string ukulele tuned to an open G chord.

Basic mandolin rhythm playing in Brazilian music can be divided into two camps: one-bar-phrase and two-bar-phrase patterns. In general, one-bar patterns are used in slower tunes, and two-bar patterns in faster tunes.

Check out Figure 12-6(a) for a typical one-bar choro rhythm pattern. I demonstrate this pattern on Track 73 Part 1 using the D minor chord that you can find in Figure 12-7.

Figure 12-6(b) shows a traditional two-bar Brazilian rhythm pattern commonly used in faster tempos. Notice that the first bar in this pattern has more of an on-the-beat type of feel, whereas the second bar is more off the beat (syncopated). This 'cycling' two-bar feel is a big element in Brazilian rhythms. I play these rhythms on Track 73 Parts 2 and 3, again using the D minor chord from Figure 12-7.

Just to make things even more challenging, choro musicians flip the measure around so that the first bar is more syncopated and the second is more on the beat, as shown in Figure 12-6(c).

Figure 12-6: (a) A slow one-bar rhythm pattern; (b) a fast two-bar traditional Brazilian pattern; (c) a fast two-bar choro pattern.

Choro goes global

Jacob do Bandolim (1918–1969) is the Brazilian superhero of the mandolin: the choro mandolin is Jacob, and Jacob is choro mandolin! You can trace any of the stylistic elements that define choro mandolin back to Jacob. Here are a few modern Brazilian disciples of Jacob: Danilo Brito (www.danilobrito.com.br/en), Hamilton de Holanda (www.hamiltondeholanda.com/en), Dudu Maia (www.dudumaia.com) and Paulo Sá.

Americans Mike Marshall and Marilynn Mair have done a great deal to introduce American mandolin players to this wonderful music

through books, recordings, performances and workshops. Many cities on the Pacific coast of North America have thriving choro scenes. Portland's Tim Connell (www.timconnellmusic.com) is one of the premier American mandolin players in the choro style, and was kind enough to supply some technical information for this chapter.

On the opposite side of the Atlantic, the British BMG (that is, banjo, mandolin and guitar) Federation featured choro music at the 2012 Festival and Rally, which suggests that the choro invasion of Great Britain is getting underway.

Trying out some choro chord progressions

Chord progressions in choro music can be more complex than in folk or blues, using the I/VI7/II7/V7 progression and the ii/V7/I progression (both of which I cover in Chapter 13) that are common in jazz and ragtime music.

Another chord progression commonly used in choro is called a secondary dominant. *Dominant* chords (commonly known as 'seventh chords') are chords built on the fifth degree of the scale (as shown in Figure 13-2 in Chapter 13). A *secondary dominant* is a device that can be used when moving from one diatonic chord (see Chapter 13) to another by inserting the dominant of the new chord (as if the new chord were a new key). For an example, look at the measure just prior to the Gm chord in 'Gaucho Corta Jaca' (Figure 12-7). Gm is simply the iv (four) chord in the key of Dm (see Figure 13-2b in Chapter 13) and is considered a common chord in the key of Dm. The D7 chord prior to the Gm is not in the key of Dm but sounds good and creates a feeling of pulling or leading towards the Gm (due to the F♯ note) when placed immediately before the Gm chord. This D7 is called the secondary (or artificial) dominant because it is acting like a V7 (five) chord to the Gm, as you can see in the key of Gm in Figure 13-3 (b) (in Chapter 13).

Choro tunes almost always have both major and minor key sections. For example, 'Gaucho Corta Jaca' (Figure 12-7) has two sections: the first section is in the key of Dm (harmonic), while the second section moves to the key of F major. By looking at the circle of fifths (see Chapter 9), you can see that the key signature for Dm and F major are the same (one flat). But by comparing the diatonic chords in Dm (harmonic) to those in F major, you can see and hear the differences (see Figures 13-2 and 13-3 in Chapter 13). This relationship between a major and minor key with the same number of sharps or flats in the key signature is called *relative minor* and is common in choro music.

Considering choro melody

Choro musicians have very specific ways of embellishing melodies, which come from the European classical style of playing. These methods may seem very odd to musicians coming from a bluegrass or American music background:

- Left-hand muting is used to create a short staccato effect at beginnings and endings of phrases. Runs of sixteenth notes (semiquavers), however, aren't usually muted. A short accent can be placed on the first up-beat after one in a measure. Also, you find that many melodies start on that beat.

- Pick direction can be quite different from American-style alternate picking, where the beat determines pick direction. In choro, pick direction is more to do with the accents or the overall shape of the phrase than the timing. Many choro mandolin players start each phrase on a down-stroke even though the note may fall on an up-beat, giving a stronger accent to the first note of each phrase. This technique is in stark contrast to the alternate-picking technique I cover in Chapter 5. As a general rule, if you can play the melody using all down-strokes, do so. If not, be prepared to get your pick tangled up in the strings, whether you're alternate picking or not.

'Gaucho Corta Jaca' was written by Chiquinha Gonzaga (1847–1935). Whereas most choro pieces have three parts, this has only two. The first part is in D minor, and the second part in F major. Figure 12-7 shows the chords you need to play 'Gaucho Corta Jaca'.

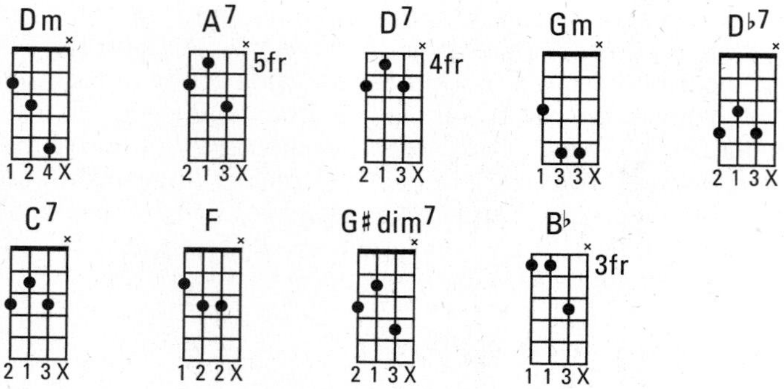

Dm A7 D7 Gm Db7

5fr 4fr

1 2 4 X 2 1 3 X 2 1 3 X 1 3 3 X 2 1 3 X

Figure 12-7: Chords for 'Gaucho Corta Jaca'.

C7 F G#dim7 Bb

3fr

2 1 3 X 1 2 2 X 2 1 3 X 1 1 3 X

For the 'Gaucho Corta Jaca' audio tracks, I'm playing a Giannini bandolim.

Listen and play along to 'Gaucho Corta Jaca' using Tracks 74 and 75 and Figure 12-8. I recorded this tune twice to demonstrate some simple one- and two-bar rhythm patterns as used in choro music. Track 74 is a bit slower and uses a one-bar pattern, as shown in Figure 12-6(a). Track 75 is a bit faster and uses the two-bar pattern from Figure 12-6(c).

Forgive me if I appear to have invented another sub-genre with my Anglo-choro phrasing. I guess this is a good example of 'you can take the boy out of the country but you can't take the country out of the boy'!

Gaucho Corta-Jaca

Figure 12-8: 'Gaucho Corta Jaca'.

Chapter 13

Swinging to Those Jazzy Rhythms

....

In This Chapter
▶ Moving to that jazz rhythm
▶ Looking at jazz chords
▶ Discovering jazzy chord progressions
▶ Blending jazz with other styles

....

*J*azz is an American form of music that has evolved from the blues and ragtime music of the early twentieth century, and continues to evolve today. With subgenres as diverse as Dixieland, gypsy swing, bebop, bossa nova and jazz-rock fusion, it's no wonder that most good musicians – including mandolin players – eventually take a close look at what some people call 'America's classical music'.

This genre of music features strong driving rhythms, lush-sounding chord changes, syncopated melodies and spirited improvisational sections where players can express themselves and play off each other in such a way that the song becomes a living, breathing organism. No accident, then, that over the years the term 'jazz' (as in 'jazz up') has come to mean 'to animate, liven up and add colour'!

Jazz presents many challenges for musicians, including complex chord changes and syncopated melodies that seem to be full of sharps and flats, but in this chapter I use a minimum of music theory and a practical hands-on approach so you can quickly start playing a variety of jazz mandolin tunes. (Most of the chords I use employ the three-string 'Jethro'-style chords that I introduce in Chapter 7.) I show you how to play the essential swing rhythm and simple chords and jazzy progressions, and how to mix jazz with other styles on the mandolin.

I don't have room to cover the involved art of improvisation skills in this chapter, but if you're comfortable with the concept, feel free to improvise on these tunes. If you're a technically minded mandolin player looking to expand your jazz horizons, take a look at http://jazzmando.com, where I contribute articles in the 'Tips and Tricks' section. You can also check out the videos about many aspects of mandolin playing (including improvisation and theory) that I've posted on www.youtube.com/donjulinlessons and http://donjulin.com for a bit more advice.

For the audio recordings that accompany this chapter, I recruit the help of a virtual bass player. These bass parts help give the music a complete feel. I play a variety of mandolins (acoustic and electric) in these recordings to illustrate the versatility of the mandolin in jazz:

- I recorded Tracks 76, 77 and 79 with a prototype Paul Newson J-model mandolin.
- I played Tracks 78 and 80 on an a solid-body Airline electric mandola strung with single strings (not pairs).
- Track 82 is the sound of a solid-body Eastwood Mandocaster.
- Tracks 81, 83, 85 and 86 feature a Kimble 2-point.

'It Don't Mean a Thing. . .': Swingin' the Melody

Swing can mean a lot of different things, but as a style and a rhythm it's central to performing jazz. Discovering how to play jazzy melodies with an authentic swing feel requires a basic understanding of *syncopation*, which is a break in the regular flow of rhythm, resulting in an accent being placed on an off-beat. Syncopation combined with a steady rhythmic pulse is what gives jazz much of its characteristic rhythmic feel.

The roots of jazz lie in ragtime and blues, both of which I describe in detail in Chapter 9, along with an example of swing rhythm, too.

Introducing swing

Swing as a musical style was very popular in the 1930s and features a steady bouncy rhythm that can include many chords or key changes, combined with syncopated melodies. You can also use the term to indicate a 'swinging' musician, one who's really 'cookin'. You may hear people say, 'We were at the club last night and, man, the cats were really swingin'!' whereas you're unlikely to hear someone say 'Christopher was swinging his butt off during his Bach oboe recital yesterday', unless Chris wants to shock his conservatory audience!

Jazz and swing styles were developed largely by horn players and so are *legato* styles, meaning that many of the notes are slurred together and not separated by a brief silence. Mandolin players need to be sure to get the maximum length out of each note so that it transitions smoothly to the next note. You can use some of the techniques that I describe in Chapter 6, such as hammer-ons, pull-offs and slides, in your jazz playing to increase this smooth legato effect.

Respecting the mighty eighth note

The eighth note (or quaver – check out Chapter 4 for an introduction to note lengths) is the cornerstone of swing, and being able to play a steady flow of them using both down-strokes and alternate picking (see Chapter 5) is crucial to getting your melodies to swing. In fact, musicians use the term *swinging eighth notes* to mean a style of playing where your melodies are mostly based on a steady flow of eighth notes.

In some forms of swing, the eighth notes that land on the down-beats (numbers) are played slightly longer than the up-beat ('ands') ones, in order to create the feeling of being laidback or smooth. As the tempos increase, this effect diminishes and eighth notes become more even. Swing should always feel loose, regardless of tempo, and never feel stiff.

Using syncopated rhythms

A steady quarter-note (crotchet) pulse supplies the foundation for the syncopated eighth-note (quaver) melodies of swing. In addition to creating a quarter-note pulse, you need to accent beats 2 and 4 in a subtle way. Being able to feel where these two beats land in jazz is very important to achieving a swing feel.

Vintage two-beat style

Older-style swing from the 1930s and 1940s is usually played in what's called a *two-beat style*. You can hear this type of rhythm in the gypsy-jazz recordings of Django Reinhardt and Stéphane Grappelli from the 1930s.

This vintage two-beat jazz style fits the mandolin and has been an influence on many mandolin players. In this style, the rhythm guitar or rhythm mandolin part consists of playing closed chords (no open strings) on all four beats, using a left-hand muting technique (see Figure 13-1). I suggest using the three-note chords from Chapter 7 when playing swing mandolin.

Figure 13-1(a) and Track 76 Part 1 demonstrate one method of playing swing rhythm where you play four short or muted strums per measure to create a short–short, short–short type of pattern. You perform this with four brisk down strums per measure (quarter notes). You need to release the pressure of your left hand on the frets immediately after each strum, muting the strings. When you do this correctly, you hear a space or silence between each chord. For the next example, in Figure 13-1(b) and Track 76 Part 2, the object is to let beats 1 and 3 ring while muting beats 2 and 4, resulting in a long–short, long–short type of sound. It may seem odd, but muting beats 2 and 4 actually creates accents on these two beats.

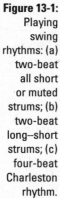

Figure 13-1:
Playing
swing
rhythms: (a)
two-beat
all short
or muted
strums; (b)
two-beat
long–short
strums; (c)
four-beat
Charleston
rhythm.

Modern four-beat style

Modern jazz started with the bebop era of the 1940s and 1950s and features a *four-beat approach* (perhaps more familiarly known as the *walking bass style*). The steady quarter-note (crotchet) responsibilities here are transferred from the rhythm guitar to the drummer and bass player. In this style, you want to play a part that contrasts the steady quarter-note pulse of the walking bass; in jazz, this type of accompaniment is known as *comping*.

Figure 13-1(c) and Track 76 Part 3 demonstrate a popular swing comping rhythm called the Charleston rhythm.

The two-beat and Charleston rhythms that I discuss are merely a starting point, so experiment with variations and accents. Jazz is a conversation among the players, so by carefully listening and responding to what is happening in the song you become part of the creative process.

Playing in all 12 keys

As you start to explore the standard jazz repertoire, you'll notice that the songs aren't all in standard mandolin keys such as D, G and A (flip to Chapter 2 for all about keys). One of the key (sorry!) reasons for this is that horn players (who created modern jazz) tend to like flat keys (for example, B♭, E♭ and A♭) as much as string players like sharp keys (such as G, D and A). In reality, the key changes as often as every few measures in most jazz tunes, and so even if the tune is in C, it may not be in C for the entire piece.

Try to learn all 12 scales in first position using open notes. I demonstrate this method in a YouTube video at www.youtube.com/watch?v=Eb-FbnWelcY. Take a look.

When you're comfortable with this method, I suggest you practise the FFcP (Four Finger closed Position) that I describe in Chapter 6, and start working your way up the mandolin's neck.

Figure 13-2 contains all 12 major scales. For a diagram of the mandolin fingerboard including note names, check out Chapter 6.

Scale	1	2	3	4	5	6	7	Octave
C major	C	D	E	F	G	A	B	C
D♭ major	D♭	E♭	F	G♭	A♭	B♭	C	D♭
D major	D	E	F#	G	A	B	C#	D
E♭ major	E♭	F	G	A♭	B♭	C	D	E♭
E major	E	F#	G#	A	B	C#	D#	E
F major	F	G	A	B♭	C	D	E	F
G♭ major	G♭	A♭	B♭	C♭	D♭	E♭	F	G♭
G major	G	A	B	C	D	E	F#	G
A♭ major	A♭	B♭	C	D♭	E♭	F	G	A♭
A major	A	B	C#	D	E	F#	G#	A
B♭ major	B♭	C	D	E♭	F	G	A	B♭
B major	B	C#	D#	E	F#	G#	A#	B

Figure 13-2: Twelve major scales.

To help out your jazz playing, also take a look at harmonic minor scales in Chapter 8 and the pure minor (Aeolian mode) and common minor (Dorian mode) scales in Chapter 11.

Simplifying Jazz Chords

Jazz chords can seem a bit like rocket science when you first encounter them, but persevere, because their lush harmony is what gives jazz its unique and complex sound. In this section, I simplify the subject, which isn't without precedence. After all, the great jazz guitarist Joe Pass taught that you can divide all chords, no matter how mysterious the chord name is, into three types when playing jazz: major, minor and dominant.

I cover chords more generally in Chapters 2, 4 and 6, but here are some brief basics. Chords are built from each note or degree of a scale. The primary notes in a chord are scale steps 1, 3 and 5, starting at any note in the scale. The first, fourth and fifth steps of the major scale produce major chords, and the second, third and sixth degrees of the scale produce minor chords. Chords that are built from scales are called *diatonic chords*.

As I explain in Chapter 2:

- Major chords tend to have a happy type of sound. Major chords in jazz are commonly followed by extensions 6, maj7 and maj9.

- Minor chords have a sadder sound owing to the flatted third note of the chord. Minor chords in jazz can be followed by extensions 6, 7 and occasionally maj7.

The *extension* (the number after the chord) indicates what additional notes of the scale are included in the chord beyond the primary three notes. (Chapter 6 gives you the primary notes of all major and minor chords.) Here are some chord examples:

- **G6:** G (root), B (third), D (fifth) and E (sixth) notes of the G scale.

- **Gmaj7:** Primary three notes and F♯ (seventh).

- **G7:** Primary three notes and F♮ (a flatted seventh).

- **G9:** Primary three notes plus F♮ (a flatted seventh) and A (ninth).

Obviously you can't play all these notes simultaneously on the mandolin. Many jazz chords contain five or six notes, and I assume that, like most mandolin players, you have only four fingers and so can play four notes simultaneously at most. In fact, I prefer to play only three notes for most of my jazz chords. When doing so, you have the freedom to choose which three notes of the chord to play. You can always reduce a chord to its primary form, thus playing D7♯9 as D7 or even simply D.

Keep in mind, however, that the extensions are the colour notes and without them the chords may sound more vanilla. But then many people love vanilla ice cream!

Diatonic chords used commonly in jazz include three types of seventh chords:

- Major seventh (or sixth chords)
- Minor seventh
- Dominant seventh

Jazz tunes can change key (or scale) frequently, but when they do so they don't always go directly to the tonic (root note) or the I (one) chord, which can be confusing. For example, say you're playing a song in the key of C major, but in the third measure you see Fm7/Bb7 as chords. Here, the song has *modulated* (that is, changed keys) to the key of E♭. (Look at Figure 13-3(a), which contains a chart of four-note (seventh) chords built from major scales, and you'll see that Fm7 is the ii and Bb7 is the V in the key of E♭.)

Coming over all dominant

Dominant chords have a moving type of sound, in that they tend to want to pull you to the next chord in the progression. They're built on the same three primary notes as major chords, but that's where the similarity ends. At a minimum, dominant chords (seventh chords) include the flatted seventh note. In jazz, dominant chords are where all the excitement lies, and you can increase that tension by altering or adding certain notes in relationship to the chord.

Dominant chords are built on the fifth step of the scale and can include altered fifths or ninths for extra tension or colour.

When you're transitioning from one key to another, the dominant chord of the new key is often used as a bridge or a way to get from one key to another. For example, if you're in the key of G and come across an E7 chord, this chord can be considered the dominant chord in the new key of A.

Altered dominant chords are one of the most important yet misunderstood elements for someone new to the jazz world but, as guitarist Joe Pass said, you can divide all chords into just three types when playing jazz: major, minor and dominant. Altered dominant chords like the D7♯9 used in 'Mr Natural' are simply dominant (seventh chords) with an added colour note (♯9 or F natural). By altering the fifth and the ninth degrees of a dominant chord, you can enter the exotic world of altered dominant chords used by all the great jazz composers. Altered G7 dominant chords include G7♭5, G7♯5 (augmented), G7♭9 and G7♯9. Remember, though, that you can reduce all of these altered dominants to the dominant chord, meaning that you can play D7♯9 as D7 or even D if you don't know the chord shape for D7♯9.

You can also build diatonic chords from a harmonic minor scale (see Chapter 8). Figure 13-3(b) shows the most common diatonic chords derived from harmonic minor scales. Only some of these chords are presented as seventh chords, while some are augmented or diminished. The good news is that songs that use harmonic minor scales rarely use chords built on the third or sixth steps of the scale, so you don't need to learn a whole new chord vocabulary to play in minor keys.

With jazz chords, don't worry too much about playing every extension; just try to determine major, minor or dominant and play what you can. Eventually your chord vocabulary grows to the point where you know many of these colourful jazz chords.

(a)

Key	I	ii	iii	IV	V	vi	vii
C	Cmaj^7 or C^6	Dm^7	Em^7	Fmaj^7 or F^6	G^7	Am^7	Bm^{7}b^5
D♭	D♭maj^7 or D♭^{6}	E♭m^7	Fm^7	G♭maj^7 or G♭^{6}	A♭^{7}	B♭m^7	Cm^{7}b^5
D	Dmaj^7 or D^6	Em^7	F♯m^7	Gmaj^7 or G^6	A^7	Bm^7	C♯m^{7}b^5
E♭	E♭maj^7 or E♭^{6}	Fm^7	Gm^7	A♭maj^7 or A♭^{6}	B♭^{7}	Cm^7	Dm^{7}b^5
E	Emaj^7 or E^6	F♯m^7	G♯m^7	Amaj^7 or A^6	B^7	C♯m^7	D♯m^{7}b^5
F	Fmaj^7 or F^6	Gm^7	Am^7	B♭maj^7 or B♭^{6}	C^7	Dm^7	Em^{7}b^5
G♭	G♭maj^7 or G♭^{6}	A♭m^7	B♭m^7	C♭maj^7 or C♭^{6}	D♭^{7}	E♭m^7	Fm^{7}b^5
G	Gmaj^7 or G^6	Am^7	Bm^7	Cmaj^7 or C^6	D^7	Em^7	F♯m^{7}b^5
A♭	A♭maj^7 or A♭^{6}	B♭m^7	Cm^7	D♭maj^7 or D♭^{6}	E♭^{7}	Fm^7	Gm^{7}b^5
A	Amaj^7 or A^6	Bm^7	C♯m^7	Dmaj^7 or D^6	E^7	F♯m^7	G♯m^{7}b^5
B♭	B♭maj^7 or B♭^{6}	Cm^7	Dm^7	E♭maj^7 or E♭^{6}	F^7	Gm^7	Am^{7}b^5
B	Bmaj^7 or B^6	C♯m^7	D♯m^7	Emaj^7 or E^6	F♯^{7}	G♯m^7	A♯m^{7}b^5

(b)

Key	i	ii^{7}b^5	III+	iv	V	VI	vii (dim)
Cm	Cm	Dm^{7}b^5	E♭ aug	Fm	G^7	A♭	B dim^7
C♯m	C♯m	D♯m^{7}b^5	E aug	F♯m	G♯^{7}	A	B♯ dim^7
Dm	Dm	Em^{7}b^5	F aug	Gm	A^7	B♭	C♯ dim^7
E♭m	E♭m	Fm^{7}b^5	G♭ aug	A♭m	B♭^{7}	C♭	D dim^7
Em	Em	F♯m^{7}b^5	G aug	Am	B^7	C	D♯ dim^7
Fm	Fm	Gm^{7}b^5	A♭ aug	B♭m	C^7	D♭	E dim^7
F♯m	F♯m	G♯m^{7}b^5	A aug	Bm	C♯^{7}	D	E♯ dim^7
Gm	Gm	Am^{7}b^5	B♭ aug	Cm	D^7	E♭	F♯ dim^7
G♯m	G♯m	A♯m^{7}b^5	B aug	C♯m	D♯^{7}	E	F♯♯ dim^7
Am	Am	Bm^{7}b^5	C aug	Dm	E^7	F	G♯ dim^7
B♭m	B♭m	Cm^{7}b^5	D♭ aug	E♭m	F^7	G♭	A dim^7
Bm	Bm	C♯m^{7}b^5	D aug	Em	F♯^{7}	G	A♯ dim^7

Figure 13-3: Diatonic seventh chords: (a) major keys; (b) minor keys.

Working with Jazzy Chord Progressions

Organising into groups or common chord progressions all the chords that mandolin players use when performing jazz helps to make sense of them. Like many other forms of music, jazz has a few common progressions that players use over and over with little variations to create hundreds or even thousands of songs. In order to be comfortable with jazz and swing music, you need to understand these basic chord progressions in a variety of keys.

Even if you're anxious to get playing jazz tunes on your mandolin straight away, when you're starting out on the instrument I strongly suggest that you read through Chapter 4 and practise the exercises on chord progressions before jumping into the ones in this section.

Keeping it moving: the 1-6-2-5 progression

The *1-6-2-5 chord progression* is a common type of jazz chord progression referred to as a *turnaround*, and is normally written as I/VI7/II7/V7. Turnarounds are great for providing a direction or movement in place of one single chord. Part of the allure of jazz is the fact that the chords are always changing, creating a forward-moving sound; the 1-6-2-5 chord progression is a major component of that moving sound. You can hear it in the swing standards 'After You've Gone', 'Sweet Georgia Brown' and 'Limehouse Blues'. (Turnarounds are also used at the ends of blues and ragtime forms – skip back to Chapter 9 for the lowdown.)

When chords are numbered with Roman numerals, upper-case indicates major chords and lower-case numerals mean minor chords (see 'Changing keys with the 2-5-1 progression' later in this chapter). The standard number seven after the Roman numeral tells you to play it as a dominant seventh chord. So the I/VI7/II7/V7 progression is based on chords built on the first, sixth, second and fifth degrees of the scale, and all except the I (one) chord are played as dominant seventh chords. In the key of C major, this progression is C/A7/D7/G7.

I wrote 'The 105 Year Old Cat' – which employs the I/VI7/II7/V7 progression – for my old cat Bonzai, who managed to antagonise dogs and raccoons for close to 20 years. At the time, he was 17, but due to the fact that cats age faster than people do, he would have been living in a aged body the equivalent of a 105-year-old person. Figure 13-4 shows you the chords for the tune.

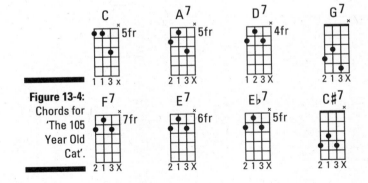

Figure 13-4: Chords for 'The 105 Year Old Cat'.

Play the melody of 'The 105 Year Old Cat' with all down-strokes to produce a lazy, laidback feel, because, after all, my cat was 105. Watch for hammer-ons and the double pull-off triplet in measure 7 (see Chapter 6 for left-hand techniques). Play the chords with the short–short pattern shown in Figure 13-1(a). See Figure 13-5 and Track 77 for 'The 105 Year Old Cat'.

The 105 Year Old Cat

Figure 13-5:
'The 105 Year Old Cat'.

Taking lessons with Jethro

Don Stiernberg (www.donstiernberg. com) started taking lessons with Jethro Burns (see Chapter 7) in Chicago as a teenager. In an interview, 'Donnie' told me, 'I wanted to be him . . . Jethro was the coolest, most positive guy I'd ever met and he became my hero the day I met him.'

During their first lesson, Jethro asked the young student to play a bit to see how best to help him. The young Stiernberg played while holding the pick wrongly and only using two fingers on his left hand to fret the notes. Jethro told the aspiring mandolin player, 'You've got all the tools', and Donnie left the lesson walking on clouds. Years later, Donnie discovered what Jethro meant: by 'all the tools', he was referring to a mandolin and a pick!

The first tunes that Jethro taught Donnie were fiddle tunes that Jethro called hoedowns. Stiernberg says that these tunes got his left and right hands working together. He followed these with standards – jazz tunes played in a chord melody style. Jethro pioneered this style on the mandolin.

Donnie says that Jethro taught 'by eye', meaning that when he was showing you something, his eyes became as big as saucers and he'd look you straight in the eye while playing. Donnie claims that by Jethro commanding his full attention through eye contact, he was able to hear these licks or chords clearly enough to then find them on the mandolin.

Getting the blues, jazz style

Jazz players have their own version of the 12-bar blues, which in true jazz fashion contains more chords. A jazz blues usually features the I/VI7/II7/V7 chord progression, beginning with bar 7 to give it a more sophisticated jazz type of sound.

Figure 13-6 shows the chords used in 'Limnology' in the key of B♭. Notice how almost all the chords are the same shape, and that by moving the chord down one fret it becomes another chord, but may not be the chord name you expect. You can play these seventh chords using only two of the three notes shown, if you prefer.

Jazz players often intentionally omit roots or fifths from chords to leave more room for the melody and to focus on the colour tones in the chord.

Figure 13-6: 'Limnology' chords.

'Limnology', as seen in Figure 13-7, is a *riff blues*, meaning that you repeat a four-bar riff or phrase three times while the rhythm section plays the 12-bar blues chord changes. Listen to Track 78 to hear 'Limnology' played twice, using the vintage two-beat style of rhythm playing in the first chorus, and the more modern four-beat style for the second chorus (from the earlier section 'Using syncopated rhythms').

Notice that while playing in the four-beat style, occasionally I just play on beat 1 and let the chord ring. This approach works well to break up the rhythm, letting it breathe a little. Also I play the melody in a lower octave first followed by a higher octave in the second chorus. See whether you can find the higher octave notes on your own. You can play the melody for 'Limnology' with alternate picking or all down-strokes.

For loads more on performing the blues on mandolin, mosey on over to Chapter 9.

Figure 13-7: 'Limnology'.

Reproduced by permission of Don Julin

Achieving a good swing feel

As I describe in the earlier section "It Don't Mean a Thing. . .': Swingin' the Melody', the swing feel relies on syncopation, and you achieve it by using primarily eighth notes (quavers) while putting accents on off-beats; playing too many quarter or half notes (crotchets or minims) in the melody results in the groove just lying there like an old dog on a hot day. In fact, you can even take a pretty square song and make it a bit hipper simply by using a few stylistic elements of swing.

Here's a list of elements you can use to transform a flat, boring melody into a hip, swingin' tune:

- ✔ **Added or subtracted notes from the original melody:** Although this makes less of a difference than the other elements in this list, subtracting notes from the melody does enable you to create drama and suspense. By adding notes, you fill out your even flow of eighth notes (quavers). When adding notes to a melody, try using other notes from the scale or key you're in or, better still, notes from the chords, called *chord tones*. I demonstrate this chord tone approach in the last four bars of 'Ode to Swing'.

- ✔ **Anticipations:** Moving a melody note that would normally be played squarely on the beat by one eighth note (quaver) earlier than written.

- ✔ **Delayed attacks:** Delaying a melody by one eighth note (quaver).

- ✔ **Shortened or lengthened notes:** Maintaining the original written notes but taking some liberties with their lengths.

- ✔ **Swing/jazz types of chord changes:** Using constantly moving chord progressions with common jazz-type chord progressions such as I/VI/II/V7 or ii/V7/I, both covered in this chapter, are primary elements of jazz.

Swingin' with rhythm changes

Rhythm changes are one of the staple chord progressions used in jazz, getting their name from the Gershwin classic 'I Got Rhythm'. This eight-bar chord progression uses a modified I/VI/II/V7 played twice, followed by any number of four-bar turnarounds. In the key of G, the basic I/VI/II/V7 pattern would be G/E7/A7/D7, but in 'Ode to Swing' (see Figure 13-8) the rhythm-changes style progression is G/G♯dim/Am7/D7. Notice that the second chord is G♯ diminished (see Chapter 7 for more about diminished chords and their uses) and the third chord is Am7 instead of A7.

Extra! Extra! Beethoven writes for *The Flintstones* shock!

'Meet the Flintstones' is the opening theme for the 1960s cartoon series, which borrowed a melodic theme from the slow middle movement of Beethoven's 'Piano Sonata No. 17 in D minor' and re-harmonised it with rhythm changes. The theme song contains elements of the old colliding with the new, much like the content of the cartoon itself.

Although 'Ode to Swing' only has one section, many tunes based around rhythm changes have a second section or bridge that involves a series of chords that follow the circle of fifths in a counter-clockwise direction. Rhythm-changes tunes with the second part are played in an AABA form (see Chapter 14). Countless numbers of tunes are based around this chord progression and its millions of variations.

To illustrate rhythm changes, I turn to one of the squarest but best-known melodies of all time. By applying some of the swing techniques from the preceding section, I attempt to make it more hip. I'm sure old Ludwig Van would roll over in his grave if he heard this version. Figure 13-8 shows one set of chords used in playing rhythm changes.

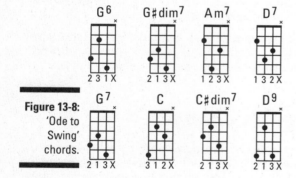

Figure 13-8: 'Ode to Swing' chords.

'Ode to Swing' (Figure 13-9 and Track 79) is a fun little experiment that demonstrates the vintage two-beat style of rhythm shown in Figure 13-1(b). (Flip to the earlier section 'Using syncopated rhythms' for more on this style.)

For extra credit, you can use the chords in Figure 13-10 in measures 3 and 4 to add variation. On Track 79, I use this variation during the third and fourth measures.

Changing keys with the 2-5-1 progression

The 2-5-1 (ii7/V7/I) progression is the hallmark progression of 1940s and 1950s jazz. This progression is commonly used as a way to move from one key to another key.

'Three Keys' uses the progression to move through three major keys. The tune starts in G major (for four bars) using the chords Am7, D7 and G major7, moving to F major (four bars) using Gm7, C7 and F major7, to Eb major (again, four bars) using the chords Fm7, Bb7 and Eb major7, and back to G major (last four bars). Figure 13-11 shows the chords.

Figure 13-9: 'Ode to Swing'.

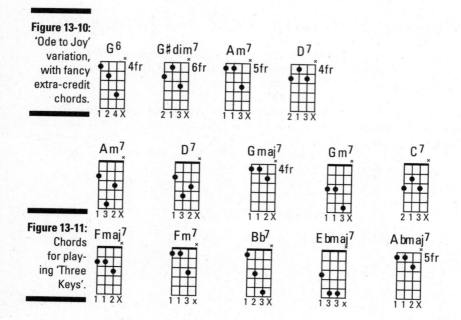

Figure 13-10: 'Ode to Joy' variation, with fancy extra-credit chords.

Figure 13-11: Chords for playing 'Three Keys'.

Play 'Three Keys' (Figure 13-12 and Track 80) with a modern comping-style rhythm (which I describe earlier in 'Using syncopated rhythms'). Perform the melody using alternate picking, being careful to use proper pick direction (measures 1 and 5 start with up-strokes).

Accompanying yourself: Chord melody

Chord melody (sometimes called *chord solo*) is a technique usually associated with jazz guitar players, where the guitarist plays chords and melody at the same time. The top note of the chord is the melody, and the player is free to harmonise the melody with chords in a jazz style.

Figure 13-13 and Track 81 demonstrate a chord melody arrangement of the New Year classic 'Auld Lang Syne'. Give it a try. Remember that the top note is the melody, so you may want to learn this first by playing only the melody. When you're comfortable with the melody, add the additional notes that make up the chords. (For a better understanding of three-string chord forms, check out Chapter 7.)

Three Keys

Figure 13-12: 'Three Keys'.

Fiddle and mandolin players

Tiny Moore and Johnny Gimble played in the Texas Playboys in the 1940s. These fiddle players doubled on mandolin and were pioneers in the development of the single-string electric mandolin, which, with the low-tuned c-string, gives the instrument an electric-guitar-like quality.

Auld Lang Syne

Figure 13-13: Chord melody arrangement of 'Auld Lang Syne'.

Mixing Things up: Jazz with Other Styles

Since its inception, jazz has been constantly evolving and has been a major influence on many other genres of music. Jazz isn't a specific list of songs but a style that you can effectively blend with other musical genres, as you'll discover in this section. Jazz has influenced rock guitarists such as Jeff Beck and Carlos Santana. Pop stars such as Sting and Donald Fagen of Steely Dan both use jazz-style chords in pop songs, and David Grisman blends jazz with folk, bluegrass, Latin and other elements to make the Dawg music I look at in Chapter 14. The rhythms, chords and tricky melodies you learn through playing jazz really have the potential to enhance your ability to play other forms of music.

Heading down to Texas: Western swing

Western swing (or *hillbilly jazz*) is a style made popular in the 1930s and 1940s by fiddler Bob Wills and His Texas Playboys. Blending rural country music and urban jazz, western swing bands use primarily string instruments instead of horns, but play big-band style arrangements to form an infectious hybrid. The origins of the style reside in the fact that these bands play standard fiddle tunes as instrumentals to add variety to a show between vocal songs. The rhythm section, however, was set up to play jazz, so blending these styles together created western swing.

Figure 13-14 shows some chords that are sort of hillbilly rhythm changes. This progression fits well over many traditional fiddle tunes and for many western swing tunes.

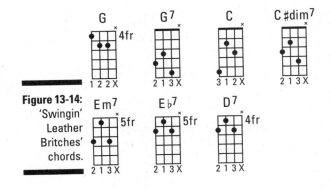

Figure 13-14: 'Swingin' Leather Britches' chords.

'Leather Britches' is an old-time fiddle tune that works well as a mandolin swing number (see Figure 13-15 and Track 82 for what I call 'Swingin' Leather Britches'). In the western swing style fiddle tunes are played slower than they would be in an old-time setting, and with a swing in the melody. As in all forms of jazz, the players feel free to improvise.

Swingin' Leather Britches

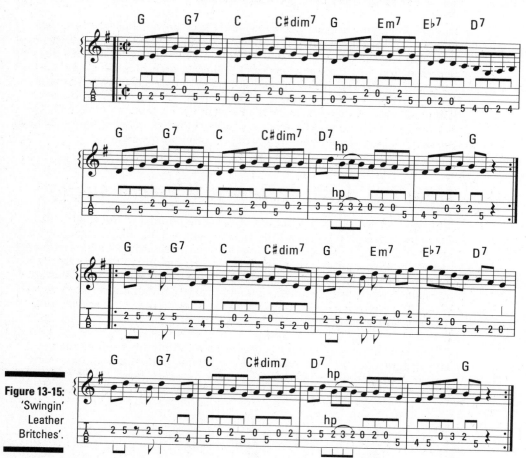

Figure 13-15: 'Swingin' Leather Britches'.

Waltzing with the Muppets

Jazz musicians love the waltz (3/4 time). Figure 13-16 shows the chords used in the jazz waltz 'Muppets on the Titanic'. Don't let the number of chords intimidate you; the piece is easier than it looks.

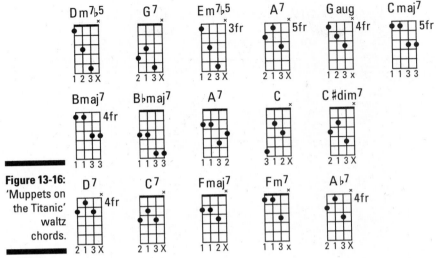

Figure 13-16: 'Muppets on the Titanic' waltz chords.

Listen to Track 83 and see Figure 13-17 for 'Muppets on the Titanic'.

For more about waltz time and time signatures, flip to Chapter 4.

Blending jazz with other genres

Jazz has had a big influence on the development of rock, funk, folk, bluegrass and jam-band music. Here I show you how to play a piece that is a blend of many styles and is fun to play on the mandolin.

'Mr Natural' is a funky, hippie bossa nova. Basically, the tune is a *long-form* blues (24 bars instead of 12) in the wonderful mandolin key of G. The piece borrows from Bill Monroe, Antônio Carlos Jobim, Miles Davis, Austin Powers and R Crumb (now that's a guest list for a party!).

Meeting Mr Natural

Mr Natural is a comic book character created by R Crumb. Along with *Keep on Truckin'* and the Fabulous Furry Freak Brothers, Mr Natural featured in the counterculture underground *Zap* *Comix* of the late 1960s and early 1970s. Mr (Fred) Natural was an unreliable guru who renounced the material world and so lived off anything he could get in exchange for his nuggets of wisdom.

Muppets On the Titanic

Figure 13-17: 'Muppets on the Titanic'.

'Mr Natural' is basically a blues in G with a little sliding around. Figure 13-18 has all the chords you need to play it.

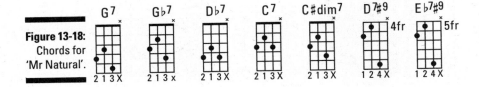

Figure 13-18: Chords for 'Mr Natural'.

Figure 13-19 shows two possible rhythm patterns for 'Mr Natural':

✔ Figure 13-19(a), demonstrated on Track 84 Part 1, is basically what some would call a gypsy-bossa. Keep an even down-up strumming pattern whilst muting with your left hand, on beats 2 and 4. Be sure not to strum too hard; it sounds much better if you lightly brush the strings.

✔ Play the Brazilian-style rhythm in Figure 13-19(b) and on Track 84 Part 2 lightly and crisply, playing only the strums marked with down-strokes. When you can play the rhythm and make the chord changes using all down-strokes, add in the up-strokes, keeping in mind that the up-stroke only brushes one string and is more of a percussion effect than a chord.

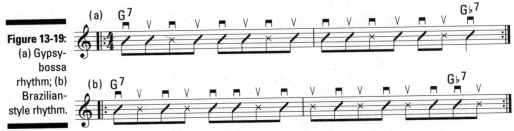

Figure 13-19: (a) Gypsy-bossa rhythm; (b) Brazilian-style rhythm.

I play 'Mr Natural' through twice – once using each rhythm – on Tracks 85 and 86 (see Figure 13-20, too).

Mr Natural

Figure 13-20: 'Mr Natural': (a) Gypsy-bossa style rhythm (Track 85); (b) Brazilian-style rhythm (Track 86).

Chapter 14

Blending Styles: Dawg Music

In This Chapter

▶ Introducing the Dawg himself: David Grisman

▶ Discovering some Dawg-style grooves

▶ Perfecting some Dawg tricks

Rarely is a musician influential enough to have a whole genre named after him, and so when that does happen dedicating a whole *For Dummies* chapter to that person seems only fair. The subject of this chapter is Dawg music: a blend of bluegrass, Latin, gypsy, swing, funk and other savoury musical ingredients prepared by the Dawg himself, mandolin guru David Grisman.

For more than 40 years, Grisman has been leaving his paw-print on some of the most influential acoustic string music around. Using spicy rhythms, lush arrangements and what musicians call 'chops' (technical skills, in other words), he created an entire genre of music intended specifically for the mandolin.

In this chapter, I introduce you to Grisman (take a bow, David), his groovy rhythm style and technique, and some of his original compositions. Believe me, if you can take on even a small piece of David's skills and innovation and put it into your own mandolin playing, you'll be barking up the right tree.

I want to thank David for allowing me to include a little Dawg music in *Mandolin For Dummies*.

Meeting David Grisman

I'll never forget the day in 1979 when my good friend Unzan handed me a cassette tape (of the first David Grisman Quintet album) and said, 'Here you go, man, this is what's happening in the mandolin world.' The sound that came out of the speakers blew me away! I bought my first mandolin the next day and started on what has turned out to be a life-long mandolin journey.

Grisman's efforts have produced some of the most memorable recordings of the last four decades by bringing together many of the world's greatest acoustic musicians and just letting them be themselves.

Groovin' to some Dawg Music

Often, rhythm is one of the first things you notice when you hear a piece of music. Grisman borrows rhythmic elements (that is, *grooves*) from musical styles that may or may not be traditionally associated with mandolin.

You can't learn grooves from a book alone. Of course, all players use books (including this one) to help, but listening and trying to imitate the music is essential to understanding different rhythms.

Bluegrass and jazz are (both) a big influence on Grisman's music, and so check out Chapters 10 and 13 for more on these genres. A basic understanding of how these two styles work comes in handy when looking at Dawg music.

In this section, I help you to start playing some less common but very cool grooves on your mandolin. As the Dawg says: 'Beyond the groove is your own musical personality.'

Heading down south: Dawg Latin

Rhythm playing is under-rated . . . it's a fine art.

David Grisman

I hope that you're ready to head down Rio de Janeiro way, because in this section I take a look at a basic Dawg samba. The Brazilian samba rhythm is counted in two time, which means that the basic pulse of the music can be counted 1, 2, 1, 2 (flip to Chapter 4 for all about counting in music).

This rhythm can be written in 2/4 time or in 2/2 (called *cut time*), but in both cases the strong (numbered) beats get broken into four equal parts. The rhythm is counted as 1 e and a 2 e and a 3 e and a 4 e and a (pronounced one eeh and ah), as I demonstrate in Chapter 4 and on Track 3.

Even though the samba originates in Brazil, don't mistake this hybrid groove for a traditional Brazilian choro rhythm (I cover choro in Chapter 12).

To demonstrate this groove, I'm going to take a look at the solo section of a Dawg tune called '16/16'. The term *solo section* (sometimes called *blowing section*) refers to the part of the song or tune where one person plays a solo (usually improvised) while the rest of the band provides the rhythm. Figure 14-1 shows the four chords needed for this solo section.

Recordings of the Dawg tunes mentioned in this chapter, along with many other great recordings featuring mandolin, are available for download at Acoustic Oasis (www.acousticoasis.com).

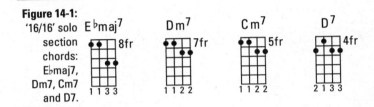

Figure 14-1: '16/16' solo section chords: E♭maj7, Dm7, Cm7 and D7.

The samba shown in Figure 14-2 can be played as a one-bar or two-bar pattern.

In general, slower grooves work better with one-bar patterns, and faster tempos work better with two-bar patterns. The Dawg samba is played with a pushed syncopated feel with upstrokes as accents. Grisman also varies the accents in different measures of the repeated chords, making it less repetitive.

Listen to Track 87 for examples of both one-bar and two-bar Dawg samba patterns, and if you can, listen to the David Grisman Quintet recordings of 'Janice', 'Barkley's Bug' and '16/16' to hear this great groove in action.

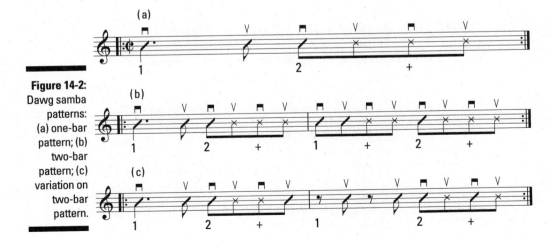

Figure 14-2: Dawg samba patterns: (a) one-bar pattern; (b) two-bar pattern; (c) variation on two-bar pattern.

Figure 14-3 shows the chord progression for the solos in '16/16'. On Track 88 I play the progression three times, as follows:

- First time, I use the repeating one-bar pattern shown in Figure 14-2(a).
- Second time, I use the two-bar pattern from Figure 14-2(b).
- Third time, I use the variation on the two-bar pattern from Figure 14-2(c).

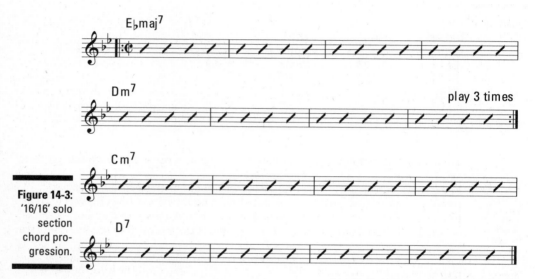

Figure 14-3: '16/16' solo section chord progression.

Reproduced by permission of Dawg Music/David Grisman.

Get up, get on up: Dawg funk

Study the masters for influence but still try to be yourself.

David Grisman

Many people of a certain generation (that is, mine!) grew up in the 1960s and 1970s listening to James Brown and popular bands that played soul or funk music. Even though the mandolin wasn't an instrument originally used in soul, by borrowing some of the rhythmic patterns that the electric guitarists played, David Grisman brought a little funkiness to the mandolin world.

Dawg's tunes 'Pneumonia', 'Dawg Funk', 'Acousticity' and 'Two White Boys Watching James Brown at the Apollo' are good examples of how funk rhythms can be used in an acoustic string group.

Figure 14-4 demonstrates the chords needed to play 'Pneumonia'. The first two chords (Em7/A7) are a very common combination called a ii/V7 (two-five) chord progression. The A7 chord actually contains a B note, making it an A9 chord, which is only a dressed-up dominant seventh chord (see Chapter 13 for more about simplifying jazz chords). This is a good example of taking a complex five-note A9 chord (A, C♯, E, G, and B) and only playing three of the chord tones (C♯, E and B) on the mandolin. (See Chapter 7 for more three-string chords.)

The next two chords (Am7/D9) are the same shape moved up five frets. The overall chord progression is basically a minor blues using the chords B and C for the turnaround. (Imagine the basic 12-bar blues chord progression covered in Chapter 9 with the Em7/A9 progression being played wherever the G7 chord is present, and the Am7/D9 progression taking the place of the C7 chord – this makes a *minor blues*. The last four bars (or six, in this case) make up the section called the *turnaround*, so for that part of the progression you play the chords B and C.)

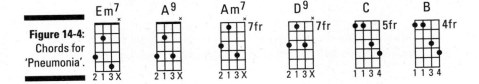

Figure 14-4: Chords for 'Pneumonia'.

Figure 14-5 and Track 89 demonstrate two separate rhythms for playing 'Pneumonia'. The first rhythm should be used for the chords Em7/A9 and Am7/D9. The second pattern should be played only over the chords B and C.

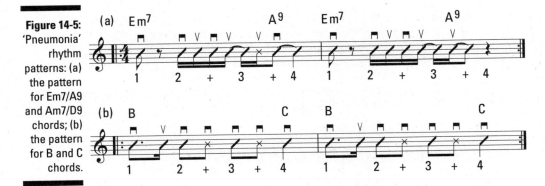

Figure 14-5: 'Pneumonia' rhythm patterns: (a) the pattern for Em7/A9 and Am7/D9 chords; (b) the pattern for B and C chords.

Figure 14-6 shows the chord progression for the solo section of 'Pneumonia'. Notice the rhythm accents in the last two measures. Listen to Track 90 and then play along with it to catch a good dose of 'Pneumonia'!

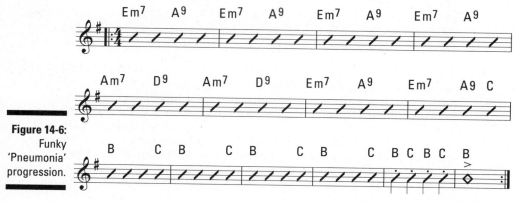

Figure 14-6:
Funky
'Pneumonia'
progression.

Reproduced by permission of Dawg Music/David Grisman.

For more Dawg tunes and techniques, I suggest that you get hold of *David Grisman Teaches Mandolin* from Homespun Tapes (www.homespuntapes.com).

Accenting Your Grooves, Dawg-Style

Don't feel limited to the basic part.

David Grisman

Of course, you're not restricted to playing grooves in the same old way, and so use the ones I present in the preceding section just as a starting point. When you're comfortable playing the rhythm parts while changing chords, start experimenting with your own variations.

In this section I show you a couple of specific techniques that Grisman uses to add some sparkle to his mandolin grooves.

Scratching like the Dawg

I try to figure out what the mandolin can do that sounds good . . . that I can play.

David Grisman

Did you know that the mandolin is also a percussion instrument? With a little practice, your rhythm patterns can include the percussive sound of the pick coming across the strings without sounding any particular pitch.

By muting specific beats with your left hand while maintaining a rhythm pattern with your right hand, your rhythms have an added dimension. In written music, this muted sound is notated with an 'x' attached to the stem, replacing the note head. I show you how to mute the strings in Chapter 6.

Stretching out with one long chord

It's not the part, it's the mojo.

David Grisman

One of the many interesting aspects of David Grisman's rhythm-playing style is the tendency to play a chord on beat one for the duration of the entire measure. This chord acts as an *accent* (or marker) and can be used to mark bar 1 of a new section or beat one in a bar, or be played once for each chord change.

The important point is that the chord is played on the beat and held until the sound falls away. In music that's more *syncopated* (that is, music that has accents on the off-beat), defining the 'one' (or first) beat of the measure or pattern as a way of marking one specific spot in the groove is important. Syncopation loses effectiveness if there isn't some part of the rhythm that is clearly on the beat. James Brown was known for his band's funky syncopated grooves, which almost always included a clearly defined 'one'.

The next Dawg song pulls together many of the elements that I discuss in this chapter and Chapter 13, including a two-beat style swing rhythm, and features a rhythm section accent. 'Swang Thang' was recorded on the *Jazz/Folk* CD (released on the Acoustic Oasis label) and features Jim Hurst on guitar and Sam Grisman on bass. Figure 14-7 shows the chords needed to play 'Swang Thang'.

Figure 14-7: 'Swang Thang' chords.

'Swang Thang' is in a swing style (which I describe in Chapter 13) and in an AABA form. This form is common in jazz, where the A section (which is usually an eight-bar section) is repeated one time, followed by the B section (which often is in a different key), before the A section returns one more time. Each person who plays the melody or an improvised solo plays for the entire AABA form (listen to Track 91 and see Figure 14-8).

Swang Thang

Figure 14-8:
'Swang
Thang'
melody.

The A section of 'Swang Thang' is in the key of D minor, and the B section moves to F major. 'Swang Thang' also has an intro and an ending that are one octave apart and almost identical (see whether you can spot the difference).

At the end of the B section is a rhythmic accent where the rhythm section players would continue to play the chords, but instead you follow the rhythm figure written below the standard notation. If you're not sure how to follow the musical roadmap symbols (coda, D.S. and so on), take a quick look at Appendix B.

Part IV

Purchasing and Caring For Your Mandolin

In this part . . .

You explore buying mandolins, including what to pay, what styles are available, how to identify a better mandolin and where you can find mandolins for sale. After you have a mandolin, the quest for accessories begins and I help you sort out what you really need and what's extra. I also suggest easy ways to change strings, as well as giving tips on the care and maintenance of your mandolin.

Chapter 15

Selecting and Buying a Mandolin

· ·

In This Chapter

▶ Investigating the different types of mandolin

▶ Deciding what to spend

▶ Assessing mandolin quality

▶ Choosing where to buy

· ·

Although buying a mandolin can be almost as much fun as playing one, the experience can be full of mystery and surprise for someone new to the world of mandolins. You have loads of options for style, price, brand, type of wood, type of finish and where to buy, and so I consider all these issues in this chapter.

I hope to make the selecting and buying experience as fun and stress-free as possible, and so I also present a few pitfalls to watch out for. I help to ensure that you're able to make a good decision about purchasing your first mandolin and, when ready, move up with confidence to a better-quality instrument.

If you're shopping for a mandolin these days, you're going to be spoiled for choice. My best piece of advice is to search out an experienced mandolin player to give you a hand.

Exploring the World of Mandolins

Here's the fun part. In this section, I take you on a tour that features some very cool mandolins. I cover a few basics in Chapter 1, but read on for a full-scale introduction to some of the models on the market. Take it easy, though. Exposure to too many mandolins can bring about the onset of MAS (the symptoms of which I detail in the nearby 'Suffering from Mandolin Acquisition Syndrome' sidebar).

Suffering from mandolin acquisition syndrome

Mandolin acquisition syndrome (MAS) affects most mandolin players at one time or another. Symptoms include, but aren't limited to, dreaming about mandolins, becoming obsessed with differences in species of spruce, reading about different types of varnish and French polishing techniques and, even worse, imagining owning a matching set of mandolins. Although some claim that MAS goes away upon acquiring the dream mandolin, most people with this disorder only experience a short-lived remission and are soon in the throes of full-blown MAS again.

Finding out about F-style mandolins

F-style mandolins have a carved top and back (sometimes referred to as a *flat back*, although in reality the back is arched, not flat) and a decorative scroll near the neck. Some F-style mandolins also have decorative body points (see Chapter 1). As a result of the ornamentation and extra carving, F-style mandolins are more difficult to build than the A-style (which I describe in the next section) so tend to be more expensive. Some people even refer to the scroll of an F-style as nothing more than an expensive strap hanger!

The most popular F-style mandolin is the F5 (which you can see in Figure 15-1), originally designed by the Gibson company in the 1920s. The F5 features a decorative scroll, f-shaped soundholes and, in some cases, a decorative headstock (see Chapter 1 for descriptions of the various parts of the mandolin). The F5 mandolin was the first mandolin to utilise structural features like an elongated neck, internal (tone bar) bracing, and an adjustable bridge. These modern innovations, designed to enhance projection and playability, are now standard on many of today's mandolins.

The F5 was originally intended for the classical concert stage, but has since become the standard look and sound for a mandolin used in a bluegrass band (check out Chapter 10 for more on playing bluegrass music).

Figure 15-1:
A typical
F5-style
mandolin.

Assessing A-style mandolins

A-style mandolins are pear-shaped with a carved back (although some inexpensive models use pressed (steamed) wood or plywood) and don't have the decorative scroll of the F-style (see the preceding section). They're a bit easier to build because of the simpler contour of the body.

The A5-style mandolin (which you can see in Figure 15-2) has f-shaped soundholes and many of the other structural innovations used in the F5, so it actually sounds very much like an F5 (although some people do argue that the decorative scroll on the F5 helps it to produce a different sound). An interesting fact about the Gibson A5 is that it was developed at the same time as the F5, but was not put into production, leaving only one (very valuable!) 1920s Gibson A5 in existence. Over time, other mandolin makers have adopted the A5's innovations, and the A5-style mandolin is now very popular.

In general, A-style mandolins are a bit lower in price, and, unlike the F5-style, they don't shout 'bluegrass music'. A-style mandolins are popular in old time and blues, and with players of a variety of other styles.

Figure 15-2:
A typical
A5-style
mandolin.

Rounding out F- and A-style mandolins

The F5- and A5-style mandolins that I describe in the preceding two sections have f soundholes, but you can also buy F- and A-body-style instruments with round soundholes (as you can see in Figure 15-3). The round- or oval-soundhole mandolins produce a mellower sound well suited for jazz, Irish and even some classical music that doesn't require great volume. Traditional oval-hole mandolins are built with shorter necks and transverse bracing (internal bracing that runs parallel to the bridge). Some people call the sound 'tubby', and most musicians agree that mandolins with round soundholes produce less volume with a sweeter tone and more *sustain* (the amount of time for which the sound continues).

Figure 15-3:
Mandolins
with round
soundholes:
(a) F style;
(b) A style.

Tossing around pancake and other flat-top mandolins

Originally manufactured for the US army and navy to be used by soldiers, this flat-top model (which you can check out in Figure 15-4(a)) has been imitated by many builders. This style is commonly referred to as the 'pancake'. These simple, inexpensive mandolins can have a surprisingly good tone and seem to sound good in most music except bluegrass.

In addition to the 'pancake', instrument makers Martin, Vega, Harmony and others made a variety of flat-top mandolins, a Washburn example of which you can see in Figure 15-4(b). Two interesting variant models from the early 1900s were the Vega Cylinderback, which featured a flat top but a back bent into a shape resembling a cylinder, and the Martin, which featured a sharp kink or bend in the top. These types of flat-top mandolin are no longer in production, but so many were produced around the turn of the last century that you can easily find them for sale online or from reputable used-mandolin dealers.

Figure 15-4:
Two flat-top
mandolins:
(a) 'pancake';
(b) vintage
flat-top.

Plugging in with electric mandolins

Electric mandolins come in two basic types:

✔ Acoustic/electric mandolins that are designed to plug into a PA system or dedicated acoustic amplifier and still maintain some of the acoustic qualities of a traditional mandolin (see Figure 15-5(a)). These mandolins can be fully functioning acoustic instruments, and feature piezo pick-ups. (A *piezo pick-up* is a very small crystal that, when attached to the inside of the mandolin body, is able to turn into electric energy the vibrations caused by picking a note. This energy is then transmitted through a cable to a sound-amplification system.)

✔ Electric mandolins that are designed to plug into a guitar amplifier (see Figure 15-5(b)). These instruments usually feature magnetic pick-ups and can even have solid bodies like an electric guitar. If this type of thing appeals to you, you may want to set aside some extra money for an amp and some effects pedals.

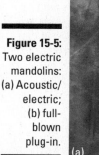

Figure 15-5: Two electric mandolins: (a) Acoustic/ electric; (b) full-blown plug-in.

Bandying about with a bandolim

A bandolim is a Brazilian mandolin (see Figure 15-6). A large body of music called choro comes from Brazil and features the bandolim as a primary instrument. These instruments are hard to find outside Brazil and have a very unique sound. I don't suggest a bandolim as your first purchase, but if in a few years you're bitten by the choro bug, you may need to get one.

Noticing Neapolitan mandolins

Often called the 'bowl back' or 'taterbug', the Neapolitan was the original design for the mandolin in northern Italy around 1800 (see Figure 15-7). Thousands of them seem to be in circulation, and you can find them at garage or car boot sales, on eBay and in your uncle's attic.

Unfortunately, the vast majority of Neapolitan mandolins are best used as a decoration hanging above the fireplace. Although professional Neapolitan mandolins exist, they're relatively hard to find and quite expensive. In my opinion, a Neapolitan doesn't make a good choice as a first mandolin.

Figure 15-6:
A Brazilian
bandolim.

Figure 15-7:
A
Neapolitan
mandolin.

Spending the Right Amount

In this section, I provide some basic price ranges of mandolins. As a general rule, get the best mandolin you can afford. If you do your homework before purchasing a mandolin, you can then be sure to buy an instrument that holds its value over time:

- ✔ **Entry level:** You can find entry-level mandolins in the £120–200 (US$120–200) range in both new and used condition.

  Steer clear of the eBay £/US$40-buy-it-now model even if the description says that it's a great mandolin (flip to the later section 'eBay' for more info).

- ✔ **Good student model:** Depending on your budget and commitment to becoming a mandolin player, you may want to start with what's considered a decent student model. You can find these instruments in the £250–500 (US$300–700) range.

- ✔ **Professional model:** You can buy professional mandolins for as little as £650 (US$800), but they can also cost many times that much (pro players invest many thousands of pounds in their mandolins). Many professional mandolins today are handmade in small shops.

At any level of mandolin purchase, you get more mandolin for your money with an A-style or a flat-top than with an F-style (check out the earlier section 'Exploring the World of Mandolins' for more on these different types).

Discovering What Makes One Mandolin Better than Another

The word 'better' is always a bit subjective, but the many variables in instrument production techniques can have huge effects on the tone, volume, looks and playability of a mandolin. In this section, I walk you through a few of these variables.

Barking up the right tree: Types of wood for mandolins

Wood is by far the most popular material for mandolin construction. Mandolins can be made from a variety of woods, but the industry standard is to use maple for the back and sides and spruce for the top of the instrument. Other types of wood are also beginning to gain a foothold in the market, including redwood and cedar for tops, and walnut for backs and sides. (You can even buy mandolins made from carbon fibre!)

With wood mandolins, the important thing is that the wood is solid wood and *not* laminated wood. Laminated wood (plywood) doesn't resonate like good quality solid wood.

Polishing off the types of finish

Most mandolins are finished with one of two substances:

- **Lacquer:** Lacquer used in finishing mandolins is the nitrocellulose variety. The good news is that lacquer is far more durable than varnish (see next bullet point), but it can't match the acoustic qualities that varnish provides. Most factory-made instruments feature lacquer (check out the later section 'Trade (or factory) mandolins' for more info on this type of mandolin).

- **Varnish:** Mandolin producers use a variety of types of varnish. Varnish is a more labour-intensive, expensive finish than lacquer and has better acoustic properties, but it's quite soft and begins to show wear much earlier than lacquer. You can find varnished mandolins in small-shop instruments and individually made instruments (I describe both types in the later section 'Making it up: Types of mandolin manufacture').

Getting comfortable: Mandolin playability

Playability is an overall term that describes how well an instrument functions in three areas when making music:

- **Ease of play:** This aspect refers to how easy you find getting a good sound from the instrument. The amount of pressure needed to properly fret notes with left-hand fingers (known as the *action*, which I discuss in the later section 'Putting a Mandolin Through its Paces' and in Chapter 18) is very important, and the size and shape of the neck also has a big impact on playability. Another element is how hard you need to pick a note to get a full sound.

- **Volume:** This aspect is very important for the mandolin player. By nature, the mandolin is a fairly quiet instrument, and so in order to blend with other instruments you need a loud mandolin. In general, higher quality mandolins tend to have a higher maximum volume.

- **Tone:** This aspect is very subjective, but one point that mandolin players can agree on is the need for a well-balanced tone. The hallmarks of a *well-balanced* tone are that all four pairs of strings are close to the same volume, and the sound doesn't get noticeably louder or softer as you play higher up the fretboard.

A good mandolin set-up can have a major effect on tone, *intonation* (playing in tune), volume and ease of play (I describe mandolin set-up in Chapter 18). Many mandolin sellers can provide a good set-up on new and used instruments. Don't be afraid to ask.

Making it up: Types of mandolin manufacture

Mandolin manufacturing falls into three categories: trade (or factory) made mandolins, small shop mandolins and individually made mandolins.

Trade (or factory) mandolins

Trade or factory mandolins are made using mass production techniques. The tops and backs are carved or pressed by machines and assembled by unskilled workers. Many of these factory-made mandolins are built in Asia and feature a high degree of decoration, including cheap inlays, shiny finishes and a fair amount of bling.

Think twice about purchasing an inexpensive mandolin with a lot of decorative flourishes. The acoustic performance of a mandolin is the most important point to consider, and highly decorated inexpensive instruments are designed to attract the inexperienced buyer!

Factory instruments can be perfectly acceptable choices for beginner and intermediate players (although some can be virtually unplayable), but they require extensive setting up. Get the retailer to set up your mandolin if you opt for an entry-level factory model, or you run the risk of getting a mandolin that is painful to play and listen to. (For more on setting up a mandolin, check out Chapter 18.)

Factory brands include The Loar, Kentucky, Michael Kelly, Fender, Epiphone, Ashbury, Rogue, Eastman and others.

Small-shop instruments

Small-shop instruments, in general, are higher quality and use acoustic tuning, not used in factory instruments. Small-shop instruments are made in limited quantities. Skilled craftspeople carry out most of the work by hand and they pay a great deal of attention to the acoustic properties. This small-shop model of quality manufacturing is used both in the West and Asia.

These mandolins are suitable for serious students or pro players and last for many years, maintaining a fair resale value. Some small-shop brands include Weber, Gibson, Collings and Northfield.

Individually produced instruments

Individually made mandolins are more common today than ever before. These mandolins can be carved with traditional hand tools or using modern robotics. At the present time, hundreds of individuals around the world are making mandolins, and the quality ranges from crude to exquisite. The price of these instruments varies greatly based on the maker.

Most of these individually produced instruments are made on a special order basis, allowing the customer to have input in elements such as wood type and finish type, and even to take part in the acoustic tuning of the instrument. Prices for these instruments can run anywhere from £1,200 to £20,000 (US$2,000–30,000).

Aging well: New versus used mandolins

Mandolins don't really wear out, and so buying a used one can be a good choice, but be aware that because of the number of mandolins currently being produced and the low cost of Asian manufacturing, a new mandolin can cost even less than a used one. The inexperienced mandolin buyer is most likely best served buying something new, but if an older, worn mandolin is what you're after, use similar guidelines to purchasing a used car: bring someone along who can help you make an educated decision, or ask for a 48-hour trial period during which you can take the instrument to a pro or a luthier (maker of stringed instruments) for inspection.

Locating Mandolins for Sale

In this section, I review a variety of places to purchase mandolins. I examine the pros and cons of each type of mandolin seller to help you avoid the mistakes commonly made by first-time mandolin buyers.

Buying in bricks-and-mortar shops

These shops are your conventional, often high-street, stores stocked with instruments for sale and staffed by real human beings. If you're lucky, the salespeople may be very knowledgeable about the products they're trying to sell you. Bricks-and-mortar outlets can range from pawn shops to speciality instrument stores.

Rock-and-roll guitar shops

Most rock-and-roll guitar shops occasionally have a mandolin or two in stock. In most cases, none of the employees can play the thing or tell you how to tune it; often the only thing this group know about mandolins is that Led Zeppelin used them – dude! My advice is to stay away from these establishments if you're looking for a good mandolin.

A mandolin is *not* a little guitar, and just because the salespeople know a fair amount – or even a lot – about guitars, doesn't mean that they know anything about mandolins, except that they have one for sale and you're a potential customer.

Pawn shops

The people at pawn shops are likely to know nothing about mandolins. Pawn shops may be good places to buy used tools or maybe a radio, but only the very savvy mandolin buyer should consider going shopping for a mandolin in a pawn shop.

Acoustic instrument speciality shops

If you're going the bricks-and-mortar route, these shops are the ones for you. Acoustic instrument shops routinely have anywhere from 10 to 50 mandolins in stock, ranging in quality from beginner instruments to handmade top-of-the-line stuff. Another sign that you're in the right place is a large inventory of acoustic guitars, banjos, fiddles and exotic acoustic instruments. Most of these shops have knowledgeable staff who can help you make the right purchase.

Ask the salesperson to play a variety of mandolins for you so you can listen to them and decide which sound you prefer. And feel free to try them out for yourself.

The only downside is that speciality acoustic shops are hard to find and sometimes require travelling some distance, but in most cases they're worth the extra hassle.

Going online

Online shopping refers to buying or selling products via the Internet. One advantage of buying this way is that the seller may have fewer overheads through not needing a shopfront and employees, which can result in lower prices. One disadvantage of this type of shopping is that you can't put the instrument in your hands before making a decision.

Internet stores

Online acoustic instrument shops are relatively new kids on the block. Some of these sellers have an actual showroom that you can visit but, by making the inventory available on the Internet, they make long-distance purchases possible. Although not as good as going to a specialist shop in person (flip to the earlier section 'Acoustic instrument speciality shops'), this approach can be a great way to get the mandolin of your dreams.

Most of these online stores contain a variety of new and used instruments in many price ranges, and many also offer free set-up and a 48-hour approval period.

eBay

Buyer beware! Only consider eBay if you're a very savvy, experienced mandolin buyer. Some reputable sellers use this type of site, but the risks for the beginner are too great. Many of the instruments aren't properly represented, because the seller is misinformed, and you may not be able to get your money back if the deal goes bad.

Mandolin Café classifieds

The Mandolin Café (www.mandolincafe.com) features a classified ads section that's a goldmine of mandolins currently for sale. The site features new and used mandolins being sold by individuals, mandolin builders and some of the best retailers that specialise in mandolins.

Always use your best judgement, but I've bought and sold many instruments through this site and never had a bad experience. Most sellers offer a 48-hour approval period. If, for whatever reason, you decide not to purchase the instrument, you need to pack it carefully and foot the bill for return shipping.

Putting a Mandolin through Its Paces

When you've done the research that I describe in the preceding sections in this chapter, and you have one or more mandolins in mind that you're considering purchasing, before you pull the trigger you need to take a few more steps to ensure that you're buying a solid product. Here's a list of questions to ask yourself before buying your first mandolin:

- ✔ **Do you like the sound?** Mandolins can vary greatly in sound so you need to love the sound of your new instrument.

  You're going to be spending many blissful hours playing your mandolin, and so its sound is of the utmost importance.

- ✔ **Can you see any cracks in the top and back?** Changes in humidity are the number one cause of this problem, and cracks can be expensive to fix. Inspect where the top and back meet the sides to make sure that they're not coming unglued.

✓ **How's the action?** The most important element in your first mandolin, assuming it isn't cracked or damaged, is to make sure that the action is set up properly. As I discuss in Chapter 18, the *action* is the height of the strings above the fretboard:

- If the action is too high, you need to press down harder, which makes your mandolin difficult to play.

- If the action is too low, the strings rattle and buzz.

Mandolin strings tuned up to pitch are much stiffer than guitar or banjo strings and need to be set up so that they're easy to play.

✓ **Is the neck straight?** Look down the instrument's neck to see whether it's straight or looks like a banana or a rollercoaster: straight is good, banana or rollercoaster is bad.

✓ **Does the bridge fit properly to the top?** Inspect the contact point where the bridge feet meet the mandolin top (see Chapter 1 for the parts of a mandolin). This contact should be an airtight fit. If you can see air or light in that area, the bridge isn't fitted properly and you'd need to have it adjusted or shaped by a qualified repair shop.

✓ **Are the tuners usable?** Turn each of the tuners to see whether they move easily. You shouldn't require pliers or the strength of a professional shot-putter to make adjustments to the tuners.

Upgrading to a better instrument

After you've played mandolin for a while, you may want to look into upgrading to a better instrument. A better instrument gives you better tone, easier playability, more dynamics and better aesthetics. The best advice I can give when looking for a better instrument is to play as many of them as you can. When you meet other players, ask if you can play their instruments. Some musicians may be very possessive of their investments and reluctant to let you handle them, but if you explain that you're looking to upgrade and haven't experienced many fine instruments yet, most let you play for a few minutes. Make arrangements to visit speciality acoustic music shops and play every mandolin you can, regardless of price. This way you can see, hear and feel the differences in mandolins.

Hundreds of independent mandolin makers are building student models and pro-level mandolins, and so when looking to upgrade be prepared to encounter unfamiliar-name brands in both new and used mandolins. Another current dynamic in the mandolin world is the increasing quality of Pacific Rim manufacturers. In the last few years, some mandolins coming from China offered good value.

Chapter 16

Building Your Accessories Kit

Remember when you were a kid and you were so proud of your bike that you wanted the shiny bell that mounts on the handlebars, the streamers and the playing cards held on by pegs in the spokes? Well, some people never really grow up, and they're called mandolin players. In fact, certain musicians go to such great lengths with accessories that they spend more on the 'bling' than on the mandolin itself. In this chapter, I introduce you to the world of mandolin accessories, dividing these extras into three types: basic necessities, educational tools and flashy bits and pieces.

You can purchase the items I describe in this chapter from online suppliers such as Elderly Instruments (www.elderly.com), Greg Boyd's House of Fine Instruments (www.gregboyd.com), The Mandolin Store (www.themandolin store.com), Hobgoblin Music (www.hobgoblin.com) and, of course, music shops specialising in mandolin accessories.

Gathering Together the Must-Haves

Buying your first mandolin is only the beginning. After you have an instrument, you soon find out about all the accessories you need. I suggest you start your accessories collection with the items mentioned in this section. You may then want to explore further the world of mandolin accessories such as those I describe in the later section 'Bringing on the Bling'. But be warned that trying to keep up with the latest and greatest gadgets can lead to an intervention and possibly a 12-step programme to wean you off your new addiction.

Picking extra picks

One thing you certainly need is extra picks. They can get misplaced in a variety of ways and end up anywhere from being buried in the sofa to getting to the back of the refrigerator (yes, this actually happened to me).

Picks come in a variety of shapes, colours, materials and thicknesses. Try as many as possible before settling on one style or brand. In fact, most picks are fairly inexpensive, and so buy a dozen or so different styles at first and experiment.

Most mandolin players eventually end up with a fairly thick non-flexible pick, because mandolin strings are fairly stiff, and a big part of mandolin playing requires you to pick up and down rapidly.

When you've been playing for a while you may want to look at some boutique varieties. These picks are becoming popular and feature attributes such as bevelled edges and polished space-age secret materials. Some of the popular boutique pick brands are BlueChip, Wegen, Red Bear and V-Picks.

Clipping on an electronic tuner

No matter how good their musical ear, all mandolin players really need to own a clip-on-style tuner to keep their instrument in tune; they're very easy to use and quite reliable. Electronic tuners vary in price, but most tuners cost less than £20 (in the UK) or $30 (in the US). Flip to Chapter 2 to find out more about how to use an electronic tuner.

Don't delay, get an electronic clip-on tuner today, and make your mandolin sound as beautiful as it can sound.

Strapping on the mandolin

Most players use a mandolin strap to support the instrument. Many mandolin players use a braided soft-leather strap, although other material is available if you have an issue with using leather. A good handmade braided leather strap costs about £30 (in the UK) or $45 (in the US), and a simpler style can cost around £10 or $15. My favourite mandolin strap is a rawhide boot lace.

Some mandolin players, such as those with Italian bowl-back mandolins, play without straps.

Protecting your mandolin

Essentially, you can buy three types of case for your mandolin to keep it protected: hard shell, soft shell or gig bag. Each style of case has advantages and disadvantages.

Hard cases

Hard cases (by which I mean an instrument case and not your toughest mates) offer great protection for your mandolin. The most popular types of hard case are wood-framed ones covered in a scuff-resistant vinyl type of material, usually lined with a synthetic furry fabric. These cases offer a fair amount of protection but can be a bit heavy. They usually cost £50 to $100 (in the UK) or $60 to $120 (in the US). A type of hard case growing in popularity is the lightweight moulded case. These cases are made of a sturdy polystyrene foam material with a strong canvas outer shell. They're also lined with the furry material. These modern, lightweight cases are very protective and cost £45–70 or $60–90.

If you have a very valuable mandolin and travel with it, you need to go to the next level in protection. Fibre-glass or even carbon-fibre mandolin cases are virtually indestructible and offer the best protection of all. Many professional touring musicians use these cases, which can cost £350 ($500) or more.

Soft cases

Soft cases aren't really soft but made of a pressed cardboard type of material. Many inexpensive instruments are sold new with this style of case. Thanks to modern improvements, you don't see this style of case as often as, say, 20 or 30 years ago.

These cases offer little protection and in my opinion are best avoided or replaced with a more modern style case or gig bag.

Gig bags

Gig bags range from a flimsy nylon bag that resembles a tennis racquet bag to a hard-leather-exterior bag lined with thick foam padding. Gig bags have the advantage of being lightweight, and most have shoulder straps to make carrying your mandolin very easy.

This type of bag is ideal for when you're travelling on crowded buses or you need to get to a gig on a bicycle. They're also a good choice when going to a music festival, because often you need to walk a long distance to get from one jam or stage to the next.

Stringing along your mandolin

Of course, extra strings themselves are a necessary accessory, but you can also buy tools to make the task of changing your strings easier.

Having some extra strings

Always keep an extra set of mandolin strings handy, because you can break a string and need a replacement at any time.

You should also plan to change your strings periodically. New strings sound much better and are easier to get in tune, and so ideally you want to keep them fresh. Strings tarnish over time even if you've kept them in their packaging.

I suggest that you buy your strings from an acoustic music shop or online from a store specialising in stringed instruments (such as www.juststrings.com).

Mandolin strings can cost anywhere from £6 to £30 (in the UK) or $8 to $40 (in the US) per set. The more expensive types are popular with classical players, but most mandolin players use the less expensive strings.

Winding the strings

Little devices called string-winders save you a lot of time and make changing strings easier. *String-winders* are tools consisting of small a rectangular wrench that fits over the tuner button. Attached to this rectangular wrench is a handle. By cranking that handle, the tuner winds the string on the peg much faster that you can do by hand.

Mandolin tuner buttons are positioned very close to each other, and a string winder fits nicely into these tight quarters.

You need to make quite a few turns of the mandolin tuner shaft to get enough string wrapped around the post, and a string-winder makes short work of the job.

Cutting and trimming the strings

Another gadget that you need when changing strings is a good sharp pair of wire-cutters. This tool is very helpful for removing old strings and trimming new ones. Chapter 17 contains a step-by-step guide to changing mandolin strings.

Buying Extras that Improve Your Playing

Accessories don't come only for your mandolin itself (see the preceding section). You can also purchase extras that in one way or another help to improve your performances.

Keeping steady with a metronome

A metronome produces a steady click or beep that you use to make sure you're playing in time. My favourite metronomes are electronic models with a single percussive sound. Some fancy models even use different-pitched sounds for each beat. Metronomes range in price from £10 to £140 (in the UK) or $15 to $200 (in the US).

A metronome is necessary if you want to sound good. Many musicians don't use metronomes, but then again most of the good ones do.

Taking lessons from books and DVDs

A never-ending sea of instructional mandolin material seems to be available today. The obvious first choice is, of course, *Mandolin For Dummies* (have you heard of it?), but after that you have loads to choose from.

Some DVDS are designed to get you off to a good start, and others relate to particular styles of music. Some focus on demonstrating songs by an artist or licks specific to an artist or a genre of music. For instance, you may find that one DVD teaches bluegrass tunes while another demonstrates basics such as holding the pick, common chord shapes or left-hand fingerings.

Check whether one or more of your favourite mandolin players have instruction DVDs available that pass on their songs or techniques.

Leaning on a music stand

If you plan on learning to play music by using sheet music or songbooks, a music stand is a must. Even if you're the type of person who commits the tune to memory after you learn it, a music stand is still a good idea. Even people who don't read music at all use music stands to hold folders containing lyrics or chord changes to songs.

Here are some music stand options:

- **Cheap lightweight wire-frame collapsible stands** are good if you need to have a portable stand. The downside is that they support only sheet music or small folders. These cost around £13 (in the UK) or $18 (in the US).

- **Medium-duty collapsible stands** can be very lightweight (and when made of new materials, very strong) as well as quite durable. These stands hold more weight than a wire stand and sell for around £25 or $35.

- **Heavy-duty non-collapsible stands** are still the best way to hold sheet music or songbooks. The problem is that they're heavy and bulky. You see orchestra players and music-school students using this type of stand when performing concerts or recitals. These are the most expensive music stands, costing around £35 or $50.

Recording made easy

The ability to record audio easily is of great value to the mandolin player.

Having the facility to record yourself and listen back to see what you really sound like is invaluable. In addition, many musicians bring portable digital recorders to jam sessions to record the tunes, so that they can learn them at home later and be ready for the next jam session; others record lessons and review them at a later date. These little pocket-sized recording devices range in price from £79 to £250 (in the UK) or $99 to $299 (in the US) depending on brand or options, and you can purchase them at music stores or through online dealers like Amazon.

Playing along with backing tracks

A growing world of free play-along tracks is available online, and you can buy tracks for most musical styles:

- **American folk styles:** Homespun Tapes (www.homespuntapes.com) and Musix (www.musixnow.com) offer a variety of instructional CDs and videos, along with many play-along tracks.

- **Choro:** For the Brazilian music lover, ChoroMusic.com (www.choromusic.com) has a series of choro play-along CDs.

- **Jazz:** Jamey Aebersold (www.jazzbooks.com) has been marketing play-along products for years that range in style from traditional to modern jazz.

✔ **Pop and rock:** GuitarBackingTrack.com (`www.guitarbackingtrack.com`) is designed for guitar, but you can also play mandolin along with many of your favourite pop music hits.

If you're a do-it-yourself person, you may want to record your own rhythm tracks with your newly purchased portable digital recorder (see the preceding section). This method is great because you discover how to play solid rhythm as well. All you need to do is record the chords for the tune, in the style of the tune, for a few times consecutively, playing through the song without stopping. Play it back, try playing along, and good luck!

Yet another route is to use a fairly simple software program called Band-in-a-Box from `www.pgmusic.com`. This software allows you to type in any chord progression you want and then assign a style to the rhythm section. With thousands of styles available, you can create tracks for just about any song you're working on, slow the tempo down until you have the notes right, and gradually increase speed until you're playing at the desired tempo. If you're an iPhone user, you may want to visit the App Store for the latest apps designed to do the same thing (they cost less).

Slowing down the music

A great way to learn how to play by ear is to reduce the speed of the music. When a tune is playing very slowly, hearing all the notes and articulations becomes much easier.

Today you have a really easy way to do this by using the Amazing Slow Downer from Roni Music (`www.ronimusic.com`). This software enables you to slow the music down without changing the pitch, while also setting loop points so you can hear a passage over and over until you can play it perfectly.

Using a webcam for online lessons

Online lessons via Skype or other video-conference software is becoming more popular as Internet speeds increase. In fact, I teach the majority of my mandolin students in this way (`www.donjulin.com`).

You have plenty of options to choose from as regards buying webcams, and the price seems to keep dropping along with that of most high-tech gadgets. Logitech (`www.logitech.com`) is a popular manufacturer of webcams and makes models that work with PCs or Mac platforms.

Bringing on the Bling

As well as basic mandolin accessories, you can also choose to enter the world of optional add-ons, which range from instrument stands to silencers and other learning aids. Some of these items are a bit more expensive than strings or picks, and not all mandolin players need or indeed want every item that I describe in this section. I divide these accessories into ones that you attach to your mandolin and ones that work independently.

Attaching accessories to your mandolin

You can dress up your mandolin in all sorts of ways, although a serious intention lies behind the items I discuss in this section. Try some out and decide whether they really do improve the sound of your instrument or are nothing more than go-faster stripes for mandolins.

Tone-Gard

The Tone-Gard (www.tone-gard.com) is a device designed to isolate the back of a mandolin from your body while playing, producing more volume and enhancing the tone. The Tone-Gard is a lightweight metal frame with rubber and leather pads that attach to the back of your mandolin. Some mandolins exhibit more benefit from this device than others, but in general the Tone-Gard seems to do what it claims.

Armrests

An armrest is a wooden mandolin accessory that you attach to the rim of the top, on the bass side of the strings at the point where your forearm is in contact with the mandolin body. Armrests attach to the mandolin with a small clamp, in a similar way to how a chin rest attaches to a violin, and are usually made of exotic hardwood and polished very smooth.

Some people believe that armrests improve tone by keeping the forearm from dampening the vibrations of the top. Another reason to buy an armrest is that it protects the finish from sweat and skin oils (some delicate varnish finishes react to sweat).

Grommets/silencers

Silencing the sympathetic vibration of the mandolin strings behind the bridge is a fairly common practice, and can be done with a simple piece of felt placed where the strings come into contact with the bridge or by weaving a leather shoelace through the strings.

The hip, stylish way to accomplish this deadening of overtones is by using little black rubber grommets. They fit perfectly between the strings, deadening the overtones while adding a customised look to your mandolin. The most popular place to buy these grommets is RadioShack (www.radioshack.com).

Tuners

All mandolins come with tuners or tuning keys, but some mandolin players feel the need to change their tuners. Some very expensive tuners claim to offer better performance along with a stylish look (for example, Waverly – www.stewmac.com or Alessi – www.alessituningmachines.it).

Tuners that have ivoroid (synthetic pearl) or ebony tuner buttons can have an effect on the look of your mandolin. The metal base is available in gold or silver and is usually matched in colour with the tailpiece.

Tailpieces

Many musicians replace the lightweight stock tailpiece with a heavier cast tailpiece. Much debate takes place over whether this does anything for tone. One thing for sure is that a decorative cast tailpiece changes the look of your mandolin. Popular tailpieces are produced by Allen, James, Weber, AXL and Orrico.

Truss rod covers

A truss rod is a threaded steel rod that runs through the neck that you use for adjusting the neck if it begins to bow or warp. The truss rod cover is a simple or decorative plate on the headstock of the mandolin, which when removed allows you access to the truss rod.

A way to dress up your baby is to get a fancy truss rod cover made of mother of pearl or some other decorative material.

ToneRite

The ToneRite (www.tonerite.com) is a device designed to make the mandolin sound more open and broken in. Musicians know that older instruments can sound better and newer instruments tend to be a little cold or stiff sounding. The common belief is that, as the instrument vibrates from being played, tone and resonance are improved. (Many experiments have been done placing mandolins and guitars in front of large loudspeakers for extended periods of time.)

The ToneRite attaches to the strings of the mandolin near the bridge, vibrating the mandolin. You can read many testimonials at the Tonerite website and discussions on the effectiveness of this device at www.mandolin.com.

Making life easier in other ways

In this section I take a quick look at a few more accessories, from expensive to downright cheap.

Instrument stands

If you find yourself often looking for a place to set your mandolin down, look into buying a mandolin stand. Basically, you can choose from two types of mandolin stand:

- ✔ Stands that support the instrument in a cradle-like manner: you set the mandolin into the stand.
- ✔ Stands that support the instrument from the neck: you hang the mandolin from the stand.

Humidifiers and hygrometers

Humidity is a big concern among all musicians who play instruments made of wood. If the humidity drops too low, the wood can dry out and crack, leaving a scar on the instrument and a hefty repair bill.

A *hygrometer* measures the humidity in your mandolin case. If you live in a climate with variable weather conditions, you can find that winter is much dryer as a result of the heating systems used in buildings. Your hygrometer indicates when you're in the danger zone and need to humidify your instrument. Most experts say that 40 per cent humidity is ideal.

If you get measurements below 40 per cent humidity, consider getting a humidifier that fits in your case. Instrument *humidifiers* are made of absorbent material that you saturate with water and then place in the instrument case.

Better yet, get a room humidifier designed to treat the room where you keep your mandolin and any other wooden instruments.

Microfibre cloths

Most mandolin manufacturers recommend using a microfibre cloth to clean your instrument. These cloths are available from a variety of sources and are intended for cleaning delicate surfaces.

I don't recommend using a liquid polish to clean your mandolin. Although some music shops sell guitar polish – which is just regular furniture polish with water added, and said to be safe to use on most mandolins – guitar finishes tend to be much tougher than mandolin finishes, and some cleaners can damage certain mandolin finishes. I suggest that you play it safe, get a microfibre cleaning cloth and leave it at that.

Chapter 17

All Change: Replacing Your Mandolin's Strings

1 can promise you one thing: the first time you change the strings on your mandolin is sure to be an adventure (a bit like changing your first nappy but less smelly – unless it all goes very wrong!). After many years of changing sets of mandolin strings, I can do so in about ten minutes. If you follow the directions I lay out in this chapter, your first few times may well take about half an hour.

I show you how to remove your mandolin's old strings and how to re-string with new ones. I also discuss how often to do this job and all about choosing the right strings, where to do the work and the basic tools you need.

Preparing to Change Your Strings

If you want to ensure a stress-free experience, you don't want to go full-steam ahead into changing your mandolin's strings without a little preparation. This section lets you in on a few pieces of useful information before you start.

Knowing when to change strings

You change the strings on your mandolin for two main reasons: because a single string breaks and you need to replace just one; or all the strings are old and no longer sound good, and you want to replace the entire set.

Strings that wear coats (but not jackets)

The latest innovation in string technology is the introduction of coated strings. These are traditional strings with a very thin coating that prevents oxidation or dirt build-up on the strings. Each string manufacturer seems to have its own secret coating formula. Coated strings cost more than traditional uncoated strings but tend to last two to five times longer.

Mandolin strings don't last forever, and periodically you do need to change the set. How often this job rolls around depends on the type of strings you use and your ability to keep the strings clean and free from dirt and sweat (check out Chapter 18 for some tips on general mandolin maintenance). In general, if the strings feel a bit sticky, making slides difficult, or when they start to become discoloured and you notice that tuning isn't as easy as before, you want to change your set of strings. Any rust or corrosion on the strings is also a good indication that you need a new set.

Always keep an extra set of strings in your mandolin case, just in case you break a string.

Selecting the right strings

The correct choice of strings for your mandolin depends on the style of your instrument and the type of music you play. Not all mandolin strings are created equal.

You can find mandolin strings at quality acoustic music shops but may have difficulty at rock-'n'-roll guitar shops. Depending on where you live, ordering online from a speciality supplier of strings may be your best option.

Types of strings

In this section, I break down strings into a few basic categories based on the material used in making them, and list them from cheaper to more costly types. All modern mandolin strings have a steel core with windings of different material used for the g- and d-strings:

✔ **Bronze-wound or phosphor-bronze-wound strings** are the brightest and loudest of the string types and are used by many top bluegrass, Celtic and old-time players. They age faster than other types and are fairly inexpensive, so changing them often is a good idea.

✔ **Nickel- or stainless-steel-wound strings** are a bit mellower than bronze-wound and last much longer. Nickel strings cost about the same as bronze. If you're going electric, nickel is a good choice when using a magnetic pickup.

The longer life of nickel strings is partly because they start out a little duller than bronze, but also because nickel doesn't oxidise at the same rate as bronze.

✔ **Silk and steel strings** have silk or synthetic fibres between the steel core and the outer winding of the string, which reduces the overtones, making the strings less bright sounding. The outer winding on some of these strings is silver coated for a less hard sound. These strings are popular with Brazilian choro players and some gypsy jazz players. They tend to cost more than bronze or nickel strings.

✔ **Flat-wound or tape-wound strings** are the most expensive type of mandolin strings and are very similar to violin strings. The outer winding is totally smooth, leaving a very fast and slippery-feeling string (no annoying finger squeaks with these strings). Classical mandolin musicians and some players of jazz and other styles prefer these strings. They last much longer than the other types of strings.

Gauge of strings

Strings are available in different gauges or thicknesses. Some mandolins sound better with heavier, stiffer strings, but heavy strings can snap other mandolins in half. Here are some general guidelines:

✔ If you have a modern carved top (Gibson-style) instrument, you can try any type of string without worrying about causing damage.

✔ If your mandolin is a vintage flat-topped mandolin, use light-gauge strings.

✔ If you play a bowl-back mandolin, you need very light strings as a result of the mandolin's lightweight construction. Most people use flat-wound strings on bowl-back mandolins (see the preceding section on types of strings).

Removing the Old Strings

Before you can put on a new set of strings, you have to remove the old dull or rusty ones. Any workbench covered by an old piece of carpet or blanket makes a perfect string-changing workstation. As tools, gather together wire-cutters, needle-nosed pliers, an electronic tuner and a string-winder. Here's my step-by-step guide to removing mandolin strings:

1. **Remove the tailpiece cover.** If your mandolin has a (Gibson-style) stamped tailpiece, you need to remove the tailpiece cover in order to access the loop ends of the strings (if the loop ends are exposed already, you don't have a tailpiece cover). These covers slide on to the base of the tailpiece and can get stuck on pretty firmly. If you can't slide the cover off, you can carefully lift up the cover to remove it. Figure 17-1 shows a common Gibson-type mandolin tailpiece.

(a)   (b)

Figure 17-1: Removing the tailpiece cover: (a) cover attached; (b) cover being removed.

Don't remove all the strings at once! Repeat: don't remove all the strings at once! (I'd repeat this warning for a whole page if I could.) If you do, the bridge falls to the floor, scattering pieces of mandolin bridge everywhere. After you find all the pieces, re-assemble them and manage to get new strings on the mandolin, you still need to place the bridge properly to achieve good intonation (I describe this procedure in Chapter 18).

2. **Loosen both g-strings.** Use your string-winder to loosen the tension on both the g (fourth) strings (see Figure 17-2).

3. **Unhook the loop ends.** The loop ends of the strings are attached to small hooks on the tailpiece (as Figure 17-3 shows).

Figure 17-2: Loosening the g-string with a string-winder.

4. **Remove the string from the tuning peg**. Unwrap the other end of the string from the tuning peg by using a pair of needle-nosed pliers. This process is a bit like taking a fish off a hook (though less slimy; see Figure 17-4).

Figure 17-3:
Unhooking
the loop
ends.

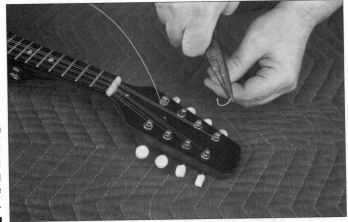

Figure 17-4:
Removing
the string
from the
tuning peg.

Be extremely careful at this point because the wires are sharp! The part of the string that has been wrapped around the peg acts like a spring and may bite you upon being released from the peg. Remember that the string is about the diameter of a sewing needle and can poke you and make you bleed.

5. **Dispose of the used strings**. Sharp mandolin strings have a way of embedding themselves into furniture and carpets, which can turn your house into a mini-minefield of sharp wires. Best to have a lined waste bin near you while you remove the strings, and to dispose of them as soon as possible.

Re-stringing Your Mandolin

Are the old g-strings off your mandolin as I describe in the previous section? I hope so, because here I talk you step by step through re-stringing your prized mandolin one course (pair) of strings at a time:

1. **Unpack both g-strings.** Uncoil the strings and lay them flat on your workstation (which I describe in the preceding section).

2. **Fasten one g-string to the tailpiece.** The most popular tailpiece today is a stamped two-piece (Gibson-style) tailpiece. Don't let the extra four tines fool you. In the old days when this tailpiece was invented, you had to wind your own loops: by running the fresh winding under the second tine and turning a 90-degree angle, the winding stayed in place. Fortunately, today you can ignore that feature (see Figure 17-5).

   Some modern tailpieces are decorative, but attaching the strings can be trickier. If your mandolin has a modern tailpiece, try bending the loop in order to hook it to the tailpiece (take a look at Figure 17-6).

   If you find that you need to bend the loop in order to get it to hook onto the tailpiece hook, curl the loop part of the string around a pencil. The curve of the pencil is round enough not to kink the string and cause a weak spot that may break under tension (see Figure 17-7).

3. **Thread the free end of the string through the tuning peg.** When you've hooked one string to the tailpiece, keep a little pressure on it so that it doesn't unhook itself. I use one hand to keep the string taut and the other hand to thread the other end of the string through the hole in the tuning peg (check out Figure 17-8).

Figure 17-5:
Fastening the loop end to the tailpiece.

Figure 17-6:
A modern
tailpiece.

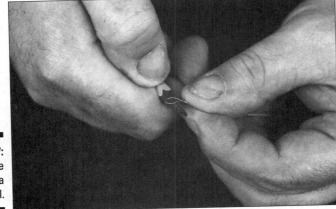

Figure 17-7:
Bending the
loop with a
pencil.

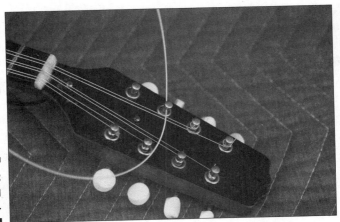

Figure 17-8:
Threading
the peg.

4. **Leave some slack.** The ideal amount of slack allows two or three revolutions of the string around the tuning peg. I find that about one fist of slack (see Figure 17-9) is just the right amount. If you leave too little, the string slips out of the tuning peg; too much and you can end up with too many windings for the peg.

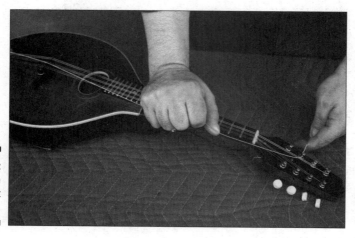

Figure 17-9: Getting the right amount of slack.

5. **Tie the string to the tuning peg.** You want to secure the string to the post so that it doesn't slip when the string is tuned to pitch. When the string is threaded through the tuning peg, bring the free end around in the opposite direction to which the post is going to turn when tightening the string.

Wind the string around the peg until you reach the string, passing under the string. Now lift up on the free end of the string, and begin tightening the tuning peg with your string-winder. As Figure 17-10 shows, the string winds over itself, which locks the string in place and prevents it from slipping.

6. **Tighten the string.** Wind the string so that it meets the peg on the centre of the headstock. As you wind it, guide the string so that it winds down towards the headstock. Tighten the string and, as you do so, be sure to guide it into the right slot in the bridge and at the nut. When you have the string fairly tight, you can use an electronic clip-on tuner to guide you to the correct pitch. If you've left the right amount of slack, you end up with two or three revolutions when the string is tuned to pitch (take a look at Figure 17-11).

Figure 17-10:
Wrapping or tying the string.

7. **Trim the excess string.** When the string is tuned up, trim off the excess with a set of wire-cutters (see Figure 17-12).

8. **Return to step 2.** Repeat all the steps while putting on the second g-string. Continue by removing the d-strings and follow the same procedure. Keep repeating this process until you've replaced all the strings.

When the job is complete, put the old strings in the rubbish bin, and all your tools away, and remember to replace the cover if you have a two-piece tailpiece. Now re-tune all the strings as I describe in Chapter 2. New strings stretch a bit, and so it may take a few minutes of re-tuning before they stabilise.

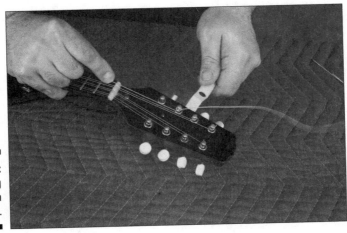

Figure 17-11:
A string wound on the peg.

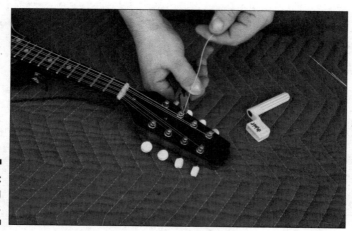

Figure 17-12:
Trimming
the excess.

Chapter 18

Caring For and Repairing Your Mandolin

In This Chapter

▶ Carrying out everyday mandolin care

▶ Repairing and adjusting your mandolin yourself

▶ Bringing in the experts

As with all musical instruments, your mandolin wants and needs loving care and attention in order to keep it in good condition. If you look after it well, it repays you with many years of faithful, great-sounding service.

This chapter covers standard maintenance and repair issues for your mandolin. Although some of these procedures are quite easy and don't require special tools or skills, others are more advanced and so best carried out by a trained professional.

Maintaining Your Mandolin's Health

A healthy mandolin is a happy mandolin, but unfortunately your beloved eight-string companion can get out of adjustment from time to time. Mandolins are a bit like people in that some preventive maintenance dramatically lowers the number of trips to the doctor's. In this section, I point out a few precautions that help keep your mandolin out of the doctor's surgery.

Wiping down your mandolin

Keeping your mandolin clean is one simple action that helps maintain its good health.

Get in the habit of wiping down the strings with a microfibre cloth whenever you set the mandolin down. The oils on your fingers corrode the strings and shorten their life expectancy.

Wiping down the mandolin itself is also a good idea. Fingerprints can dull the finish, and the oils from your hands or whatever you've been touching can damage the surface. For more on cleaning your mandolin, including some precautions to take, turn to Chapter 16.

One of the best ways to keep your mandolin clean is to wash your hands before you begin to play.

Controlling the climate

Keep your mandolin away from extremes of cold, heat and humidity.

The cold temperature alone isn't really harmful to the mandolin, but going from cold to warm too quickly can destroy the finish. If your mandolin is subject to below-freezing temperatures, be sure to let it warm up, while still in its case, for many hours. If the case feels cold to the touch, don't open it!

Heat can be even more dangerous. Never leave an instrument in a car for long during the summer months. The boot may seem like a safe place to keep your mandolin, but the heat inside a locked car can reach well over 38 degrees Celsius (100 degrees Fahrenheit). This type of heat can cause major problems such as glue joints coming undone or, worse, the wood becoming flexible and warping or caving in.

Humidity is also a big concern for the mandolin player. Wood is an organic material that interacts with moisture from the surrounding air: it swells and contracts depending on its moisture content. This change in shape and size puts a great stress on the instrument.

What do frogs and mandolins have in common?

I remember being a young boy playing outside on a summer's day, when I came across a frog. Being a boy, I was playing with my new friend the frog, carrying him around with me. Just then, I heard the voice of my mother calling me, and so I ran up to the house with the frog in my hands. 'C'mon, Don, we need to go to the store,' my mother said. 'Can I bring my frog?' I asked. 'Okay, as long as you put him in a container so he doesn't jump around the car.' I found a nice plastic bowl and even put some water in it for him.

Off we went to the shopping plaza, where we parked the car on the hot tarmac. You can probably guess the rest of the story (that frog never had the chance to be kissed and turn into a prince). Think of your mandolin as a frog, and don't leave it in a hot car.

When it gets too dry through low humidity, wood shrinks leaving the perfect condition for the formation of cracks and failure of the joints and seams. With too much humidity, not only does the wood swell, but its susceptibility to bending and permanent deformation increases. (Heat and moisture are used in the bending of the rims when making mandolins, because they make the wood more flexible.)

The best way to deal with heat, cold and humidity for your mandolin is just as you do for yourself, because as a general rule if you're comfortable, your mandolin's also comfortable. Controlling the temperature and humidity in your house (or at least one room with proper heating) helps to keep your mandolin healthy for many years. For more on humidity problems and solutions, check out Chapter 16.

Getting a good case or bag

Protecting your mandolin when transporting it is the primary argument for having a good case. You should also use a case when you aren't going to be playing the mandolin for extended periods. But wait! Surely, the only reason you wouldn't play a mandolin for an extended period is that you bought another one and now have two or three (or ten) mandolins, right? I discuss case and bag options in Chapter 16.

Keeping an instrument stand handy

I recommend keeping the mandolin near you in an accessible place, so that you can practise often and quickly without a lot of fuss. The problem is that keeping it available also risks leaving it open to accidental damage. Although 'storing' your mandolin on the sofa may work if you live alone and are very careful not to sit on it, if you have housemates or children, don't leave the mandolin lying out where it can easily be crushed.

The best option is to have an instrument stand in your living room, so that you can pick up your mandolin and play for a few minutes whenever you want to throughout the day (I talk more about mandolin stands in Chapter 16).

If you have young children, you may want to keep the mandolin (or perhaps the kids) in a case or a designated room, but this solution makes picking the mandolin up and playing it at any time more difficult. If necessary, assess your living situation, determine the danger level and come up with a plan.

Setting-up Your Mandolin Yourself: Only for the Brave

Many mandolins ship from the factory or even from some small independent builders in need of a good set-up, and if there's one thing any mandolin requires to live up to its potential, it's being set up properly.

Setting up your mandolin doesn't mean framing it for taking the last piece of pie that you know darn well you ate yourself, but includes adjusting the action, intonating by positioning the bridge, and in some cases carrying out fretwork. If you're handy with a few tools and measuring devices, you may be able to do some of this basic set-up work yourself. If you've never done this type of work but think that you want to give it a try, get some instruction first from a qualified set-up professional. In addition, you can buy instructional DVDs on this topic, and an ever-growing list of YouTube do-it-yourself videos are available to help in this process, too. Most mandolin players can perform the basic set-up tasks of adjusting the bridge but take the more advanced jobs to a pro.

Even a great guitar technician may do a terrible job on a mandolin set-up. The shorter scale, and the stiffness of the double strings of the mandolin require much more precise tolerances than a guitar.

In this section I cover a few easy jobs that you may want to try yourself with a few basic tools. Stewart-MacDonald (www.stewmac.com) and Tonetech (www.tonetechluthiersupplies.co.uk) are suppliers of speciality tools and parts used in the making and repairing of string instruments. Some of these tools are quite expensive but can make the job much easier. Also, Frank Ford, at Gryphon Stringed Instruments in Palo Alto, California, has a wealth of additional information on set-up and other issues about the care and feeding of a mandolin, available online at www.frets.com.

If you're even a little intimidated or feel uncomfortable at the thought of carrying out the set-up procedures, leave them to the pros and go to your acoustic music speciality shop. Believe me, a good mandolin set-up technician is a great friend to have.

Adjusting the action

Action describes the distance by which you have to press the strings down in order to get a fretted note to ring properly. Mandolin strings are very tight when tuned up to pitch, and so having the action low makes your mandolin easier to play and causes less pain to your fingertips. However, if the action is too low, the strings buzz and rattle against the frets.

Many mandolins built since the 1920s have adjustable bridges with two thumbwheels that you use to raise or lower the overall height of the bridge. You can adjust these thumbwheels in two ways:

✔ Loosen the tension on the strings until you can turn the screws with your thumb.

✔ Use a screwdriver with a wide flat tip inserted near one of the thumbwheels, between the bridge base and the bridge top. Carefully turn the handle until it takes enough pressure off the thumbwheel by lifting the bridge top so that you can adjust the thumbwheel. Figure 18-1 demonstrates this method.

Most mandolin players like their action to be about 1.5 millimetres (0.06 of an inch) high at the twelfth fret. You can measure this distance with metal feeler gauges or a rotary depth micrometer. Although a bit pricy, these micrometers take all the guesswork out of the job. Some very experienced luthiers and set-up technicians can set the action by eye, but I prefer to measure it. Figure 18-2 shows this measuring tool.

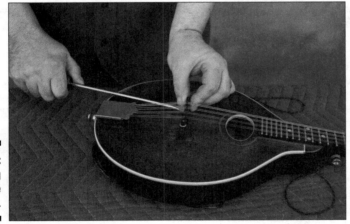

Figure 18-1:
Adjusting the bridge height.

Tackling the truss-rod adjustment

Some mandolins have an adjustable steel rod running the length of the neck, called a *truss rod*. This steel rod is designed so that by turning the nut on the threaded end of the rod, you can adjust the straightness of the neck. A bowed fretboard makes for high action and poor intonation. If your mandolin neck has a bow to it, a truss-rod adjustment (which somehow sounds more unpleasant than it is) may be able to straighten the neck.

Figure 18-2:
A rotary
depth
gauge.

The truss rod screw or nut is located in the headstock, under a cover plate. You have to remove a few small screws to access the truss-rod adjustment screw. After you've removed the cover, determine what type of tool you need to make the adjustment. Some truss rods require an Allen key (or wrench), and others a thin-walled socket wrench. You can purchase truss-rod adjustment tools from luthier supply stores.

If your mandolin's neck is bowed forwards, turn the rod to the right. A very small amount can make a big difference, and so only turn this rod about one-eighth of a turn at a time. If the neck is back-bowed or bent backwards, making the strings buzz against the frets, try loosening the truss rod by turning it to the left.

Some modern mandolin builders are putting a two-way adjustable truss rod in the neck. This type of rod pushes or pulls the neck in either direction, thus making this whole process easier. Check out Figure 18-3 for a view of the truss-rod adjusting procedure.

Slotting the nut

The action (or string height) at the first fret is very important for getting your mandolin to play easily and in tune. This measurement is overlooked quite often in lower-priced mandolins, but I've also seen many expensive mandolins that are very hard to fret because of this problem. If you think that your mandolin is hard to play on the frets nearest the nut, you may want to measure the action at the first fret. I use a rotary depth gauge (as shown in Figure 18-2) for this job.

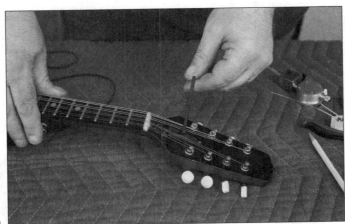

Figure 18-3:
Truss-rod
adjustment.

I like the action at the first fret to be about 0.3 of a millimetre (0.012 of an inch) for the e-string and about 0.38 of a millimetre (0.015 of an inch) for the g-string, with the a- and d-strings being somewhere in the middle (see Figure 18-4). You can get different-sized metal files made specifically for slotting the nut. Try to find files that are slightly larger than the string you're slotting. For instance, if your e-string is 0.254 or 0.28 millimetres (0.010 or 0.011 of an inch), look for a file that's about 0.33 of a millimetre (0.013 of an inch).

Cutting or deepening the nut slots can be a little risky, and so go slowly. One swipe too many with a file and the nut is ruined.

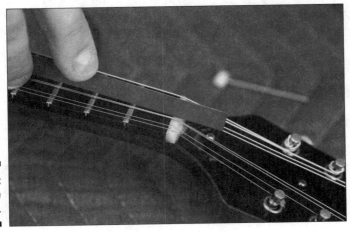

Figure 18-4:
Filing the
nut slots.

Setting the bridge: Intonation

Mandolin bridges are held in place by the downward pressure of the strings; they aren't glued down. In order to get the mandolin to play in tune all the way up and down the neck, the bridge must be in the correct location.

The term *intonation* refers to how well the instrument plays in tune. You can check this aspect by using an electronic digital tuner while moving the bridge very small amounts. (Chapter 2 contains much more on tuning.) Below are step-by-step instructions to set the intonation on your mandolin:

1. **Tune the mandolin using an electronic tuner so that all the open (that is, unfretted) strings are in tune.**

2. **Fret each of the strings at the twelfth fret (the octave, which I explain in Chapter 2) and observe the reading on the tuner:**

    • If the tuner is reading flat or lower than it should, move the bridge towards the neck a small amount.

    • If the tuner is reading sharp or higher than the open string, move the bridge back towards the tailpiece a bit.

A millimetre or two (say, 0.06 of an inch) can make a huge difference, and so be careful not to move the bridge too far. Notice that in Figure 18-5, the open string and the twelfth fret are both in tune.

Figure 18-5:
Adjusting intonation with a tuner.

(a)   (b)

3. **Check that the bridge is upright and not leaning one way or the other. If the bridge is leaning, carefully set it straight.**

Sometimes, however, the bridge needs to be at a slight angle to get the best intonation on all the strings. And, sometimes, adjusting a bit for one pair of strings might throw one of the other pairs off, so repeat as necessary to get as close to perfect as you can for all the pairs.

Attempt the more involved set-up procedures that I mention in this section only if you're confident with your handyman skills. A professional set-up technician has the special tools and experience to carry out these procedures.

Turning to the Professionals

Whereas the preceding section covers some jobs that you can take on if you're confident and nimble-fingered enough, in this section I describe those repair scenarios for which you really do need to hand over your mandolin to a pro.

Dressing or replacing the frets

Over time, all mandolin frets wear down. As they do so, they develop flat spots where the strings hit the frets. These flat spots make it difficult to get a clean note and also affect the intonation. The remedy to this problem is to have the frets dressed or replaced.

Fret dressing involves filing the frets flat to remove the grooves worn by the strings, after which the top edges of the frets are re-crowned or rounded and polished. This procedure normally costs around £80 ($100).

In some cases, replacing the frets is a better option than dressing them. In *re-fretting*, as it's called, the expert removes the frets, planes the fingerboard flat and installs new frets, which are then levelled, crowned and polished. This procedure averages around £180 (or $250).

If you're having frets replaced, you have the option of changing the fret size. Traditionally, mandolins used very small-gauge fret wire, but modern builders are using larger-gauge wire with good results. Fret size is a personal preference, and much debate and discussion revolves around this topic. My preference is for larger frets, because they seem easier to play and allow you to slide from note to note with less effort.

Repairing cracks

Repairing cracks and re-gluing open seams (where the back or top separates from the sides) are jobs best left to the professionals. The most important thing that you need to do yourself if you find a crack or a separated seam on your mandolin is to loosen the strings – immediately. If you don't, the crack or separation will continue to get bigger and will eventually distort the shape of the wood, causing more damage and necessitating a far more expensive repair. You need to get any crack that goes completely through the wood, no matter how big, repaired without hesitation. Cracks just to the finish don't cause structural concern, though, and you therefore don't have to repair them.

The most common place to see cracks on a mandolin is on the top around the f-shaped soundholes. These cracks run with the grain of the wood and are usually caused by lack of humidity (or someone sitting on your mandolin). Repairing a crack – if you catch it early, and it just needs gluing – costs only around £15 (or $20) per inch. If crosspatches or cleats are needed to stabilise the crack, a repair will cost more, depending on the hourly rate of the repair shop. The average hourly rate is £40 (or $65) per hour.

For seam separations, most shops charge by the hour for gluing seams back together, and can accomplish the task in one or two hours. If you leave it too long to get your mandolin repaired, though, and the top or back becomes warped or bent, be warned – this repair could get very costly.

Part V
The Part of Tens

The 5th Wave   By Rich Tennant

"Here's a nice G major paisley chop chord."

In this part . . .

1 present a list of tips and helpful info so that you can get the most out of your mandolin experience. Also, you get to meet some of the greatest mandolin players of the past and present to inspire you, and you discover how to connect with the mandolin community in your home town or halfway across the world via the Internet.

Chapter 19

Ten (or so) Tips on Becoming a Good Mandolin Player

*P*laying mandolin can become a major source of happiness for you. Although at the beginning things can seem difficult and even frustrating, the more you practise, the easier it gets and the more fun you have.

Watching a musician sit and make beautiful music together with total strangers can be a bit of a mystery for the novice, but when you start to understand this new shared musical language, you begin to see how these sessions can happen. I promise you from experience that being part of the music is one of the best feelings you can ever have.

In this chapter, I provide several tips that help you reach your goals as a mandolin player.

Listen to Mandolin Music

The number one thing that you can do for yourself in your quest to become a good mandolin player is listen to mandolin music. Fortunately, in today's world of instant digital downloads you can easily get hold of great new and old mandolin music to listen to.

Listen to a variety of mandolin players in a variety of styles so you can begin to form an opinion on what you want your playing to sound like. I'm always amazed when I meet new mandolin students and ask, 'So who are your favourite mandolin players?' and they answer, 'I don't know; I don't really listen to mandolin music'! Do yourself a favour and start building a library of great mandolin music.

Get a Good Teacher

Even with a book as good as this one, you can still benefit from a mandolin teacher. A good teacher can spot problems in your playing and offer a way to correct them, and also hold you accountable for lessons and progress, just as a trainer at the gym does when you're trying to get in shape.

Ideally, your mandolin teacher should teach the type of music you're interested in playing. For example, a good bluegrass player may not be your best choice if you want to play classical music. Importantly, *don't* settle for a guitar teacher who can play a little bit on the mandolin. If no reputable mandolin teachers are within driving distance of you, look online. Skype or Internet teleconference lessons are becoming more common, along with downloadable lessons and even online schools where you have the ability to interact with other online students or teachers.

Keep Your Mandolin Nearby

Getting at your mandolin needs to be easy. For example, if you need to go to a certain room in your house, close the door, get the mandolin out of its case, set your music up on your music stand and get a cup of your favourite hot beverage, you may never get to play the mandolin. Everyone leads busy lives, and the best way to add a new thing into your schedule is to make doing so easy.

Get a good mandolin stand and leave your instrument on it, in a main room of your house, as often as possible. If doing so is difficult, perhaps because you have young children in the house, use a separate room, but try to make access to your mandolin as easy as possible.

Practise whenever you have a few spare minutes. You don't need to wait until your scheduled practice time. A few five- to ten-minute sessions per day can have a great effect on your progress. They may even relieve a bit of stress.

Play Your Mandolin Every Day

Music is a language, and in order to be fluent at any language you need to speak it often. Therefore, try to play your mandolin every day. This can be structured practice time working on new songs or techniques, playing your favourite songs just for fun, or putting on some recorded music and trying to play along by ear (check out the later section 'Develop a Musical Ear' for more). Almost any time you spend with the mandolin in your hands helps your playing develop.

Find People to Play Music With

Playing music with other people is a special experience, and so don't underestimate it. At first, most new musicians are a bit shy about playing with others, because it can be a bit intimidating. But most musicians are willing to slow down a bit, if necessary, to let a beginner sit in or play along. Try to find someone who likes a similar style of music and is roughly at or slightly above your skill level.

Finding musicians to play along with may be easier than you think. Many different places hold open-mic nights where amateur musicians can get on stage and perform in front of each other. Remember that loads of musicians learn to play together through a church group. Bluegrass festivals also offer a great opportunity to network and jam with others.

Many people say that the best part of some bluegrass festivals is the parking lot picking and not the main stage acts! So when you go to a festival, be sure to bring your mandolin with you.

All musicians were beginners at one point, and most remember how they progressed when more seasoned players let them play along. Many of them are willing to return the favour and help out the next new musician. Having good etiquette is important, however. If you happen upon a hot jam of seasoned players, for example, you might want to just observe or quietly play chords around the perimeter. My rule here is that if my playing wouldn't add anything to the jam, I just watch. You earn the respect of the other players this way and, as you improve, your time will come to join in.

Practise with a Metronome

Learn to love your metronome! Timing is by far the hardest part of discovering how to play music. Metronomes are totally unforgiving and can be frustrating at first, but *don't give up*! If you can't seem to figure out how to use the metronome, get a basic lesson in music counting from any music teacher (it doesn't matter what instrument the teacher plays for this aspect). I offer some metronome practice exercises in Chapter 4.

The right note played at the wrong time is still wrong. The wrong note played at the right time may sound good. Timing is more important than playing the right notes!

Go to Mandolin Camps or Workshops

Mandolin camps seem to be popping up all over the world lately. These camps can be great for helping mandolin players to gain experience playing with other people and to study with some of their heroes. Mandolin camps feature many diverse styles ranging from bluegrass (which I discuss in Chapter 10) to classical or choro (Brazilian). Mandolin camps, symposiums and conferences are all great ways to get a huge dose of mandolin in a small amount of time. The Mandolin Café (www.mandolincafe.com) publishes a list of these mandolin camps.

If a weekend-long camp seems out of your comfort zone, try attending a mandolin workshop. These are often held in music shops and normally last a few hours. Workshops may be very focused on a specific style or be more general, and some are designed specifically for beginners. Many of the top stars of the performing and teaching world give workshops. Spending a few hours with a good teacher in a group of like-minded mandolin enthusiasts can be a great experience.

Practise Slowly Using Good Technique

Practising slowly with good left- and right-hand technique builds up a good foundation. When the time comes to play fast, you already have the technique needed to be fast and accurate.

Playing slowly is much tougher than it seems. When you play in slow-motion, you hear the beginning, middle and end of each note. Some of the fastest mandolin players suggest that the key to playing fast is the ability to play slowly.

Use your metronome to help you practise slowly (flip to the earlier section 'Practise with a Metronome').

Develop a Musical Ear

Developing a good musical ear is an essential skill for the mandolin player. Even though this attribute can seem difficult to acquire at first, over time it proves to be one of your most valuable tools.

Slowing down a recording is a great way to learn by ear. In the last few years some very affordable software programs have been developed that have the ability to slow down a recording without altering the pitch. If you decide to begin discovering songs or licks from favourite CDs or MP3s, this approach can become really useful. The most common brand of this type of software is the Amazing Slow Downer, available online at www.ronimusic.com. The Mac/PC version costs $50, and the iPhone version costs $15.

Acquire Some Music Theory

Basic music theory isn't as difficult as some people tell you, and learning a bit can be very helpful in becoming a good mandolin player. You don't need to start analysing the chord progressions in Bach chorales or trying to figure out why John Coltrane played what he did; for some types of music, a very basic understanding of scales and common chord progressions can take much of the mystery out of discovering new tunes. You can choose from loads of books and websites that explain music theory.

The layout of the strings on the mandolin is symmetrical, meaning that the relationship of all adjacent strings is always the same, whereas on a guitar the relationship between the second and third string is different than the relationships between all of the rest. Banjo is even less symmetrical. So, on the mandolin, a D scale using the second and third strings can become an A scale (first and second strings) or a G scale (third and fourth strings) just by moving your fingers over one string and playing the same finger pattern. The same applies to chords, licks and even complete melodies, and therefore makes applying a bit of theory to a mandolin much easier than to a guitar, banjo or ukulele.

Record Yourself

Recording yourself playing is a valuable tool and has become easy and afford-able, with good quality results. You can make decent recordings on many mobile phones, but if you don't have one of these buy yourself an easy-to-use handheld recorder. Here are two main reasons why you may want to record yourself:

- ✔ **You can tell which part of your playing needs work.** Have you ever heard a recording of your voice and thought to yourself, 'Do I really sound like that?' The answer is yes, but you didn't know until you heard the recording. The same thing happens when you play music: you have a mental idea of what you think you sound like that may not be the whole truth. In the days of analogue recording, people would say 'The tape doesn't lie.'

- ✔ **You can chart your progress.** When you feel that you're not making any progress (which happens to everyone from time to time), go back and listen to a recording of yourself from a few months before. This review almost certainly confirms that you're getting better. If not, you may want to check out a few of the points I make earlier in this chapter and see whether you need to change your approach.

Try to record your private lessons and any workshops you attend. Most teachers allow and even encourage you to do so.

Have Fun!

The main thing to remember while you're learning to play the mandolin is to have fun! Playing music can bring you and others great joy, and so don't let the day-to-day scheduled practice sessions become a drag. Make sure to learn some songs that you really like, so you want to hear them over and over again.

Don't make the mistake of simply learning songs in a lesson book, playing them correctly once and saying, 'Okay, been there, done that, on to something new.'

Chapter 20

Ten Mandolin Players You Need To Know

*I*n this chapter, I present ten players who made a difference in the world of the mandolin. These musicians aren't only the best at what they do, but are also among the most influential mandolin players of all time. Some invented new styles, some are pushing the envelope and creating the next mandolin sound, and others follow in the tradition of the great classical mandolin players. All these masters are amazing and all mandolin players need to hear their music.

Bill Monroe (1911–1996)

Bill Monroe – the father of bluegrass – didn't only play the mandolin with an energy that's rarely been duplicated, but also invented an entire musical genre. By blending old-time fiddle tunes of Scottish and Irish origin with blues from the American South and throwing in some gospel-style singing, Bill created the sound known as bluegrass (which I discuss in more detail in Chapter 10). Many people believe that bluegrass is a very old musical style, but in fact these elements weren't blended together to form this uniquely American musical form until the 1940s.

For most of his career, Bill played a Gibson F5 mandolin. He wrote hundreds of songs and instrumentals, among the most famous of which is 'Blue Moon of Kentucky' recorded in 1954 by Elvis Presley. Bill is the only person inducted into the Bluegrass Hall of Fame, Country Music Hall of Fame *and* the Rock and Roll Hall of Fame. His style influenced nearly all American mandolin players, and current disciples of his style include David Grisman, Sam Bush, Ronnie McCoury, Mike Compton, Frank Wakefield, Ricky Skaggs, Roland White and many others.

Chris Thile (born 1981)

Chris Thile started playing mandolin at age 5 and by 12 had won the prestigious national mandolin contest at the Walnut Valley Festival in Winfield, Kansas. Chris's technique and imagination have put him at the front of the current pack of mandolin players. He has a certain charisma and performance style along with a skill level that makes incredibly difficult playing seem easy, such that he has inspired a whole new generation to start playing.

Chris's musical style ranges from bluegrass to Bach, with a touch of Radiohead. At 8 years old, Chris along with brother and sister Sean and Sara Watkins formed the band Nickel Creek. Nickel Creek continued for 17 years, winning one Grammy and being nominated for others. Chris's current band is Punch Brothers, and he can also be seen in a variety of side projects featuring many of today's elite performers, including Edgar Meyer, Yo-Yo Ma and Mike Marshall (check out the later section 'Mike Marshall (born 1957)') among many others. His 2011 recording *Sleep With One Eye Open* with Michael Daves is a return to his bluegrass roots.

Chris seems to have kicked down many barriers and is currently blazing a trail to which future generations of mandolin players can aspire. At the time of writing, Chris Thile is 30 years old and has a very active touring and recording schedule. Do yourself a favour and get a ticket to see this guy play when he's in your city!

Jethro Burns (1920–1989)

Kenneth C. Burns is best known for his work as Jethro of the musical comedy team Homer and Jethro. Homer and Jethro parodied popular songs with rural American humour from 1936 until Homer Haynes died in 1971. Even though most of his career was based in comedy, Jethro's mandolin playing is legendary: he was a pioneer in the world of jazz mandolin. Many people consider his 1978 recording *Back To Back* (available from Acoustic Disc) with Tiny Moore to be a landmark recording of jazz mandolin (I look at playing jazz styles on the mandolin in Chapter 13).

After Homer's death in 1971, Jethro spent much of his time perfecting the art of playing solo mandolin by playing melody and chords simultaneously. During the 1970s, he taught mandolin in the Chicago area. His most notable student or protégé is Don Stiernberg, who was a bandmate for many years and who helped to revitalise Jethro's career. Don also lives in Chicago, where he performs and teaches jazz mandolin.

Another interesting note about Jethro is that he and country music mogul Chet Atkins were married to twin sisters. Wouldn't you like to have been at those family gatherings after dinner when the instruments came out of their cases? Wow!

David Grisman (born 1945)

David Grisman has been performing, recording, teaching, producing and promoting mandolin music since 1964. He's done more for the promotion of the mandolin than anyone alive today.

Jerry Garcia (of the Grateful Dead) gave David his nickname 'Dawg' in the early 1970s. Around the same time, David and Jerry, along with Peter Rowan, Vassar Clements and John Kahn, recorded *Old and in the Way* (originally released on the Grateful Dead label and now available from Acoustic Disc), one of the first of the new generation of 'hippie' bluegrass recordings, and still the bestselling bluegrass album of all time. This album introduced traditional bluegrass to a new generation of fans.

In 1975, the David Grisman Quintet (DGQ) released its self-titled album of what was to become known as Dawg music: a complex blend of bluegrass, swing, jazz, gypsy and Latin, becoming its own unique hybrid (Chapter 14 contains the lowdown on this style). This acoustic music is instrumental and features intricate arrangements and improvised solos. The instrumentation for the original DGQ was first mandolin, second mandolin, violin, guitar and bass. I strongly suggest you find this recording and listen again and again.

David Grisman has also produced many albums and CDs. In 1990, he founded the Acoustic Disc label (www.acousticdisc.com), a boutique CD label specialising in acoustic string music. The label has released about 70 titles, including many by the greatest mandolin players of all time. David's latest venture is Acoustic Oasis (www.acousticoasis.com), a website from which you can download some of the best mandolin music currently available anywhere.

Dave Apollon (1897–1972)

Dave Apollon was a Russian-born mandolin virtuoso who emigrated to America in 1919. He found work in Vaudeville, where he was billed as 'the world's greatest mandolin virtuoso'. Dave Apollon played a variety of styles on mandolin, including Russian gypsy, Latin, ragtime and jazz (I cover playing jazz, including using Latin rhythms, in Chapter 13, and ragtime in Chapter 9). The best way to experience the mastery of Dave Apollon is to find *The Man with the Mandolin* (Acoustic Disc). This release is still in print and available in CD form or as a download.

Apollon also had a career in motion pictures, during which he starred in many musical shorts (sort of like early music videos). These *soundies* were based on Vaudeville routines and are some of the earliest films with sound. If you search the Internet you may be able to find a collection called 'Dave Apollon 7 Short Films 1933–1939'.

Jacob do Bandolim (1918–1969)

Born Jacob Pick Bittencourt, Jacob do Bandolim was a Brazilian musician, composer and choro mandolin virtuoso. *Bandolim* is the Brazilian word for mandolin, so his stage name translates to Mandolin Jacob. Choro music is an infectious blend of European classical melodies and Afro-Brazilian rhythms.

Americans were introduced to Jacob do Bandolim and choro music by two CD releases, *Mandolin Master of Brazilian Original Music* (Volumes I and II) (Acoustic Disc). Both releases are in print and fairly easy to find. Thanks in part to these recordings, choro music and the Brazilian mandolin style are experiencing renewed interest in America. Some current mandolin stars in the world of choro are Danilo Brito, Dudu Maia and Hamilton de Holanda.

Yank Rachell (1910–1997)

James 'Yank' Rachell was the master of mandolin blues (check out Chapter 9). In a career that spanned 70 years, Rachell was best known for his recordings with Sleepy John Estes. Legend has it that, when Yank was 8 years old, he traded the family pig for his first mandolin.

You can hear Yank Rachell late in his career on the 1986 recording *Blues Mandolin Man* (recently re-released on Blind Pig Records). This album features Yank backed by a full rhythm section of drums, bass and electric guitar. Yank also appeared in the Terry Zwigoff documentary film *Louie Bluie* based on the life of his friend and fellow blues musician, Howard Armstrong. A biography called *Blues Mandolin Man: The Life and Music of Yank Rachell* (by Richard Congress) is also available.

In many of his later recordings and performances, Yank played a Harmony Batwing electric mandolin that he plugged into a guitar amp. He'd tune his mandolin a minor third (in other words, three frets) lower than normal, so that when he played a G chord it sounded like an E chord. Guitar players like to play blues in E, and most mandolin players prefer the key of G, so this way of tuning down to the guitar enabled Yank and his guitar player to work together more easily.

Mike Marshall (born 1957)

Mike Marshall can play anything on the mandolin! He has it all going on – speed, tone, imagination and technique – and is one of the hardest-working players around. Mike is amazingly versatile on the mandolin, being equally comfortable with bluegrass, classical, Swedish fiddle tunes, Brazilian choro, improvisation and anything else that he chooses to play.

When Mike was a teenager in Florida he contacted his idol, David Grisman, to purchase copies of the album *The David Grisman Quintet* (on Acoustic Disc) to sell to his mandolin students. David invited Mike to look him up if he ever found himself near San Francisco. So, with a friend living in the San Francisco Bay area who knew the guys in Grisman's band, and a sister living in Las Vegas, Mike flew out for a visit and convinced his sister to give him a ride to the Bay area the next day so he could meet his heroes. Upon Mike's arrival, his friend took him over to Grisman's house, where David was working on his *Hot Dawg* CD (for A&M records) and a film soundtrack. Grisman was suffering from tendonitis and needed someone to play the rhythm parts for him. Having memorised Grisman's tunes from the first album, and being more than familiar with the quartet's style, Mike was ready and willing. Within a few days, Mike found himself in the studio with his hero, and within a few weeks he'd become a full-time member of Grisman's band, at age 19.

Mike is also well known as an instructor and co-founder (with David Grisman) of the Mandolin Symposium (www.mandolinsymposium.com), held annually in Santa Cruz, California, where over 100 mandolin students study with the world's top players for a week.

Caterina Lichtenberg (born 1969)

Hailing from Sofia, Bulgaria, Caterina Lichtenberg studied at the Cologne Academy of Music under the guidance of Professor Marga Wilden-Hüsgen. She is one the world's foremost proponents of the German classical mandolin style, and currently conducts a mandolin course at the Cologne University of Music. In 2008 she was appointed to the position of professor at the Cologne University of Music, and currently holds the sole professorship of mandolin in the whole of Europe.

Caterina has recorded nine CDs to date with a variety of ensembles. Her recordings include the music of Handel, Scarlatti, Bach and Calace, along with the tango music of Piazzolla and the Brazilian choro music of Pixinguinha. Do yourself a massive favour and check out Caterina's website (www.caterinalichtenberg.de) for a complete list of her wonderful recordings and current concert and workshop schedule.

Carlo Aonzo (born 1967)

Carlo Aonzo comes from Savona, in Italy. He first learned from his father, Giuseppe Aonzo, although he went on to graduate with honours from Cesare Pollini Conservatory in Padua, Italy, in 1993. Since then, Carlo has toured the world, performing with many top orchestras.

Aonzo's playing is based in the Italian tradition of classical mandolin, including the music of Raffaele Calace, but his wide-ranging repertoire also takes in Italian folk music, original pieces, and the music of American virtuoso Kenneth (Jethro) Burns. Carlo made his American debut in 1997 when he took first place in the national mandolin contest at the prestigious Walnut Valley Festival.

In 2006, Carlo founded the International Mandolin Academy, an annual week-long event that features an Italian classical mandolin workshop. Since 2001, he has also led a weekend-long workshop in New York city, through which he spreads his vision of Italian-style mandolin.

Carlo has many recordings available and has a very active performance and teaching schedule. Check them out on his website – www.aonzo.com.

Chapter 21

Ten Ways of Tapping Into the Mandolin Subculture

In This Chapter

▶ Meeting other mandolin players

▶ Seeing your mandolin heroes

▶ Entering the world of mandolin culture

▶ Finding more inspiration for your playing

The mandolin community is like one big happy family, perhaps in part because the mandolin isn't the world's most popular instrument (yet) and mandolin lovers need to go to great lengths to satisfy their mandolin appetites. If you run into a stranger with what looks to be a mandolin case, and if doing so seems appropriate, introduce yourself as a student of the mandolin. Don't be surprised if you're treated like a long-lost friend from school. Mandolin lovers just can't get enough mandolin.

In this chapter, I provide ten ways for you to move more deeply into the world of the mandolin.

Attending Acoustic Music Concerts

The only thing better than listening to recorded music is being present while the magic happens. An acoustic concert doesn't need to be mandolin-specific; many acts use various instruments, and mandolin may be just one. You may get exposed to musical mandolin styles that you never considered, resulting in a broadening of your mandolin horizons.

Concerts are a good place to network with like-minded musicians. If the performers are good acoustic string musicians, most likely a number of aspiring acoustic musicians are in the audience. Many concerts have an after-show reception or party where you can make new friends; some of these events are invitation-only, but many aren't. In many cases, the artist comes to the lobby to sign autographs. Keep your eyes and ears open at the end of the concert, and you may get a chance to meet a legendary performer in this way. Everyone needs to go to live music concerts in order to support live music and avoid it fading away.

Be open-minded when choosing which concerts to attend. The acoustic guitar, fiddle, Dobro, cello and the banjo are all considered cousins in the world of string instruments, and as such are related to the mandolin.

Trying Out Mandolin Workshops

Mandolin workshops certainly allow you to increase your mandolin skills (as I mention in Chapter 19), but they're also a great way to get deeper into the mandolin world. If eight people show up for a mandolin workshop in a town near you, you have the perfect opportunity to meet seven other mandolin players like yourself. Meeting other mandolin players and talking mandolin is a big part of the mandolin subculture. Discussions among mandolin players often include topics such as different types of tunes, picks, strings and so on, along with conversations about new recordings or upcoming mandolin concerts.

You may need to be prepared to drive some way to attend a workshop held by one of the mandolin greats, but doing so is worthwhile.

Visiting Mandolin Camps

For a concentrated dose of mandolin culture, consider attending a mandolin camp. These camps can be as short as a weekend or as long as a full week, and so may require you to take some time off work. In addition, going to a camp requires a financial commitment resulting from travel, tuition and accommodation fees.

The Mandolin Symposium, held each summer in Santa Cruz, California, offers six full days of the ultimate mandolin culture saturation. Started by David Grisman and Mike Marshall, this camp features loads of the world's top mandolin performers and teachers, many of whom I list in Chapter 20. This mandolin gathering features a huge selection of styles, including bluegrass, jazz, Celtic, classical, choro and blues. Each day includes lectures, classes, ensemble rehearsals, staff concerts and organised jam sessions. Over 100 mandolin enthusiasts attend each year for this great over-the-top mandolin experience.

A similar event in the UK is held by Sore Fingers Summer Schools – Europe's leading organisation for bluegrass and old-time music camps. The school offers world-class tuition for all the instruments played in bluegrass. The school runs classes, held in the Cotswolds, a few times a year, and hosts a music festival too. Check out its website at www.sorefingers.co.uk.

Another great entry in your diary would be the International Italian Mandolin Academy – a yearly week-long event which takes place in Italy, with the focus being on Italian classical music. Take a look at the website (www.acca-demiamandolino.com) for more information.

Going to Acoustic Music Festivals

Attending an acoustic music festival requires you to load up the car with a tent, sleeping bag and, of course, your mandolin, and drive a long distance to attend a weekend-long event – while hoping it doesn't rain. Festivals can vary greatly in size and musical content. Larger festivals can have three or more stages happening all day long, and so you need to plan out your day to see the bands that appeal to you.

Take some sunscreen, a hat, an umbrella or rain poncho, maybe a folding chair and plenty of water to any outdoor concerts you attend.

When you decide to go to one of these events, don't worry about sleep (festivals can be a bit noisy, so you may not have much choice, anyway!). You can track down some of the best music in the campsite or even where people have parked their cars. Most of the campsite pickin' goes on pretty late at night, and sometimes into the wee hours, so don't be in too much of a hurry to get to bed. Campsite music can vary greatly from one festival to the next, ranging from the featured performers you saw on the main stage earlier that day to the festival-goer who only knows three songs and has had too much to drink. In either case, these events are great places to chat and play with other like-minded musicians.

If you aren't into outdoor camping, several great indoor festivals take place, which are usually held in convention centres and hotels. Among the well-known events are Wintergrass in Belleview, Washington state, USA, and the International Bluegrass Music Association's annual event in Nashville, Tennessee, in the USA. Almost everyone who attends these events is a musician, so you find music being played everywhere and at all hours, in the lobby or hotel rooms rather than around the campsite.

Joining a Jam Session or Orchestra

Playing with other people is the best way to improve as a player and to network with other musicians, even if some of them don't play mandolin. Public jam sessions and mandolin orchestras enable you to meet like-minded players.

Ask people who work at local music stores if they know of any jam sessions or open-mic nights in your area. *Open-mic nights* are events where amateurs can get on stage and play a few songs. Playing in front of your peers can be an amazing experience and do wonders for your confidence. Even if you're not ready to perform in public yet, you may meet someone to begin playing with. This type of playing can be good for you, because sheet music is rarely used: all the playing is by ear!

In contrast to an informal jam session is the organised mandolin orchestra. Yes, you did read that right! Believe it or not, community mandolin orchestras are currently making a comeback. A mandolin orchestra is similar to a traditional string orchestra, with the big difference that the instruments are plucked and not bowed. In most cases, parts are written for first and second mandolins, mandola, mando-cello, guitar and bass. Finding this type of group can be like finding the mother lode or a rich seam of mandolin culture. Where else can you come across 20 or 30 mandolin players in one room? Ask around – a mandolin orchestra may be located in your area. If not, start one!

Mandolin orchestras usually rely on the players being able to read music.

Reading Mandolin Magazines

Mandolin-focused magazines are great places to dive deeper into the world of mandolins. Here are a few options:

- ✔ *Mandolin Magazine* (www.mandolinmagazine.com) is a quarterly publication featuring a wide range of mandolin styles.
- ✔ *Bluegrass Unlimited* (www.bluegrassmusic.com) is published monthly and covers all things bluegrass (as I do in Chapter 10).
- ✔ *The Fretboard Journal* (www.fretboardjournal.com) is a quarterly oversized magazine with extremely high-quality photos and stories relating to guitars and mandolins.

If you like treasure hunts, try to find issues of the now out-of-print (1976–1984) *Mandolin World News*.

Making Use of the Internet

The Internet is a great place to pick up mandolin-related info. Here are some of my favourite websites:

- **The Mandolin Café** at www.mandolincafe.com is the mandolin player's home in cyberspace. Developed and run by Scott Tichenor, this website is an absolute wealth of everything mandolin. The site features stories and interviews with many of the greatest mandolin players of today, along with mandolin-related news. The website hosts a vibrant discussion forum covering everything from playing advice to reviews of new instruments. Some of today's top performers and educators give advice or share sage knowledge about mandolin playing. The classified ad section of the Mandolin Café is one of the best places in the world to find, among other items, new and used mandolins for sale in all price ranges.

- **Jazzmando.com** at www.jazzmando.com specialises in jazz techniques for mandolin. Jazz is popular among mandolin players; after all, one of the all-time mandolin greats, Jethro Burns (see Chapter 20), specialised in playing jazz. Music-theory buffs can find much instructional material on this website, along with reviews of innovative mandolins by rising stars in the mandolin-building world.

- **Mandohangout.com** at www.mandohangout.com is a relative newcomer to mandolins, although the hangout.com site concept has been around for a while for banjos, fiddles and flatpickers. This site features mandolin discussion forums, links to lessons and a place where mandolin players can post videos of themselves playing, allowing other mandolin players to comment.

- **Mandolinmoments.com** at www.mandolinmoments.com is another new kid on the block, coming from Oslo, Norway. This website links to stories from other mandolin sites as well as creating new ones about all things mandolin. The site is relatively small and looks at the mandolin from a European perspective.

- **Acousticoasis.com** at www.acousticoasis.com is an online digital record shop. Imagine a small family-owned record shop that carries only very cool acoustic music. Now imagine that the shop is owned by a mandolin player who's been a major player in the acoustic music scene for over 40 years, and you start to get the picture. With a growing library of titles and independent artists, this division of the Acoustic Disc record label is an oasis of good mandolin music. Music downloads are available in different sound qualities ranging from standard MP3s to full studio-quality files.

Joining a National Organisation

The Classical Mandolin Society of America (CMSA) is a national organisation with a mission to promote and support the art of classical mandolin playing in North America. Started by Norman Levine in 1986, the CMSA provides grants and scholarships for mandolin education and recruitment. It also publishes a quarterly newsletter, *Mandolin Journal*.

CMSA holds a yearly conference where mandolin players (not all classical) gather to study with some of today's finest classical mandolin players and teachers. The conference activities include masterclasses, faculty concerts, lunchtime concerts by CMSA member ensembles, late-night jamming (or sight-reading events), and the final night concert where attending members can participate in the En Masse Orchestra of over 100 mandolins! Every mandolin player needs to experience the sound of 100 mandolins tuning simultaneously at least once in a lifetime!

Across the Atlantic, the British BMG (that is, banjo, mandolin and guitar) Federation is a great source for mandolin networking in the UK. The Rally is one of the BMG's main events and consists of a weekend-long event featuring workshops and competitions. The Summer School is the other event organised by the BMG, and is a weekend event (held yearly) that includes classes and performances on mandolin, guitar and banjo.

Exploring Your Own Town

When you start to look around for mandolin activity, you may be surprised to find that it really does exist. You can make a mandolin connection at the hairdresser's, at the supermarket, or at church. Looking for mandolin culture is a bit like hunting morel mushrooms. At first you don't see any mushrooms, but after a while you start to see them in the same patches of woods that seemed empty before. Go out and explore (for mandolin contacts, not mushrooms, unless that's your bag too!).

Spreading the News

Telling other people about your new-found joy may influence them to take up the mandolin as well. By doing so, you potentially increase the number of mandolin players in your community. I can't imagine anything negative about having more mandolin players in a community. My motto is: mandolins heal the world!

Part VI

Appendixes

The 5th Wave   By Rich Tennant

SUDDENLY, JAKE, REALIZED HE AND HIS MANDOLIN HAD STUMBLED INTO A UKULELE PUB.

In this part . . .

1 present a list of 96 great mandolin chords (just look up any chord you don't know), a guide to standard musical notation and a complete track list to help you get the most out of the audio tracks.

Appendix A
Chord Charts

*I*n this appendix, I provide you with 96 invaluable chords that come in handy in a variety of musical situations and genres. Whether you're playing a Beatles' tune or a bossa nova, look here when you need a few extra chords that you don't use every day.

This appendix is intended to be an all-purpose chord chart. If you need only one way to play, for example, A♭ major 7, I present a version that's practical and fairly easy to play.

You can play any chord in a variety of *inversions* (that is, in different ways with different fingerings — see Chapter 7 for more details), and certain inversions work better with certain styles of music. For example, I show you the chop chords that bluegrass players use in Chapter 10, and jazz and swing chording in Chapter 13.

If you're just starting out, flip to Chapter 4 where I give you five easy chords to kick-start your playing.

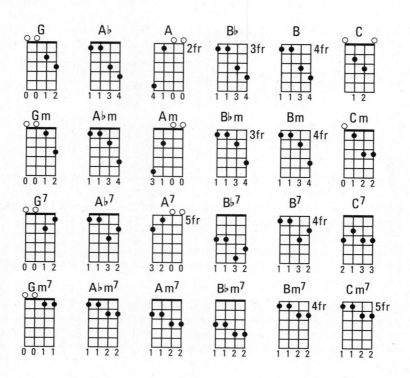

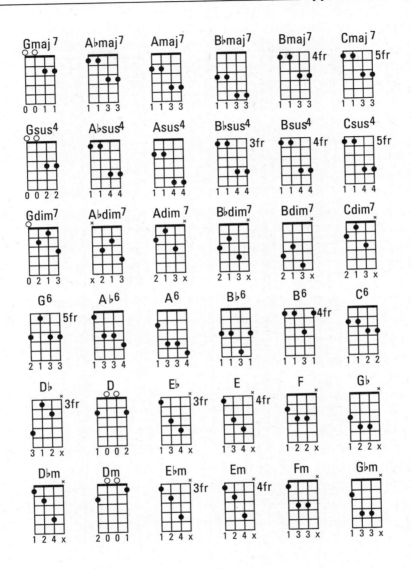

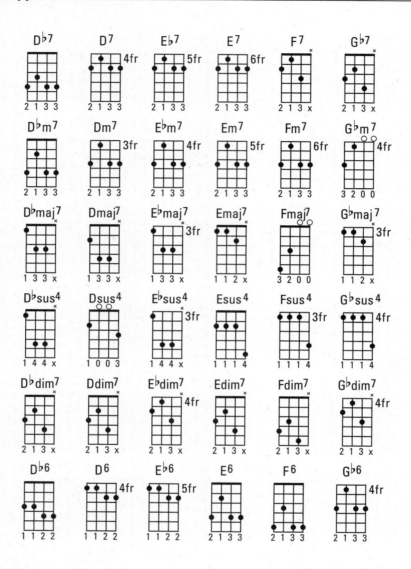

Reading Standard Musical Notation

· ·

Getting to grips with musical notation is a great idea because it enables you to read music written for other instruments and to communicate effectively with other musicians. So, in this appendix, I lead you gently into the world of written music, providing a practical hands-on guide that you can refer back to again and again while reading standard notation. I describe the staff – where the notes are written – some signs and symbols to follow so that you never get lost in a song, and the notes themselves and how to play them.

Meeting the Musical Staff

The *musical staff* doesn't refer to the wonderfully tuneful people at *For Dummies* HQ (grovel, grovel!) but to the series of five parallel horizontal lines with a space between each one. Notes of different pitches are written on or between these lines. Conveniently, higher notes are placed higher on the staff and lower notes lower on the staff.

In this section, I provide a basic understanding of the staff and where the range of the mandolin is written. In addition, I describe a few signs and symbols that are included at the beginning of a piece of music and apply to the entire piece that you're playing, giving you an idea of the overall feel of the music.

Starting at the beginning: Treble and bass clefs

Musical instruments range from very low in pitch (for example, tuba and string bass) to very high in pitch (such as piccolo and glockenspiel), and so people use more than one staff to accommodate all the musical possibilities. Most musical instruments fit into the range of the *treble clef* or *bass clef,* which are the symbols at the beginning of every line of printed music (see Figure B-1). Some instruments (such as piano) have such a large range of notes that the musician is required to read both treble and bass clefs.

Mandolin music is written in the treble clef. If you decide to explore the lower-voiced instruments in the mandolin family (mandola, mando-cello), you may find a need to look into the bass clef or even alto clef (viola clef), but for now I focus on the treble clef.

Treble clef

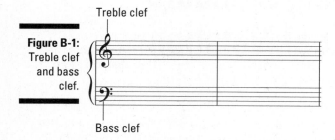

Figure B-1: Treble clef and bass clef.

Bass clef

Signing in with the key signature

The *key signature* is placed at the beginning of a piece of music (see Figure B-2) in the form of a series of sharp or flat symbols written on the staff, indicating the notes that you need to play *sharp* (one fret higher) or *flat* (one fret lower). For example, if you see a sharp (♯) symbol on the top line (F), you know to play all F notes in this song as F sharp.

Time signature   Time signature

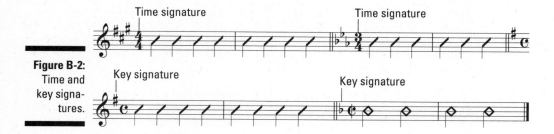

Figure B-2: Time and key signatures.

Key signature   Key signature

Each key or scale has a unique number of sharps and flats, and so by looking at the key signature, you can tell what scale or key the song is in. For a description of major and harmonic minor scales see Chapter 8, and see Chapter 13 on jazz.

Timing is everything: Time signatures

The *time signature* indicates the pulse or rhythm of the music. Time signatures look like fractions (for example, 3/4 and 2/4). They're placed on the staff, in the upper left corner of the *score* (sheet of music), near the treble clef and the key signature (check out the two preceding sections and Figure B-2).

The top number in a time signature tells you how many beats are in each measure. The bottom number indicates what duration of note equals the beat. (Chapter 4 has lots more about counting beats, time signatures and the names of notes.) Here are some example time signatures:

- 2/4: The top number (2) indicates that the music has a beat of '1, 2, 1, 2' and so on. The bottom number (4) shows that the beat is written as a quarter note (a crotchet) and that two quarter notes (crotchets) are used per measure.

- 3/2: The top number (3) indicates a pulse of '1, 2, 3, 1, 2, 3' and so on. The bottom number (2) tells you that the beat is written as a half note (a minim) and that three half notes (minims) are used per measure.

- 5/8: The top number (5) indicates a pulse of '1, 2, 3, 4, 5, 1, 2, 3, 4, 5' and so on. The bottom number (8) shows that the beat is written as an eighth note (a quaver), and so five eighth notes (quavers) are used per measure.

Musicians often use shortcuts to refer to certain time signatures. For example, 4/4 (four quarter (quaver) notes in a measure) is the most commonly used time, and is sometimes called (logically enough) *common time* and indicated by a letter C as Figure B-2 shows. Another common shortcut is to use the symbol ₵ to indicate *cut time* (see the nearby sidebar 'Musician lingo: Cut time').

Getting the speed right: Tempo

Printed sheet music often includes a suggested *tempo* (speed) at which you need to play the music. In the past, Italian words were used to describe this aspect of a piece of classical music, but today most tempos are indicated with metronome markings. Metronomes measure the tempo in beats per minute (bpm) and have become the global standard. Chapters 16 and 5 contain more on buying and using metronomes, respectively.

TECHNICAL STUFF

Musician lingo: Cut time

Cut time is in fact 2/2 time, but musicians use the term in situations where something is written in 4/4 time but you really only feel two beats per measure instead of four (which all sounds more complex than it really is). When you start applying this type of counting to music, it begins to make more sense.

Below is a short list of Italian tempo terms along with the modern-day metronome markings:

- ✔ *Largo* = 40–60 bpm
- ✔ *Larghetto* = 60–66 bpm
- ✔ *Adagio* = 66–76 bpm
- ✔ *Andante* = 76–108 bpm
- ✔ *Moderato* = 108–120 bpm
- ✔ *Allegro* = 120–168 bpm
- ✔ *Presto* = 168–200 bpm

Figure B-3 shows how composers and songwriters display tempo markings on a musical score.

Figure B-3: Tempo markings and style markings.

Knowing the style

When you're to play the music in a specific genre or style, the composer can choose to include words indicating that style, which can be anything from heavy metal to bossa nova or hornpipe. These styles appear in the upper left corner of the music near the tempo marking (see Figure B-3).

Not all written music has a style marking, and to find markings useful you need to acquire a good knowledge of many different styles (to help with this aim, check out the musical genres that I cover in Part III).

Following the Musical Directions

Reading music is a bit like reading a map or following motorway signs. Most music consists of a few small parts that get repeated and linked together to form a complete piece. In this section, I introduce you to a number of signs that give directions on where to go next in the music:

- **Repeat signs** (as in Figure B-4) are covered in more detail in Chapter 4. They're indicated by a thick vertical double-bar line with two dots. The basic idea is that you repeat the music in the frames any number of designated times, and only once if no number of repeats are indicated.

- **First and second endings** are indicated by a horizontal bracket over a measure or measures, with a small number at the corner of the bracket (see Figure B-4).

- **D.C. (*Da Capo*)** is a marker instructing you to repeat from the beginning.

- **D.S. (*Dal Segno*)** instructs you to repeat a passage starting from the sign (*segno*).

- **Sign (*Segno*)** (Figure B-4) is used together with D.S. (see preceding bullet point) instructing you to repeat a passage from the sign.

- **Coda** is a passage that brings a piece of music to an end. The coda symbol looks like a set of crosshairs.

- **Fine (final)** is a directive to end the piece after you've played all the written repeats.

- **D.C. al fine (*Da Capo al fine*)** means repeat from the beginning and play to and stop at the word *fine*.

- **D.C. al Coda (*Da Capo al Coda*)** means repeat from the beginning to the words 'to coda' and then play the coda.

- **D.S. al fine (*Dal Sengo al fine*)** means repeat from the sign and play to the word 'fine', stopping at 'fine'.

- **D.S. al Coda (*Dal Segno al Coda*)** means repeat from the sign to the words 'to coda' and then play the coda.

Figure B-4 shows an example of these roadmap symbols in action. The following list of instructions explains how and why composers use these symbols (without them, music would require many more pages to print):

1. **Start at the beginning (upper left corner) and play through to the third line until you reach the repeat sign (double bars with double dots) under the first repeat bracket.**

2. **Jump to the double repeat bars at the beginning of the third line, playing the third line a second time but this time skipping over the measure containing the first repeat bracket and going directly to the measure under the second repeat bracket.**

3. **Follow the D.S. al Coda sign, which directs you back to the sign (*segno*) at the beginning of the second line.**

4. **Play from the sign through the second line until you reach the 'to coda' sign at the end of the last measure in the second line.**

5. **Jump directly to the coda (crosshairs) at the beginning of the fourth line and play until you reach 'fine' at beat one of the last measure in the fourth line and stop at 'fine'.**

When you can follow all this perfectly, reward yourself with a beverage!

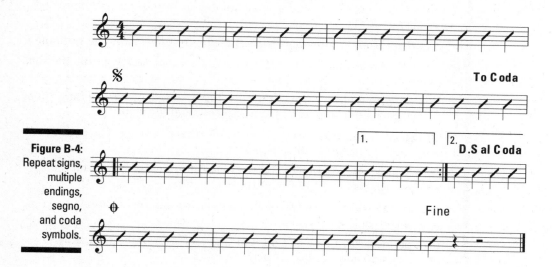

Figure B-4:
Repeat signs,
multiple
endings,
segno,
and coda
symbols.

Noting the Musical Notes

The notes are clearly the most glamorous part about reading music. Melody is king, and notes make up melodies. In this section, I help get you started learning how to read musical notes.

Pitching in with high and low notes

The term *pitch* in music relates to how high or low a sound is. Music is made up of a series of pitches ranging from very low to very high. These pitches are organised into scales and given letter names ranging from A to G (I discuss scales in Chapter 8). Here, I explain how to tell the name of a note placed on the staff (see the section 'Meeting the Musical Staff').

Lines and spaces

Notes can be placed on the lines or the spaces of the staff. Starting at the bottom and working your way up, the lines represent the notes E, G, B, D and F. Many people memorise the notes on the lines by the mnemonic 'Every Good Boy Does Fine'. The spaces from bottom to top are F, A, C and E, which forms the word 'FACE'.

When I was first learning to read music, someone usefully pointed out that if you read alternately upwards line-space-line-space, the notes are actually in alphabetical order (see Figure B-5(a)).

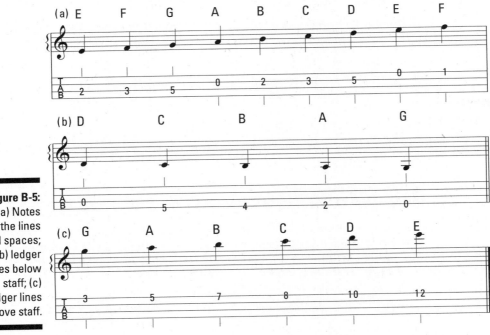

Figure B-5:
(a) Notes on the lines and spaces;
(b) ledger lines below staff; (c) ledger lines above staff.

Ledger lines

Ledger lines are the extra staff lines that extend above or below the staff to accommodate notes in the higher or lower range of the mandolin. The notes continue in alphabetical order, alternating between lines and spaces (see Figure B-5(b) and (c)).

Sharps, flats and naturals

Sharps (♯) and flats (♭) – but not naturals (♮) – can appear in the key signature or in the staff placed just prior to the affected note. When sharps or flats are in the key signature, you play the indicated sharps or flats for the entire piece of music or until another key signature is presented. If the sharp or flat symbol is used on the staff to affect only one note, it's called an *accidental*, meaning that the note stays a sharp or flat for the remainder of that measure only (see Figure B-6):

✔ **Sharp:** Move the indicated note one half step or one fret higher in pitch.

✔ **Flat:** Move the indicated note one half step or one fret lower in pitch.

✔ **Natural:** Negate any sharps or flats that have been applied to this note by the key signature or by any accidentals.

All three accidentals can be placed prior to a note in a measure of music.

Figure B-6: Accidentals.

Discovering note duration

Music is a combination of sounds (pitches) and silence arranged in rhythmic patterns. The lengths of the sounds and the lengths of the silences between them is the rhythm. For each possible length note an equal length rest exists (see Figure B-7 for note and rest values). Chapter 4 includes some basic music counting examples and exercises.

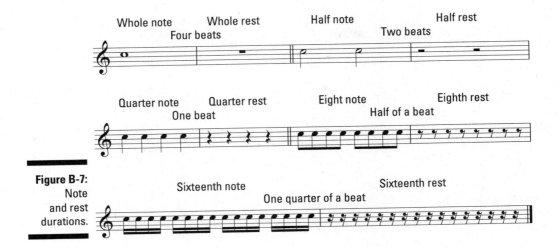

Figure B-7:
Note
and rest
durations.

Dotting and tying notes

Dots and ties perform essentially the same job: they make the notes longer, but in slightly different ways:

➤ A dot after a note increases the length of the note by one half. For example, a dot after a half note (minim) increases the length by a quarter note (crotchet), resulting in a note that has the duration of three quarter notes (crotchets).

In Figure B-8(a), the dots appear next to quarter notes (crotchets), making the length equal to one quarter note (crotchet) and one eighth note (quaver) (or three eighth notes (quavers)).

➤ When notes are tied, you add their length together. The sign to indicate a tie is an arch between the notes.

In Figure B-8(b), the quarter note (crotchet) is tied to eighth notes (quavers) and equals three eighth notes (quavers).

Although they look a bit different, examples (a) and (b) sound identical.

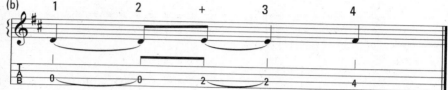

Figure B-8:
(a) Dotted
notes; (b)
tied notes.

Getting louder and quietening down: Dynamics

Dynamics are a set of musical terms for describing how loudly or quietly to play the piece of music. Below are some common Italian words used to indicate dynamics, their abbreviations and the English translations:

- ✔ **Pianissimo (pp):** Very soft
- ✔ **Piano (p):** Soft
- ✔ **Mezzo-piano (mp):** Medium soft
- ✔ **Mezzo-forte (mf):** Medium loud
- ✔ **Forte (f):** Loud
- ✔ **Fortissimo (ff):** Very loud

A gradual change in volume is indicated as follows:

- ✔ **Crescendo (cresc):** Gradually get louder
- ✔ **Diminuendo (dim):** Gradually get quieter

Hairpins look like stretched out 'greater than' or 'less than' symbols. They indicate gradual changes in volume called *crescendos* (<; louder) and *diminuendos* (>; quieter): check out Figure B-9.

Figure B-9:
Hairpins
used as
crescendos
and diminu-
endos.

Crescendo (louder)   Diminuendo (quieter)

Articulating your playing

Articulation refers to the performance technique that affects a single note or the transition between multiple notes or sounds. Articulation varies between instruments, so I address only articulations that apply to the mandolin. These articulations are covered in more detail in Chapter 6.

Slur

Rather than an insult to your reputation, a *slur* is a curved line connecting two or more notes, directing you to play the slurred notes without separation. Hammer-ons, pull-offs and slides (see Chapter 6) are slurring techniques for mandolin where only the first note is plucked; you play slurred notes by using specific left-hand techniques (see Figure B-10).

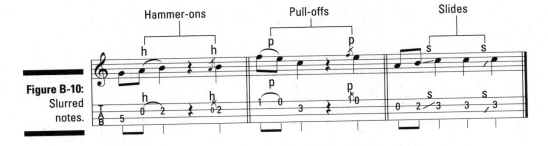

Figure B-10:
Slurred
notes.

Staccato

Staccato is a shortening of notes to allow a bit of silence between each one, which you achieve with left-hand muting techniques (see Chapter 6). A dot directly above the note indicates staccato (see Figure B-11(a)).

Figure B-11:
(a) Staccato;
(b) accents.

Accents

Accent symbols are written over notes that you need to play more loudly than surrounding notes. Figure B-11(b) shows the small wedge-shaped symbol (>) indicating an accented note.

A note can be marked with an accent and the staccato marking, meaning to play it more loudly than the surrounding notes with a shortness to the note that allows for a brief silence before sounding the next note.

Tremolo

Tremolo is the rapid back-and-forth right-hand picking of a note to create a sustained effect (I cover this technique in detail with a variety of examples in Chapter 5). Tremolo is indicated by slash marks on the stems of the notes that you need to play with tremolo (see Figure B-12).

Figure B-12:
Tremolo.

Appendix C

Audio Tracks

• •

I perform every music example in *Mandolin For Dummies* as an audio track available with this book, giving you a true multimedia experience. Wherever you see the 'PlayThis!' icon in the margin, I demonstrate the technique or song on a variety of mandolins so that you can hear what different makes and models sound like.

If you've purchased the paper or e-book version of *Mandolin For Dummies*, you can find the tracks – ready and waiting for you – at www.dummies.com/go/mandolin. (If you don't have internet access, call 877-762-2974 within the U.S. or 317-572-3993 outside the U.S.) If you have the enhanced e-book version, you'll find the audio tracks right there in the chapters.

Discovering What's on the Audio Tracks

Table C-1 lists all the tracks along with the associated figure number, so you can quickly look up any tracks you like the sound of. The first number is always the chapter containing that figure.

Table C-1		Audio Tracks
Track Number	**Figure Number**	**Track Title or Description**
1	2-5	Sound of the mandolin's four open strings.
	n/a	Basic counting.
2	4-4	Eighth notes (quavers).
3	4-5	Sixteenth notes (semiquavers).
4	4-6	Whole notes (semibreves) and half notes (minims).
	4-7	Dots and ties.
5	4-9	Repeat signs.
6	4-10	Playing the rests.

(continued)

Table C-1 (continued)

Track Number	Figure Number	Track Title or Description
7	4-11	Counting exercises.
8	4-22	Simple strumming patterns.
9	4-24	Strumming patterns with chords.
10	4-26	'Ode to Joy' theme.
11	4-27	'Down in the Valley'.
12	4-28	'Go Tell Aunt Rhodie'.
13	4-29	'Skip to My Lou'.
14	4-30	'Red River Valley'.
15	5-5	Basic alternate picking.
	5-6	Crossing strings while alternate picking.
	5-7	Alternate picking a syncopated phrase.
	5-8	Alternate picking an off-beat phrase.
16	5-9	Down-stroke technique.
17	5-10	Jig picking pattern.
18	5-11	Cross-picking forward roll.
	5-12	Cross-picking reverse roll.
19	5-16	Four-stroke tremolo.
	5-17	Six-stroke tremolo.
	5-18	Eight-stroke tremolo.
	5-19	Twelve-stroke tremolo.
20	n/a	Free tremolo.
	n/a	Slow tremolo.
21	5-20	Four notes per string exercise.
	5-21	Three notes per string exercise.
	5-22	Two notes per string exercise.
22	5-23	String-skipping on the g-string.
	5-24	String-skipping on the d-string.
	5-25	String-skipping on the a-string.
	5-26	String-skipping on the e-string.

Track Number	Figure Number	Track Title or Description
23	5-27	Two-measure pattern using only two strings.
24	5-28	Dividing the beat by two.
	5-29	Dividing the beat by three.
	5-30	Dividing the beat by four.
	5-31	Dividing the beat by six.
25	5-32	Rest exercise one.
	5-33	Rest exercise two.
	5-34	Rest exercise three.
26	5-35	Dynamics exercise one.
	5-36	Dynamics exercise two.
27	5-37	Tremolo exercise.
	5-38	Trying out tremolo on a song.
28	6-3	A left-hand finger exercise.
29	6-4(a); (b)	Note-to-note slide; single-note slide as embellishment.
	6-5(a); (b)	Note-to-note hammer-on; single-note hammer-on as embellishment.
	6-6(a); (b)	Note-to-note pull-off; single note pull-off as an embellishment.
30	6-7	Jethro-style super pull-off.
	6-8	Hammer-on pull-off combination.
	6-9	Muting fretted and open notes.
31	7-14(b)	Jazz chord progression using Jethro-style three-string chords.
32	7-15(b)	Jazzy blues chord progression using Jethro-style three-string chords.
33	8-4	'The Flop-Eared Mule' mandolin version.
34	8-8	'Simple Gifts' melody.
35	8-11	'Minuet in G' melody.
36	8-13	'Skiffle Mando' rhythm.
	8-14	'Skiffle Mando' melody.

(continued)

Table C-1 (continued)

Track Number	Figure Number	Track Title or Description
37	8-18	'Waltz Ukrainian Style' melody.
38	8-19	'Bighorn River Sunset' arrangement for solo mandolin.
39	8-22	'Angelina Baker' in the low octave.
	8-23	'Angelina Baker' in the high octave.
40	8-26	'Poor Wayfaring Stranger' mandolin arrangement.
41	9-1	Three old-time strumming patterns.
	9-2	Melodic strumming for old-time fiddle tunes.
42	9-4	'The Arkansas Traveller'.
43	9-5	'The Girl I Left Behind Me'.
44	9-6	'Soldier's Joy'.
45	9-9	'Waltz of the Little Girls'.
46	9-11	'White Hair and Wisdom'.
47	9-14	'Stone's Rag'.
48	9-17	'Eight String Rag'.
49	9-19	Typical 12-bar boogie-style bass line.
50	9-21	Basic 12-bar blues chord progression.
	9-22	Quick to the four with a turnaround.
51	9-23(a)	First basic eight-bar blues progression in the key of G.
	9-23(b)	Second basic eight-bar blues progression in the key of G.
	9-23(c)	Eight-bar blues progression using a few more chords as a turnaround.
52	9-26	'Workin' That Riff'.
53	9-28	'Three Shots of Rye Whiskey'.
54	9-30	'Country Boy Blues'.
55	9-33	Slow blues rhythm.
	9-34	'Slow Cookin' blues.
56	10-2	Bluegrass 'chop' rhythm.

Track Number	Figure Number	Track Title or Description
57	10-4	'Whiskey Before Breakfast', old-time fiddle version.
	10-5	'Whiskey Before Breakfast', bluegrass style.
58	10-6	Some Bill Monroe rhythmic patterns.
59	10-7	'Bury Me Beneath the Willow' melody.
60	10-8	'Uncle Bill' using down-strokes.
61	10-13	Double-stop crawl.
62	10-14	'Kickin' Mule'.
63	10-15	'Bury Me Beneath the Willow', instrumental break.
64	11-1	Straight eighth notes (quavers), as used in reels; eighth notes, as used in jigs; lilt or hornpipe.
65	11-6	'The Drunken Landlady'.
	11-7	'The Drunken Landlady' with triplets.
66	11-8	'Hag at the Churn'.
	11-9	'Hag at the Churn' with triplets.
67	11-10	'A Fig for a Kiss'.
	11-11	'A Fig for a Kiss' with slip jig triplets.
68	11-12	'Little Stack of Wheat'.
69	12-1	'O Sole Mio'.
70	12-2	'Torna a Surriento'.
71	12-3(a)	Triple glide stroke with d-string as bass.
	12-3 (b)	Triple glide stroke with g-string as bass.
	12-4	Excerpt from 'La Fustemberg Variations'.
72	12-5	An excerpt from 'Sonatina in C Major'.
73	12-6(a)	Choro rhythm, slow.
	12-6(b)	Choro fast rhythm 1.
	12-6(c)	Choro fast rhythm 2.
74	12-8	'Gaucho Corta Jaca' with one-bar slow rhythm pattern.
75	12-8	'Gaucho Corta Jaca' with two-bar faster rhythm pattern.

(continued)

Table C-1 *(continued)*

Track Number	Figure Number	Track Title or Description
76	13-1(a)	Swing rhythm: two-beat, all short or muted strums.
	13-1(b)	Swing rhythm: two-beat, long–short.
	13-1(c)	Swing rhythm: four-beat Charleston rhythm.
77	13-5	'The 105 Year Old Cat'.
78	13-7	'Limnology'.
79	13-9	'Ode to Swing'.
80	13-12	'Three Keys'.
81	13-13	'Auld Lang Syne' chord melody arrangement.
82	13-15	'Swingin' Leather Britches'.
83	13-17	'Muppets on the Titanic'.
84	13-19(a)	Gypsy-bossa rhythm pattern.
	13-19(b)	Choro rhythm pattern.
85	13-20(a)	'Mr Natural' played with gypsy-bossa pattern.
86	13-20(b)	'Mr Natural' played with choro pattern.
87	14-2	Dawg samba rhythm patterns.
88	14-3	'16/16' solo section chord progression.
89	14-5	'Pneumonia' rhythm patterns.
90	14-6	Funky 'Pneumonia' solo section.
91	14-8	'Swang Thang'.

Index

FOR DUMMIES®

Making Everything Easier!™

UK editions

BUSINESS

978-0-470-97626-5

978-0-470-74737-7

978-1-119-97527-4

REFERENCE

978-0-470-68637-9

978-0-470-97450-6

978-1-119-97660-8

HOBBIES

978-0-470-69960-7

978-1-119-99417-6

978-1-119-97250-1

Asperger's Syndrome For Dummies
978-0-470-66087-4

Basic Maths For Dummies
978-1-119-97452-9

Body Language For Dummies, 2nd Edition
978-1-119-95351-7

Boosting Self-Esteem For Dummies
978-0-470-74193-1

British Sign Language For Dummies
978-0-470-69477-0

Cricket For Dummies
978-0-470-03454-5

Diabetes For Dummies, 3rd Edition
978-0-470-97711-8

Electronics For Dummies
978-0-470-68178-7

English Grammar For Dummies
978-0-470-05752-0

Flirting For Dummies
978-0-470-74259-4

IBS For Dummies
978-0-470-51737-6

Improving Your Relationship For Dummies
978-0-470-68472-6

ITIL For Dummies
978-1-119-95013-4

Management For Dummies, 2nd Edition
978-0-470-97769-9

Neuro-linguistic Programming For Dummies, 2nd Edition
978-0-470-66543-5

Nutrition For Dummies, 2nd Edition
978-0-470-97276-2

Organic Gardening For Dummies
978-1-119-97706-3

11–43522

FOR DUMMIES®

Making Everything Easier! ™

UK editions

SELF-HELP

978-0-470-66541-1

978-1-119-99264-6

978-0-470-66086-7

STUDENTS

978-0-470-68820-5

978-0-470-974711-7

978-1-119-99134-2

HISTORY

978-0-470-68792-5

978-0-470-74783-4

978-0-470-97819-1

Origami Kit For Dummies
978-0-470-75857-1

Overcoming Depression For Dummies
978-0-470-69430-5

Positive Psychology For Dummies
978-0-470-72136-0

PRINCE2 For Dummies, 2009 Edition
978-0-470-71025-8

Project Management For Dummies
978-0-470-71119-4

Psychometric Tests For Dummies
978-0-470-75366-8

Renting Out Your Property For Dummies, 3rd Edition
978-1-119-97640-0

Rugby Union For Dummies, 3rd Edition
978-1-119-99092-5

Sage One For Dummies
978-1-119-95236-7

Self-Hypnosis For Dummies
978-0-470-66073-7

Storing and Preserving Garden Produce For Dummies
978-1-119-95156-8

Study Skills For Dummies
978-0-470-74047-7

Teaching English as a Foreign Language For Dummies
978-0-470-74576-2

Time Management For Dummies
978-0-470-77765-7

Training Your Brain For Dummies
978-0-470-97449-0

Work-Life Balance For Dummies
978-0-470-71380-8

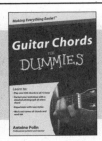

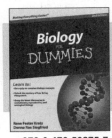

FOR DUMMIES®

Making Everything Easier!™

COMPUTER BASICS

978-0-470-57829-2

978-0-470-61454-9

978-0-470-49743-2

DIGITAL PHOTOGRAPHY

978-0-470-25074-7

978-0-470-76878-5

978-1-118-00472-2

MICROSOFT OFFICE 2010

978-0-470-48998-7

978-0-470-58302-9

978-0-470-48953-6

Access 2010 For Dummies
978-0-470-49747-0

Android Application Development For Dummies
978-0-470-77018-4

AutoCAD 2011 For Dummies
978-0-470-59539-8

C++ For Dummies, 6th Edition
978-0-470-31726-6

Computers For Seniors For Dummies, 2nd Edition
978-0-470-53483-0

Dreamweaver CS5 For Dummies
978-0-470-61076-3

iPad 2 For Dummies, 3rd Edition
978-1-118-17679-5

Macs For Dummies, 11th Edition
978-0-470-87868-2

Mac OS X Snow Leopard For Dummies
978-0-470-43543-4

Photoshop CS5 For Dummies
978-0-470-61078-7

Photoshop Elements 10 For Dummies
978-1-118-10742-3

Search Engine Optimization For Dummies, 4th Edition
978-0-470-88104-0

The Internet For Dummies, 13th Edition
978-1-118-09614-7

Visual Studio 2010 All-In-One For Dummies
978-0-470-53943-9

Web Analytics For Dummies
978-0-470-09824-0

Word 2010 For Dummies
978-0-470-48772-3

WordPress For Dummies, 4th Edition
978-1-118-07342-1